LEGAL ASPECTS OF INSURANCE

DR. P.K. GUPTA

M.Com., Ph.D.(Finance), FICWA, FCS, CFA, FIII

Reader (Finance & Risk Management)

Centre for Management Studies

Jamia Millia Islamia, Delhi

Himalaya Publishing House

ISO 9001 : 2015 CERTIFIED

First Edition : 2008
Reprint : 2023
Reprint : 2025

Published by : Mrs. Meena Pandey
for **HIMALAYA PUBLISHING HOUSE PVT. LTD.,**
"Ramdoot", Dr. Bhalerao Marg, Girgaon, Mumbai - 400 004.
Phone: 022-23860170, 23863863; **Fax:** 022-23877178
E-mail: himpub@bharatmail.co.in; **Website:** www.himpub.com

Branch Offices :

New Delhi : "Pooja Apartments", 4-B, Murari Lal Street, Ansari Road, Darya Ganj, New Delhi - 110 002. Phone: 011-23270392, 23278631; Fax: 011-23256286

Nagpur : Kundanlal Chandak Industrial Estate, Ghat Road, Nagpur - 440 018. Phone: 0712-2721215, 2721216

Bengaluru : Plot No. 91-33, 2nd Main Road, Seshadripuram, Behind Nataraja Theatre, Bengaluru - 560 020. Phone: 080-41138821; Mobile: 09379847017, 09379847005

Hyderabad : No. 3-4-184, Lingampally, Besides Raghavendra Swamy Matham, Kachiguda, Hyderabad - 500 027. Phone: 040-27560041, 27550139

Chennai : No. 34/44, Motilal Street, T. Nagar, Chennai - 600 017. Mobile: 09380460419

Pune : "Laksha" Apartment, First Floor, No. 527, Mehunpura, Shaniwarpeth (Near Prabhat Theatre), Pune - 411 030. Phone: 020-24496323, 24496333; Mobile: 09370579333

Cuttack : Plot No 5F-755/4, Sector-9, CDA Market Nagar, Cuttack - 753 014, Odisha. Mobile: 09338746007

Kolkata : 3, S.M. Bose Road, Near Gate No. 5, Agarpara Railway Station, North 24 Parganas, West Bengal - 700109. Mobile: 09674536325

DTP by : Twinkle Graphics, Delhi-110 088.

Printed at : Infinity Imaging System, New Delhi. On behalf of HPH.

Dedicated to the
Sacred Memory of my Father

PREFACE

Insurance is not a new area of academic study or profession. With the increasing dynamism of risk and the growth of professional risk management, the insurance device has become more and more popular these days. The recent liberalisation of the economy has resulted into the availability of large number of alternative products/financial services. This has paved the way for the potential and unconventional entrants to penetrate the financial market through innovative higher product profile and portfolios, resulting into a sudden spurt in the demand of insurance professionals. The study of insurance as an academic discipline *in new form* is an obvious outcome. More and more academic institutions all over the countries are offering highly specialised insurance programmes to cater to this demand.

Recently, the universities in India and abroad have introduced insurance as a specialised study both at graduate and postgraduate level. This has accentuated the dire demand for the literature on insurance in the Indian context.

This book is an attempt to conceptualise the students with the legal aspects of insurance business.

Organisation of the Text

This book has been organised into four modules.

Module 1 Introduces the readers to the legal environment of the insurance business. Chapter 1 discusses insurance as a contractual relationship in light of the Indian Contract Act, 1872. The principles of insurance and a synoptic view of the legal history of insurance are also provided. Chapter 2 gives an overview of the various provisions of the Insurance Act, 1938. Chapter 3 and 4 highlight the salient provisions of the Life Insurance Corporation Act, 1956 and General Insurance Business (Nationalisation) Act, 1972 respectively. Chapter 5 is devoted to the constitution of and regulation of insurance business by the IRDA as per Insurance Regulatory and Development Authority Act, 1999

Module 2 Chapter 6 describes the important provisions of Motor Vehicles Act, 1939 & the amended act of 1988 which include the insurance of third party risks and the functioning of MACT. Chapter 7 discusses the Marine Insurance Act, 1963 - the various principles of insurance applicable to insurance business, the provisions relating to losses and damages etc.

Module 3 Provide a brief overview of the provisions relating to insurance as contained in the various transportation Laws other those discussed in module 2. These includes Inland Steam Vessels Act, 1917 & Ammended Act of 1977, Carriage of Goods by Sea Act, 1925, Merchant Shipping Act, 1958, Indian Railways Act, 1890, Carriers Act, 1865, Carriage by Air Act, 1972, Indian Ports (Major Ports) Act, 1963, Bill of Lading Act, 1855, Indian Post Office Act, 1898, Multi Modal Transportation Act, 1993 (Chapter 8).

Module 4 Contains the various liability laws as applicable to insurance. Chapter 9 contains the important provisions of the Workmen Compensation Act, 1923 and Public Liability Insurance Act, 1991. Chapter 10 finally describes the other miscellaneous laws concerning insurance - Employees State Insurance Act, 1948, Indian Stamp Act, 1899, Consumer Protection Act, 1986, Arbitration Act, 1940 and amended act of 1986. A brief view of the functioning of Lok Adalats and Ombudsman is also given.

After the end of every chapter, "Key Terms", "Suggested Readings/References" and "Questions for Review" are also given. At the end, the book contains a glossary of important insurance terms which may useful for the readers.

ACKNOWLEDGEMENTS

I am grateful to my readers for their continued support and valuable comments. I am thankful to Himalaya Publishing House for their efforts and support in bringing out the earlier works–Insurance Risk Management (2004) and Fundamentals of Insurance (2005).

I must thank Mr. Joshi and Mr. Rawat at Delhi office of Himalaya Publishing House, who provided the various books and other reference literature which helped me to write this book.

I am indebted to my wife Rachna Gupta, my mother, brother, sisters and family members especially my beloved Tinku, Chinki and Pintoo who have made sacrifices at all levels in various forms and contexts for timely completion of this book.

I thank Prof. Furqan Qamar, Director, Centre for Management Studies, Jamia Millia Islamia for his motivation, guidance and support in all academic endeavors.

I also thank my Ph.D. supervisor, Dr. B.L. Surolia, who has provided me presentation skills which, I feel is the most important tool in any literary work.

I would be failing in my duty if do not thank my colleagues and staff of various libraries who have helped at various stages in provision of statistics and other information required for the book.

The last but not the least, my thanks are due to the academicians at various institutions and insurance companies who provided me an idea as to contents and other valuable suggestions.

New Delhi, **P.K. GUPTA**

July, 2006

BRIEF CONTENTS

Module 1

Module 2

Module 3

Module 4

CONTENTS

Module 2

Module 3

Module 4

Module 1

Legal Framework of Insurance Business

Historical Perspective

The Insurance Sector in India dates back to 1818 when the first insurance company was established–the Oriental Life Insurance Company at Calcutta. This was followed in quick succession with the establishment of Bombay Life Assurance Company (1823) and Madras Equitable Life Assurance Society (1829). In the general insurance business Triton Insurance Company (1850) was the first to be established. Prior to 1871, Indians were charged about 15 percent more premium as compared to Europeans. Bombay Mutual Life Assurance Society (1871) was the first company not to differentiate between Indians and Europeans in the matter of fixation of premiums. The first attempt at regulation of the insurance business in India was through the Indian Life Assurance Companies Act in 1912. This was later broad-based and the Insurance Act came into existence from the year 1928 onwards. The Insurance Act was subsequently reviewed and a comprehensive legislation was enacted called the Insurance Act, 1938. The nationalization of life insurance business took place in 1956 when 245 Indian and foreign insurance and provident societies were first amalgamated and then nationalized. The Life Insurance Corporation of India (LIC) came into existence and has since enjoyed a monopoly over the life insurance business in India. The milestones in the Insurance sector 1912 onwards can be summarised as under. The life insurance sector witnessed the following development :

1912 : The Indian Life Assurance Companies Act enacted as the first statute to regulate the life insurance business.

1928 : The Indian Insurance Companies Act enacted to enable the government to collect statistical information about both life and non-life insurance businesses.

1938 : Earlier legislation consolidated and amended to by the Insurance Act with the objective of protecting the interests of the insuring public.

1956 : 245 Indian and foreign insurers and provident societies taken over by the central government and nationalised. LIC formed by an Act of Parliament, *viz.* LIC Act, 1956, with a capital contribution of Rs. 5 crore from the Government of India.

The General insurance business in India, on the other hand, can trace its roots to the Triton Insurance Company Ltd., the first general insurance company established in the year 1850 in Calcutta by the British. Some of the important milestones in the general insurance business in India are :

1907 : The Indian Mercantile Insurance Ltd. set up, the first company to transact all classes of general insurance business.

1957 : General Insurance Council, a wing of the Insurance Association of India, frames a code of conduct for ensuring fair conduct and sound business practices.

1968 : The Insurance Act amended to regulate investments and set minimum solvency margins and the Tariff Advisory Committee set up.

1972 : The General Insurance Business (Nationalisation) Act, 1972 nationalised the general insurance business in India with effect from 1st January 1973. 107 insurers amalgamated and grouped into four companies *viz.*, the National Insurance Company Ltd., the New India Assurance Company Ltd., the Oriental Insurance Company Ltd. and the United India Insurance Company Ltd. GIC incorporated as a company.

1.1 INSURANCE SECTOR REFORMS

In 1993, Malhotra Committee, headed by former Finance Secretary and RBI Governor, R.N. Malhotra was formed to evaluate the Indian Insurance Industry and recommend its future direction. The committee was set up with an objective of complementing the reforms in the Indian Financial sector. The reforms were aimed at "creating a more efficient and competitive financial system suitable for the requirements of the economy keeping in mind the structural changes currently underway and recognising that insurance is an important part of the overall financial system where it was necessary to address the need for similar reforms."

Malhotra Committee–Purpose and Recommendations

Purpose

(*a*) To suggest the structure of the insurance industry, to assess its strengths and weaknesses of insurance companies in terms of the objectives of creating an efficient and viable insurance industry, which will have a wide reach of insurance services, a variety of insurance products with a high quality of services to the public and servicing as an effective instrument for mobilization of financial resources for development.

(*b*) To make recommendations for changing structure of insurance industry, for changing general policy frame work etc.

(*c*) To take specific suggestions regarding LIC and GIC with a view to improve functioning of LIC and GIC.

(*d*) To make recommendations on regulation and supervision of the insurance sector in India.

(*e*) To make recommendations on role and functioning of surveyors, intermediaries like agents etc. in the insurance sector.

(*f*) To make recommendations on any other matter which are relevant for development of the insurance industry in India.

Recommendations

In 1994, the committee submitted the report and gave the following recommendations now in the point form :

Structure

- Government stake in the insurance Companies to be brought down to 50%.
- Government should take over the holdings of GIC and its subsidiaries so that these subsidiaries can act as independent corporations.
- All the insurance companies should be given greater freedom to operate.

Competition

- Private Companies with a minimum paid up capital of Rs. 1 billion should be allowed to enter the industry.
- No Company should deal in both Life and General Insurance through a single entity.
- Foreign companies may be allowed to enter the industry in collaboration with the domestic companies.
- Postal Life Insurance should be allowed to operate in the rural market.
- Only one State Level Life Insurance Company should be allowed to operate in each state.
- The Insurance Act should be changed.
- An Insurance Regulatory body should be set up.
- Controller of Insurance (Currently a part from the Finance Ministry) should be made independent.

Investments

- Mandatory Investments of LIC Life Fund in government securities to be reduced from 75% to 50%.
- GIC and its subsidiaries are not to hold more than 5% in any company (There current holdings to be brought down to this level over a period of time).

Customer Service

- LIC should pay interest on delays in payments beyond 30 days.
- Insurance companies must be encouraged to set up unit linked pension plans.
- Computerization of operations and updating of technology to be carried out in the insurance industry.

Overall, the committee strongly felt that in order to improve the customer services and increase the coverage of the insurance industry should be opened up to competition. But at the same time, the committee felt the need to exercise caution as any failure on the part of new players could ruin the public confidence in the industry.

Insurance on the risks of transportation of goods is one of the oldest and most vital forms of insurance. The value of goods shipped by business firms each year cost millions of rupees. These goods are exposed to damage or loss from numerous transportation perils. The goods can be protected by ocean marine and inland marine contracts. Ocean marine insurance provides protection for goods transported over water. All types of ocean going vessels and their cargo can be insured by ocean marine contracts, the legal liability of ship owners and cargo owners can also be insured. Inland marine insurance provides protection for goods shipped on land. It includes insurance on imports and exports, domestic shipments, and means of transportation such as bridges and tunnels. In addition, inland marine insurance can be used to insure fine art, jewellery, fur and other properties.

1.2 LEGAL FRAMEWORK OF INSURANCE BUSINESS

Insurance is made available to the public through the medium of contracts that detail the rights and duties of the parties to the insurance agreement. These contracts may range from implied or oral agreements, as in the binders given by fire and casualty insurance agents, to formal written contracts issued by companies.

Most of the insurance contracts are expressed in writing even when an oral binder initiates the transaction.

Insurance contracts are complicated because of the technical nature of the subject matter, the statutory requirement that certain language be employed, and the need to avoid terms that may be construed as ambiguous. However, the need for legal clarity may lead to a contract that is beyond the comprehension of the typical insurance consumer. Furthermore, the technical nature of many contracts often distracts from the mutual understanding of its terms by the parties to the contract.

Insurance contract can broadly be classified into two categories (a) life and (b) non-life insurance. The subject matter of life insurance is life of the assured. In a life policy the life is covered for a certain amount which is payable on the maturity of the policy or on the death of policyholder which is earlier. The amount is payable on death to the nominee/legal heir of the deceased.

Non-life insurance can again be categorised according to the uncertainties and events covered by the respective policies. Some examples of non-life insurance policies are householders insurance and fire insurance. Personal accident insurance is linked to human life hence would not strictly fall in the category of non-life insurance though the characteristic of uncertainty which attracts to non life insurance is manifested even in personal accident and medical insurance policies respectively.

The primary law governing contracts of insurance is the Indian Contract Act, 1872. However, there many issues not covered by the said Act. This may relate to torts, consumer rights, transfer of property, agency issues etc.

Torts and Crimes

Torts

A tort is a private wrong. It occurs whenever someone acts or fails to act in such a manner that an individual's peace of mind or right are jeopardized. It refers to any individual's action that effectively deprives another of his right to security of person, reputation, or property. Technically, each tort is defined in terms of specific statutory or common law requirements, and these vary substantially in different jurisdictions. Negligence, assault, battery, libel, slander, trespass, fraud, and false imprisonment are examples of torts. Torts differ from crimes in that the latter are public wrongs. A crime is any act that the legislature determines to be punishable by law. The same act may include all of the elements of a particular tort and a particular crime, in which case there exists a public remedy in the form of punishment prescribed by law and a private remedy that is often in the form of monetary damages.

Torts are important in insurance because they are a major source of loss covered by liability insurance. The automobile insurance policy is essential because it provides for payment of judgments awarded by the courts in negligence cases as well as the costs of litigation or claims settlement. The comprehensive personal liability insurance policy covers losses arising from negligent conduct unrelated to the care, custody, or control of the automobile or to business pursuits. The comprehensive general liability insurance policy covers losses occurring as a direct result of negligence in many business situations.

Crimes

Some crimes that are recognized by statute are specific to insurance, while others are relevant to insurance law because they are crimes committed to obtain funds illegally from insurance companies. A few example of crimes are:

(*a*) *Rebating* : passing of commission/incentives by agents to prospective insureds to purchase on insurance policy.

(*b*) *Twisting* : inducing an individual to terminate are life insurance policy in order to buy another to the disadvantage of the insured.

(*c*) *Filing of false claims* : attempt to collect money from an insurance company when there is no loss or the padding or inflation of claims by procuring excessive and fraudulent estimates of damages.

(*d*) *Unlicensed insurance activity* : Unlicensed person engaging in any insurance transaction that requires licensing (guilty of a misdemeanor).

(*e*) *Defamation* : publication of material that might tend to lessen public confidence in the institution of insurance.

(*f*) *Asson* : felonious burning of property of another to defraud an insurance company.

(*g*) *Homicide* : when the beneficiary of a life insurance policy swindles the insured for the purpose of obtaining the proceeds of the policy or otherwise.

(*h*) *Breach of trust* : agents using or mingling the client's insurance premiums with their own funds.

(*i*) *Unfair discrimination* : charging of different rates by a single insurance company to similar risk class.

(*j*) *Conspiracy* : dishonest agent conspires with his client to defraud the insurance company by misrepresentation, by filing false claims or falsifying documents.

Indian Contract Act, 1872

Insurance contracts are agreements between insurance companies and insured for the purpose of transferring from insured to the insurer a part of the risk of loss arising out of contingent event. Therefore all the provisions of Indian Contract Act, 1872, in general are applicable to insurance contracts. Under Section 10 of the Indian Contract Act, following conditions are necessary to form a valid contract:

(*a*) Agreement between two parties

(*b*) Lawful object

(*c*) Capacity to contract

(*d*) Consideration

(*e*) Possibility of performance etc.

Offer and Acceptance

The offer for entering into insurance contract generally come from the insured (proposer). The insurance company may also propose to make the contract. In order to constitute a valid acceptance, offer and its acceptance must fulfil the requirements as prescribed by the Indian Contract Act, 1872. Whether the offer is made by the insurer or insured, the moot point is acceptance.

Any act that precedes it is an offer or a counter-offer. All that precede the offer or counter-offer is an invitation to offer. In insurance, the publication of prospectus, the canvassing of the agents are invitations to offer. When the proposer proposes to enter the contract it is an offer and if there is any alteration in the offer that would be a counter-offer. If this alteration or change (counter-offer) is accepted by the proposer, it would be an acceptance. In absence of counter-offer, the acceptance of offer will be an acceptance by the insurer. At the moment, the notice of acceptance is given to other party, it would be a valid acceptance.

On acceptance of the proposal by the insurer, a valid and binding contract comes into existence. If the insurer indicates a higher premium than the normal as per proposal or conditions of acceptance are different from the standards ones, such indication tantamounts to a counter-offer which the proposer may or may not accept. It is necessary that in order to make a binding contract of insurance, the parties must agree upon every material term affecting the agreement.

In case of Life insurance a valid and binding contract comes into existence upon payment of first premium. When a proposal form duly filled in by the proposer is accepted by the insurer, the acceptance communicated to the proposer is in reality a counter-offer indicating that the proposal will be accepted on payment of the premium and communication of the assent of the proposer to special terms, if any. Unless the proposer assents to or complies with the terms of insurer no contract would come into existence.

Every contract of insurance must be in writing and must comply with the provisions of the Indian Stamp Act. An oral or informal contract gives the insured a right to call for a stamped policy, even after the loss insured against has occurred in view of the Indian Stamp Act, 1899.

An issuance of a policy may some time takes time after acceptance of risk in view of underwriting and administrative procedures. The issuers may issue a cover note for a stipulated period which is also a valid evidence of contract.

Legal Object

For a valid contract, the object of the agreement should be lawful and must not be prohibited by any law. Any subject matter of contract that is (*i*) not forbidden by law, or (*ii*) is not immoral, or (*iii*) opposed to public policy, or (*iv*) which does not defeat the provisions of any law, is lawful. The subject matter of insurance in the proposal form and also the consideration should be legal. If there is any contract to defraud the insurer rather than based on round principles of indemnity, the contract is void.

Mistake and Misrepresentation

A contract of insurance is a contract uberrimae fidei, *i.e.*, is based on the principle of utmost good faith. If utmost good faith is not observed by either party insurer or insured the contract may be avoided by the other.

Capacity to Contract

The rules laid down under the Indian Contract Act, 1872, defining the contractual capacity of the parties apply generally to insurance contracts in the same manner as they apply to other types of contracts.

Every person is competent to contract (*a*) who is of the age of majority according to the law, (*b*) who is of sound mind, and (*c*) who is not disqualified from contracting by any law to which he is subject.

The capacity of an insurer to enter into contracts of insurance depends upon its constitution.

A minor is, therefore, incompetent to contract, and a contract with a minor is a nullity; but under certain circumstances, an insurer may issue a policy on the life of a minor. Under the system of deferred assurance policies, the insurance contract is with a parent or legal guardian, who is competent to contract.

Consideration

For insurance contracts, consideration is in the form of premium to be paid by the insured and a promise to pay, compensate or indemnify in accordance with the terms and conditions incorporated in the policy, on the part of the insurer. A premium is the price for the risk undertaken by the insurers. It is the consideration receivable by the insurers from the insured in exchange for their undertaking to pay the sum insured in case the event insured against takes place.

Amount of premium is not the criteria, but a contract without payment of premium is void.

Free Consent

Parties entering into the contract should enter into the contract by their free and genuine consent. The consent shall be free with it is not caused by : (1) coercion, (2) undue influence, (3) fraud, or (4) misrepresentation, or (5) mistake. When there is no free consent except fraud the contract becomes voidable at the option of the party whose consent was so obtained. In case of fraud, the contract would be void. The proposal for free consent, must sign a declaration to this effect, the person explaining the subject-matter of the proposal to the proposer must also accordingly make a written declaration on the proposal.

The proposer must full disclose all material information and sign a declaration in the proposal. Also, the insurer must full disclose the product details to the proposer.

Examples of Material Circumstances in Marine Insurance

1. Concealing the nationality of the insured when such nationality is of importance [*Associated Oil Carriers Ltd. v. Union Ins. Society of Canton* (1917) 2 K.B. 184].
2. The fact that the ship had developed a leak before the insurance was effected [*Russel v. Thorton* 1859 20 L.R. Ex. 9].
3. The fact that the goods carried on the ship are grossly over-valued when the ship is insured. [*Ionidies* v. *Pender* (1874) L.R. 7. Q.B. 531].

Discharge of Contract

A contract terminates in the following situations :

1. **Performance :** *When all the terms of the contract* in terms of performance have been carried out. Payment of premium and payment of claim by respective parties.

2. **Release :** *When one party to the contract* agrees to excuse performance by the other party after breach of the contract by the latters. Denial of a claim by insured on account of fraud.
3. **Discharge :** (*a*) ***Discharge by implied consent or impossibility of performance:*** *The law does not compel a man to do the impossible thing. Contract* is discharged when performance becomes impossible :
   (*i*) Due to destruction of the subject-matter;
   (*ii*) Due to death or incapacity of the promisor in a contract for personal services;
   (*iii*) Due to subsequent change of legislation;
   (*iv*) Due to non-existence or cessation of a state of affairs, the existence or continuance of which formed the basis of the contract; and
   (*v*) Due to such an alternation of circumstances as to bring about complete frustration of the commercial object.

   (*b*)***Discharge by tender :*** *Where on party is ready and willing to perform his promise and has offered to do so at the right time and place, but the other party does not accept performance, the contract* is discharged by tender or 'attempted performance'.
4. **Void Contracts :** *When an agreement is discovered to be void.*
5. **Breach of Contract :** *When a contract has been broken.* Where the insured has committed such a breach the insurer can terminate the contract of insurance.
6. **Novation :** *If the parties to a contract* for it or rescind or later it, the original contract need not be performed.

Agency

The law relating to agency is part of the Indian Contract Act. An agent is defined as "a person employed to do any act for another, or to represent in dealings with third persons."

The person for whom such an act is done or who is so represented is called the Principal. Section 226 of the Contract Act states that "Contracts entered into through an agent, an obligation arising from acts done by an agent, may be enforced in the same manner, and will have the same legal consequences as if the contracts has been entered into and the acts done by the principal in person". A contract of agency may be made in writing or verbally. When it is in writing, it is in the form of power of attorney. Following provision]s are worthnoting :

- An agent cannot lawfully employ another to perform acts, which he has expressly or implied undertaken to perform personally, unless by ordinary custom of trade or from the nature of the agency, a sub-agent must be employed. This involves the general maxim of law that a delegatee cannot

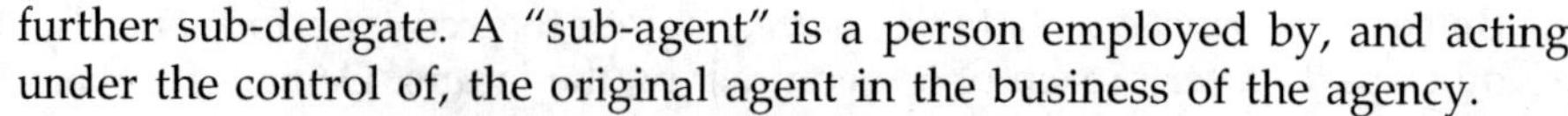

further sub-delegate. A "sub-agent" is a person employed by, and acting under the control of, the original agent in the business of the agency.

- Where a sub agent is properly appointed, the principal is, represented by the sub-agent and is bound by and responsible for his acts as if he were an agent originally appointed by the principal.
- The agent is responsible to the principal for the acts of the sub-agent.
- The sub-agent is responsible for his acts to the agent, but not to the principal, except in cases of fraud of wilful wrong.
- If an agent does something on behalf of the principal but without his knowledge or authority, the principal may elect to ratify the action or to disown it. A principal ratifying any unauthorized act done on his behalf ratifies the whole of the transaction of which such act formed part.

In an agent deals on his own account in the business of the agency, without first obtaining the consent of his principal and acquainting him with all material circumstances which have come on his own knowledge on the subject, the principal may repudiate the transaction, if the case shows either that any material fact has been dishonestly concealed from him by the agent or that the dealings of the agent have been disadvantageous to him.

If an agent does a criminal act, the principal is not liable to the agent, either upon an express or an implied promise, to indemnify him against the consequence of that act.

Where an agent does more than he is authorized to do, and what he does beyond the scope of his authority cannot be separated from what is within it, the principal is not bound to recognise the transaction.

In the absence of any contract to that effect, an agent cannot personally enforce contracts entered into by him on behalf of his principal nor is he personally bound by them.

Termination of Agency : An agency is terminated by the principal revoking his authority; or by the agent renouncing the business of the agency; or by the business of the agency being completed; or on the death of either the principal or the agent.

Agent's Duty : An agent is bound to conduct the business of his principal according to the directions given by the principal, or in the absence of any such directions, according to the custom which prevails in doing business of the same kind at the place where the agent conducts such business. When the agent acts otherwise and any loss is caused, he must make it good to his principal, and if any profit accrues, he must account for it.

Misrepresentations made or frauds committed by agents acting in the course of their business for their principals have the same effect on agreement made by such agents as if such misrepresentations or frauds has been made or committed by the principals; but misrepresentations made or frauds committed by agents in matters which do not fall within their authority, do not affect their principals.

1.3 LAWS CONCERNING INSURANCE

Insurance Act, 1938

Insurance Act, 1938 is the primary law that governs the insurance business in India. It provides for the registration and licensing of insurers, payment of premiums, alteration and other policy matters, powers of governments, accounts, audit and other reporting requirements, mode of deposits and investments, constitution of claim settlement authorities.

Insurance Regulatory and Development Authority Act, 1999

The Insurance Regulatory and Development Authority Act, 1999 provides for the establishment of an Authority to protect the interests of holders of insurance policies, to regulate, promote and ensure orderly growth of the insurance industry and for matters connected therewith or incidental thereto and further to amend the Insurance Act, 1938, the Life Insurance Corporation Act, 1956 and the General Insurance Business (Nationalisation) Act, 1972.

Life Insurance Corporation Act, 1956

Life Insurance Corporation Act, 1956 and the regulations made thereunder deals with the formation of Life Insurance Corporation–its functions, powers, capital, transfer of business, conduct of business and other related matters.

General Insurance Business (Nationalisation) Act, 1972

It deals with the formation of GIC and amalgamation of insurers existing prior to the promulation of the Act. It describes the powers and functions of GIC, powers of Central Government and other related issues.

Motor Vehicles Act, 1988

Motor Vehicles Act, 1988 provides for compulsory insurance of motor vehicles. The Act provides that no motor vehicle can be used in a public place unless there is in force in relation to vehicle a policy issued by an authorised insurer. This policy covers the insured person's liability in the event of death, bodily injury of certain persons or damage to property of third persons.

The Inland Steam Vessels Act, 1917 and the Amended Act, 1977

The Act provides that the provisions of chapter VII of the Motors Vehicles Act, 1955 regarding insurance of mechanically propell vessels against third party risks are applicable to steam vessels. The Act maker it compulsory for the owners of operators of inland vessels to insure against legal liability of death, bodily injury or damage caused to the property of third persons and passengers.

Marine Insurance Act, 1963

Marine Insurance Act, 1963 (based on Marine Insurance Act 1906) codifies the law relating the conduct of marine insurance business in India. The provisions of the Act *inter-alia* includes provisions relating to basic insurance principles (Indemnification, insurable interest, utmost goodfaith, subrogation and contribution, valuation, losses, warranties, return of premiums etc.

The Carriage of Goods by Sea Act, 1925

The Act defines the minimum rights, liabilities and immunities of a shipowner on loss or damage to cargo. The act deals with three aspects of a shipowners liabilities towards cargo owner:

(*i*) the circumstances when the shipowner is deemed to be liable for loss or damage to cargo unless he proves otherwise;

(*ii*) the circumstance when the shipowner is exempted from liability, *i.e.*, when loss or damage is caused by events outside his control, *e.g.*, perils of the seas;

(*iii*) the limits of liability of a shipowner for loss of or damage to cargo calculated in monetary terms per package or unit of cargo.

The Merchant Shipping Act, 1958

This Act also provides a certain protection to shipowners. For example, the liability of a shipowner can be limited to certain maximum sum for certain losses, provided the incident giving rise to such claim has arisen without the actual fault or privy of the shipowner.

These claims may relate to loss of life, personal injury or loss of or damage to property on land or water. The Act also confers the obligation on the shipowner to send his ship to sea in a seaworthy and safe condition.

The Bill of Lading Act, 1855

This Act defines the character of the Bill of Lading as an evidence of the contract of carriage of goods between the shipowner and the shipper, as an acknowledgement of the receipt of the goods on board the vessel and, as a document of title. The bill of lading is one of the various documents required in connection with settlement of marine cargo claims.

The Indian Ports (Major Ports) Act, 1963

This Act defines the liability of Port Trust Authorities for loss of or damage to goods whilst in their custody and prescribes time limits for filing monetary claim on, or suit against, the Port Trust Authorities.

The Indian Railways Act, 1890

The Indian Railways Act, passed in 1890 was amended in 1961 and the amendment came into force from 1st January, 1962. The Act deals with various aspects of Railway Administration. However, Chapter VII is relevant to Marine Insurance practice as it deals with the responsibility of Railway Administration as carriers. This Chapter makes provision, *inter alia*, for the following:

(*a*) rights and liabilities of railways as carriers of goods:

(*b*) procedure for notification of claims for compensation for losses.

The Railways Claims Tribunal Act, 1987 provides for formation of tribunals to deal with claims for cargo loss, personal injuries, excess freight, etc. and prescribes procedures thereunder.

The Carriers Act, 1865

The Act defines the rights and liabilities of truck owners or operators who carry goods for public hire in respect of loss or damage to goods carried by them.

The Act also prescribes the time limit within which notice of loss or damage must be filed with the road carriers.

The Indian Post Office Act, 1898

This Act defines the liability of the Government for loss, misdelivery, delay of or damage to any postal articles in course of transmission by post.

The Carriage by Air Act, 1972

This Act gives effect to the provisions of the Warsaw Convention, 1929 and the Hague Protocol, 1955 relating to international carriage of passengers and goods by air.

The Act defines the liability of the air carrier for death of or injury to passengers and loss of or damage to registered luggage and cargo.

The Act also prescribes the maximum limits of liability for death, injury, damage etc. and also prescribes the time limits within which claims have to be filed on the air carrier.

The provisions of the Act also apply with some changes, to domestic carriage, that is, carriage within India.

Multi Modal Transportation Act, 1993

The Act provides for registration of multi-modal transport operators engaged in transportation of goods under more than one mode of transport, i.e., by rail/road and sea. The Act prescribes limits of liability of the operator, contents of documents to be issued by them, notice of loss, etc.

Workmen's Compensation Act, 1923

The Act provides for the payment by employers to their workmen of compensation for injury by accident, arising out of and in the course of employment. The object of this legislation has been stated as follows:

The growing complexity of industry in this country, with the increasing use of machinery and consequent danger to workmen, along with the comparative poverty of the workmen themselves render it advisable that they should be protected as far as possible, from hardship out of accidents.

It provides certain benefits to employees in case of accidents during employment, sickness, maternity etc.

Employees State Insurance Act, 1948

The Employees' State Insurance Act, 1948, has been described as an Act "to provide for certain benefits to employees in cases of sickness, maternity and employment injury and to make provision for certain other matters in relation thereof "Under the Act, the Employees' State Insurance Corporation has been set up to administer the Insurance Scheme.

The Scheme is applicable to industrial employees as defined in the Act. The Act operated in certain industrial areas as notified by the Government from time to time. It is intended that the Act will be eventually extended to all industrial areas in the country. Under the scheme a fund is maintained consisting of contributions from the employees, employers and the Government. From this fund the following expenses are met:

(*i*) Sickness benefit, maternity benefit, disablement benefit, dependants' benefit (death) and medical treatment

(*ii*) Establishment and maintenance of hospital, dispensaries, etc. for the benefit of the insured persons and their families.

(*iii*) Administration of the Scheme.

The Indian Stamp Act, 1899

The Indian Stamp Act requires that a policy of insurance be stamped in accordance with the schedule of rate prescribed.

The Consumer Protection Act, 1986

The Act applies to all goods and services unless specifically exempted by Central Government. The provisions of the Act are compensatory in nature.

It enshrines the following rights of the consumers:

(*i*) The right to be protected against the marketing of goods which are hazardous of life and property;

(*ii*) The right to be informed about the quality, quantity, potency, purity, standard and price of goods so as to protect the consumer against unfair trade practices;

(*iii*) The right to be heard and to be assured that consumers interest will receive due consideration at appropriate forum;

(*iv*) The right to seek redressal against unfair trade practices or unscrupulous exploitation of consumers;

(*v*) The right to consumer education.

Under Section 2(e) of the Act, the insurance is recognised as services. Chapter 32 of the Act elaborates various consumer rights.

Arbitration and Conciliation Act, 1996

Arbitration means the reference of a matter in dispute to the judgment of a person selected by the parties to the dispute. Arbitration thus is a private process of resolution of disputes and it is commonly resorted to because it is less formal, less expensive and less time consuming than proceedings in a court of law.

An arbitration condition is incorporated in a majority of "Non-marine general insurance policies."

The main objectives of the Act, *inter alia*, are:

(*i*) To comprehensively cover international and commercial arbitration and conciliation as also domestic arbitration and conciliation;

(*ii*) To make provision for an arbitral procedure which is fair, efficient and capable of meeting the needs of the specific arbitration;

(*iii*) To provide that the arbitral tribunal gives reasons for its arbitral award;

(*iv*) To minimise the supervisory role of courts in the arbitral process;

(*v*) To permit an arbitral tribunal to use mediation, conciliation or other procedures during the arbitral proceedings to encourage settlement of disputes;

(*vi*) To provide that every final arbitral award is enforced in the same manner as if it were a decree of the court.

1.4 INSURANCE CONTRACTS – IMPORTANT FEATURES

The principle functions of an insurance contract are :

(1) to define the risk that is to be transferred

(2) to state the conditions under which the contract applies and

(3) to explain the procedure for settling losses.

Nature of Contract

An insurance contract as four attributes:

(*a*) *Entirety* : all the terms and conditions are to be found in the policy document. If the terms and conditions are oral or not stated explicitly they are difficult for parties to prove.

(*b*) *Personal* : the contact follows the person, the insured, rather than property.

(*c*) *Unilateral* : After the insured pays the premiums the performance is obligatory on one party, i.e. the insurer.

(*d*) *Aleatory* : performance is conditioned upon an event that may or may not happen

1.4.1 Elements of Insurance Contract

The four basic elements to every insurance contract are:

(*a*) **Application :** An application is required for every contract of insurance. In the application, which is an offer to enter into a contract, the prospective insured sets forth the facts and figures required by the insurance carrier's underwriting department. The application may be brief and oral, or of any length and in written form. In life insurance, the application itself becomes a part of the contract.

(*b*) **Binders :** A binder is a memorandum specifying some of the details of the property or liability policy to be issued by the company. It is memorandum of insurance issued pending delivery of the formal policy. The binder may be oral or written and may be given either by an agent or a company. A broker, not being an agent of an insurance company, cannot issue binders. The binder is usually a temporary document and ordinarily would remain in force no more than ten days. For example, in automobile insurance a car buyer wants immediate coverage. By binding the insurance company to the risk, the agent need not wait for the insurance to become effective.

Binders are not used in life insurance. Given the long term nature of the contract and the insurer's inability to cancel a life insurance policy, the life insurer requires an opportunity to examine the application (and possible the applicant) before being bound to a lifetime contract. However, in place of binders the life insurance agent can provide the applicant with a receipt (assuming the first premium installment is paid) that will provide varying insurance benefits depending on the nature of the receipt.

(*c*) **Policy Forms :** are formal written contract of insurance that sets forth all of the terms of the agreement. The policy had two parts:

(*i*) *Heading :* It is the declaration page and identifies the risk by specifying the name of the issued, the address location of the risk, period covered by the policy, description of the subject being insured, the amount of insurance the amount of the premium, and any warranties of representations made by the insured.

(*ii*) *Body :* It is the contract itself containing the various clauses pertaining to agreements exclusion and condition.

(*iii*) *Back :* It specifies the rights of the insured and the duties of the insurer. The condition, and stipulations define the rights and duties of the parties aside from injury agreement.

Standardization of policy forms is an ongoing process, and most insurance contracts have uniform language for the greater part of their terms. Such standardisation makes possible economies of operation, statistical uniformity, and better communication between the insured, his agent, and the insurance company. Where language has been standardised, determination of the meaning of the words and phrases by the courts reduces the chance a misunderstanding.

(iv) *Endorsement :* An endorsement is a form that is used to modify the policy contract Endorsements may extend or restrict coverage, permit transfers of interest in property, transfer coverage, transfer coverage from one place to another, increases or decreases limits of coverage, provide for assignment of policies or changes in beneficiary designations, provide for changes in settlement options elected, or in any other legal manner permit amendments to the contract.

Endorsement are usually done by party forms or by embossing through rubber stamps of the desired alteration.

1.4.2 Maxims Applicable to Insurance Contracts

The following maxims are elemental to insurance contracts and their interpretation:

(*a*) *Uberrimac fiddi :* Utmost good faith

(*b*) *Spes successions :* hope of succession — direct and not hope of insurable interest

(*c*) *Cause proxima :* the proximate and immediate cause of loss is important

(*d*) *Pari Delicto :* parties to be equally blamed — in case of illegal policies, the premium cannot be recovered/returned.

(*e*) Salus Populist supermen by the regard for pubic interest and welfare is the highest in law

(*f*) *Rao ipsa loquitor :* the thing speaks for itself for example in case of accidents, the circumstances of the case and not more occurrence of the events has to be seen.

Key Terms

- Contract
- Indemnity
- Subrogation
- Exempted Insurers
- Crime
- Binders
- Cause Proxima

References

★ Anoop K. Kaushal and S.K. Mohanty, *Insurance Law Manual*, Universal Law Publishing Co. Pvt. Ltd. 2002.

★ Kenneth S. Abraham, *Distributing Risk — Insurance, Legal Theory and Public Policy*, Yate University Press, 1986.

★ J.E. Grieder and W.T. Breadles, *Law and the Life Insurance Contract*, Richard D. Irwin, 1968.

★ *Practice of General Insurance*, Insurance Institute of India, Mumbai, 1999.

★ *www.irdaindia.org*

★ *www.bimaonline.com*

★ *www.indiacore.com*

★ *www.insuranceinstituteindia.com*

Questions for Review

1. Briefly summarise the various legal provisions applicable to insurance business in India.
2. Write short notes on:
   (*a*) Licensing of insurance companies
   (*b*) Elements of insurance contracts
   (*c*) Maxims applicable to insurance contracts.
3. "Insurance business is partially regulated in India." Do you agree? Give reasons for your answer.

C H A P T E R

Insurance Act, 1938

Insurance Act, 1938 and Insurance Rule, 1939 primarily govern the conduct of insurance business in India. As per the preamble of the Act, Insurance Act, 1938 is an act to consolidate and amend the law relating to the business of insurance. Most of the provisions of the Act are applicable to all classes of insurance business.

2.1 DEFINITIONS

(*i*) Life insurance business is defined in the Section 2(11) and includes the contracts of insurance upon human life, which include the granting of disability, allowances, accident benefits, annuities and superannuation allowances. This business may be linked or non-linked business or both.

(*ii*) General insurance business is defined under Section 2(6-B) that includes the marine fire and miscellaneous insurance business whether carried on singly or in combination with one or more of them, *i.e.*, may be linked insurance business.

(*iii*) Marine insurance business includes the business effecting the contract of insurance upon vessels of any description, including the cargo of freights and other interests. (Section 2.13A)

(*iv*) Fire insurance is the insurance, which includes the risks insured against the fire and incidental to fire. (Section 2(6A))

(*v*) Miscellaneous insurance includes the business of effecting contracts of insurance, which are not principally, or wholly of the kind or kinds included above. (Section 2.13B)

The insurer, as defined by Section 2(9) as amended by the IRDA Act, 1999 means and includes

- An individual
- Body of individuals unincorporated
- Body corporate but not incorporated under the law of country
- Anybody corporate (not being a person specified above) standing as subsidiary company within the meaning of Indian Companies Act, 1956
- Any person who has standing contract with the underwriter who is a member of the society of Lloyds and authorized to issue cover notes and other documents to others on their behalf in conducting the insurance business,

provided they carryon business of insurance in India, or their principal place of business is domiciled in India, or established with the object of obtaining insurance business, employs a representative or maintains a place of business in India.

2.2 PROHIBITION ON CONDUCT OF INSURANCE BUSINESS

Section 2c of the Act prohibits persons to carry on insurance business until he is:

(*a*) A public company.

(*b*) A registered society under.

(*c*) A body corporate incorporated under the law of any country outside India not being in the nature of a private company. However, the central government is empowered to exempt any insurer or any person for the purpose of carrying on the business of granting superannuation allowances and annuities as per Section 211(c) or for the purpose of carrying general insurance business. Exempted insurer after the promulgation of IRDA Act, 1999 only Indian Insurance company can carry insurance business.

2.3 LICENCING

Section 3 of the Act, as ammended by IRDA Act, 1999 read together with Section 3A and 3B deals with the registration, sanctioning of license and its renewal and issuance of certificate of soundness for life insurers.

Licensing Conditions

Only Indian Insurance companies to be granted licenses : Under the Act, it is mandatory that only an Indian insurance company can carry on an insurance business in India. An Indian insurance company is a company registered under the Companies Act 1956 where the aggregate foreign equity shareholding does not exceed 26 per cent and whose sole purpose is to carry on a life, general or reinsurance business.

Two-stage Licensing Process

Stage 1 – Requisition for Registration

An application has to be made to the Authority with all the prescribed disclosure norms. Some of the important items cover :

1. Promoter's background, financial strength, share-holders' agreement and reasons for entering the sector.
2. Director's background.
3. Capital structure, initial and future.

4. Financial projections for 5 years.
5. Scenario Building and Sensitivity analyses.
6. Rural and social sector strategy.

There is no provision for appeal in the event of a second rejection. A revised application is permissible by the applicant company only after 2 years with an additional condition that this will be with a new set of promoters or for a different class of insurance business.

Stage 2 – Application for Registration

After the requisition is granted by the Authority, the applicant is required to make an application for registration. Information to be disclosed includes :

- Proof of paid-up capital of Rs. 100 crore.
- Proof of deposit.
- Marketing and distribution information. This should include information on Market Research. Product information, Distribution Strategy and Details, Sales promotion, Customer service.
- *Operations :* Information should cover underwriting, information technology, Internal controls, Personnel.
- *Investment :* Information on investment Philosophy, Strategy and ground level arrangements.
- *Reinsurance :* Information on Approach and Terms.
- *Expenditure :* This should include a description of the manner in which the expenses of administration have been estimated. These expenses will have to be distinguished between first year and renewal, fixed and variable. The proposed expenses as a percent of premium at levels of operational offices, supervisory offices and head office.

Licensing Criteria

Some of the important parameters include :

- Promoter and directors' background
- Promoter financial strength
- Volume of business and earning prospects
- Rural and social sector focus
- Product profit
- Capital structure
- Actuarial and professional expertise

- Infrastructure
- Public interest

Other Licensing Issues

An appeal can be made to the Central Government against the decision of Authority, which shall be final. The applicant company can submit a new application only after two years with the additional condition that it has to be with a new set of promoters or for a different class of insurance business. The Authority will grant more licenses to applicants for life and health insurance than general insurance. Licenses expire on the 31st day of March each year and have to be renewed each year.

Capital Requirement and Foreign Stake

Section 6 of the Act requires that minimum paid-up equity capital required for a life insurance is Rs. 100 crore and for a reinsurer Rs. 200 crore. The capital contributed can only be in the form of equity shares as preference shares cannot be issued. The incumbent, LIC, would be required to increase its equity share capital from the existing Rs. 5 crore to Rs. 100 crore within a period of six months from the date of commencement of the IRDA Act. Also, the four GIC subsidiaries would have to increase the equity share capital to Rs. 100 crore from Rs. 40 crore are resent. The GIC will not be required to bring in additional capital since its present capital base is Rs. 215 crore.

The certificate of registration of insurance business is for a period of one year only. The certificate is renewal every year. The insurance company has to apply for renewal of license by paying the requisite fee of Rs. 50,000 and along with one percent of total gross premium written directly by insurer in India during the last financial year. This application for renewal has to be made in the month of December every year.

2.4 POLICIES – PREMIUMS, CLAIMS AND RELATED ISSUES

Advance Payment of Premium

No insurer shall assume any risk unless and until the premium is received in advance or is guaranteed to be paid or a deposit is made in advance in the prescribed manner. This rule of advance payment of premium may be relaxed in circumstances specified in the rules framed under the Act.

Section 38 of Insurance Act, 1938 explains the procedure by which the insurance policy can be transferred to the transferee, and insurer being the transferee.

Assignment and Transfer of Insurance Policies

Section 38 : (1) A transfer or assignment of a policy of life insurance, whether with or without consideration, may be made only by an endorsement upon the policy itself or by a separate instrument, signed in either case by the transferor or by the assignor or his duly authorised agent and attested by at least one witness, specifically setting forth the fact of transfer or assignment.

(2) The transfer or assignment shall be complete and effectual upon the execution of such endorsement or instrument duly attested but except where the transfer or assignment is in favour of the insurer shall not be operative as against an Insurer and shall not confer upon the transferee or assignee, or his legal representative, any right to sue for the amount of such policy or the moneys secured thereby until a notice in writing of the transfer or assignment if and either the said endorsement or instrument itself or a copy thereof certified to be correct by both transferor and transferee or their duly authorised agents have been delivered to the insurer:

Provided that where the insurer maintains one or more places of business in India, such notice shall be delivered only at the place in India mentioned in the policy for the purpose or at his principal place of business in India.

(3) The date on which the notice referred to in sub section (2) is delivered to the insurer shall regulate the priority of all claims under a transfer or assignment as between persons interested in the policy: and where there is more then one instrument of transfer or assignment, the priority of the claims under such instruments shall be governed by the order in which the notices referred to in sub section (2) are delivered.

(4) Upon the receipt of the notice referred to in sub section (2), the insurer shall record the fact of such transfer or assignment together with the date thereof and the name of the transferee or the assignee and shall, on the request of the person by whom the notice was given, or of the transferee or assignee, on payment of a fee not exceeding one rupee, grant a written acknowledgment of the receipt of such notice; and any such acknowledgment shall be conclusive evidence against the insurer that he has duly received the notice to which such acknowledgment relates.

(5) Subject to the terms and conditions of the transfer or assignment, the insurer shall, from the date of the receipt of the notice referred to in subsection (2), recognise the transferee or assignee named in the notice as the only person entitled to benefit under the policy, and such person shall subject to all liabilities and equities to which the transferor or assignor was subject at the date of the transfer or assignment and may institute any proceedings in relation to the policy without obtaining the consent of the transferor or assignor or making him a party to such proceedings.

(6) Any rights and remedies of an assignee or transferee of a policy of life insurance under an assignment or transfer affected prior to the commencement of this Act shall not be affected by the provisions of this section.

(7) Notwithstanding any law or custom having the force of law to the contrary, and assignment in favour of a person made with the condition that it shall be

inoperative or that the interest shall pass to some other person on the happening of a specified event during the lifetime of the person whose life is insured, and an assignment in favour of the survivor or survivors of a number of persons shall be valid.

The *Section 39* of the Insurance Act, 1938 and amendments made thereafter deals with the provisions of nomination of a policy by the policyholder.

The holder of a policy of life insurance on his own life may nominate the person or persons to whom he wants the policy money to be paid in the event of his death. He may do so either at the time of effecting the policy or at any time before the policy matures for payment. Where the nominee is a minor, the policy-holder may indicate in the prescribed manner any person to receive the money during the minority of the nominee.

Nomination by Policy Holder

Section 39 : (1) The holder of a policy of life insurance on his own life, may, when effecting the policy or at any time before the policy matures for payment, nominate the person or persons to whom the money secured by the policy shall be paid in the event of his death:

Provided that, where any nominee is a minor, it shall be lawful for the policy holder to appoint in the prescribed manner any person to receive the money secured by the policy in the event of his death during the minority of the nominee.

(2) Any such nomination in order to be effectual shall, unless it is incorporated in the text of the policy itself, be made by an endorsement on the policy communicated to the insurer and registered by him in the records relating to the policy and any such nomination may at any time before the policy matures for payment be cancelled or changed by an endorsement or a further endorsement or a will, as the case may be, but unless notice in writing of any such cancellation or change has been delivered to the insurer, the insurer shall not be liable for any payment under the policy made *bona fide* by him to a nominee mentioned in the text of the policy or registered in records of the insurer.

(3) The insurer shall furnish to the policy holder a written acknowledgment of having registered a nomination or a cancellation change thereof, and may charge a fee not exceeding one rupee for registering such cancellation or change.

(4) A transfer or assignment of a policy made in accordance with section 38 shall automatically cancel a nomination:

Provided that the assignment of a policy to the insurer who bears the rats on the policy at the time of the assignment, in consideration of a loan granted by that insurer on the security of the policy within its surrender value, or its re-assignment on repayment of the loan shall not cancel a nomination, but shall affect the rights of the nominee only to the extent of the insurer's interest in the policy.

(5) Where the policy matures for payment during the lifetime of the person whose life is insured or where the nominee or, if there are more nominees than

one, all the nominees die before the policy-holder or his heirs or legal representatives or the holder of a succession certificate, as the case may be.

(6) Where the nominee or, if there are more nominees than one, a nominee or nominees survive the person whose life is insured, the amount secured by the policy shall be payable to such survivor or survivors.

(7) The provisions of this section shall not apply to any policy of life insurance to which section 6 of the Married Women's Property Act, 1874 (3 of 1874), applies or has at any time applied:

Provided that where a nomination made whether before or after the commencement of the Insurance (Amendment) Act, 1946 (VII of 1946), in favour of the wife of the person who has insured his life or of his wife and children or any of them is expressed, whether or not on the face of the policy as being made under this section, the said section 6 shall be deemed not to apply or not to have applied to the policy.

Misstatement or Concealment [S. 45]

Section 45 provides that after the expiry of two years from the date on which a policy is effected, the policy shall not be called in question by the insurer on the ground that a statement made in the proposal, or medical officer's report, or by a referee or friend of the assured, or in any other document relating to the issue of the policy, was inaccurate or false. Thus a policy can be avoided by the insurer on the ground of a misrepresentation or suppression only within two years of the date of the policy.

Payment of Money into Court

Section 47 of the Act explains the method of payment of claim by the insurer into the court and settlement of claim by the interference of the Court. Section 47A explains the method of payment of small amounts of claims under life insurance policy.

Section 47 : (1) Where in respect of any policy of life insurance maturing for payment an insurer is of opinion that by reason of conflicting claims to or insufficiency of proof of title to the amount secured thereby or for any other adequate reason it is impossible otherwise for the insurer to obtain a satisfactory discharge for the payment of such amount, the insurer may, apply to pay the amount into the Court within the jurisdiction of which is situated the place at which such amount is payable under the terms of the policy or otherwise.

(2) A receipt granted by the Court for any such payment shall be a satisfactory discharge to the insurer for the payment of such amount.

(3) An application for permission to make a payment into Court under this section, shall be made by a petition verified by an affidavit signed by a principal officer of the insurer setting forth the following particulars, namely:

(*a*) the name of the insured person and his address;

(*b*) if the insured person is deceased, the date and place of his death;

(*c*) the nature of the policy and the amount secured by it;

(*d*) the name and address of each claimant so far as is known to the insurer with details of every notice of claim received;

(*e*) the reasons why in the opinion of the insurer satisfactory discharge cannot be obtained for the payment of the amount; and

(*f*) the address at which the insurer may be served with notice of any proceeding relating to disposal of the amount paid into Court.

(4) An application under this section shall not be entertained by the Court if the application is made before the expiry of six months from the maturing of the policy by survival, or from the date of receipt of notice by the insurer of the death of the insured, as the case may be.

(5) If it appears to the Court that a satisfactory discharge for the payment of the amount cannot otherwise be obtained by the insurer it shall allow the amount to be paid into Court and shall invest the amount in Government securities pending its disposal.

(6) The insurer shall transmit to the Court every notice of claim received after the making of the application under sub section (3), and any payment required by the Court as costs of the proceedings or otherwise in connection with the disposal of the amount paid into Court shall as to the cost of the application under sub section (3) be borne by the insurer and as to any other costs be in the discretion of the Court.

(7) The Court shall cause notice to be given to every ascertained claimant of the fact that the amount has been paid into Court, and shall cause notice at the cost of any claimant applying to withdraw the amount to be given to every other ascertained claimant.

(8) The Court shall decide all questions relating to the disposal of claims to the amount paid into Court.

Claims on Small Life Insurance Policies

Section 47A : (1) In the event of any dispute relating to the settlement of a claim on a policy of life insurance assuring a sum not exceeding two thousand rupees (exclusive of any profit or bonus not being a guaranteed profit or bonus) issued by an insurer in respect of insurance business transacted in India, arising between a claimant under the policy and the insurer who issued the policy or has otherwise assumed liability in respect thereof, the dispute may at the option of the claimant be referred to the Authority for decision and the Authority may, after giving an opportunity to the parties to be heard and after making such further inquires as he may think fit, decide the matter.

(2) The decision of the Authority under this sub section shall be final and shall not be called in question in any Court, and may be executed by the Court which

would have been competent to decide the dispute if it had not been referred to the Authority as if it wore a decree passed by that Court.

(3) There shall be charged and collected in respect of the duties of the Authority under this section such fees whether by way of percentage or otherwise as may be prescribed.

2.5 APPOINTMENT OF AGENTS

Prohibition of Payment by Way of Commission or Otherwise for Procuring Business

Section 40 : (1) No person shall after the expiry of six months from the commencement of this Act, pay or contract to pay any remuneration or reward whether by way of commission or otherwise for soliciting or procuring insurance business in India to any person except an insurance agent or an intermediary or insurance intermediary.

(1A) In this section and section 40A, 41 and 43 references to an insurance agent shell be construed as including references to an individual soliciting or procuring insurance business exclusively in the territories which Immediately before the 1st November, 1956 were comprised in a Part B State notified in this behalf by the Central Government in the Official Gazette and holding a valid licence as an insurance agent under the law of that Part B State.

(2) No insurance agent shall be paid or contract to be paid by way of commission or as remuneration in any form an amount exceeding, in the case of life insurance business, forty per cent of the first year's premium payable on any policy or policies effected through him and five per cent of a renewal premium, payable on such a policy, or, in the case of business of any other class, fifteen per cent of the premium:

Provided that insurers in respect of life insurance business only may pay during the first ten years of their business to their insurance agents fifty five per cent of the first years premium payable on any policy or policies effected through them and six per cent of the renewal premiums payable on such policies:

Provided further that nothing in this sub section shall apply in respect of any policy of life insurance issued after the 31st day of December, 1950, or in respect of any policy of general insurance issued after the commencement of the Insurance (Amendment) Act, 1950 (47 of 1950).

(2A) Save as hereinafter provided, no insurance agent or intermediary or insurance intermediary shall be paid or contract to be paid by way of commission or as remuneration in any form any amount in respect of any policy not effected through him:

Provided that where a policy of life insurance has lapsed and it cannot under the terms and conditions applicable to it be revived without further medical examination of the person whose life was insured thereby, an insurer, after giving by notice in writing to the insurance agent through whom the policy was effected if such agent continues to be an agent of the insist an opportunity to effect the revival of the policy within a time specified in the notice, being not less than one month from the date of the receipt by him of the notice, may pay to another insurance agent who effects the revival of the policy an amount calculated at a rate not exceeding half the rate of commission at which the agent through whom the policy was effected would have been paid had the policy not lapsed, on the sum payable on revival of the policy on account of arrear premiums (excluding any interest on such arrear premiums) and also on the subsequent renewal premiums payable on the policy.

(3) Nothing in this section shall prevent the payment under any contract existing prior to the 27th day of January, 1937, of gratuities or renewal commission to Many person, whether an insurance agent within the meaning of this Act or not, or to his representatives after his decease in respect of insurance business effected through him before the said date.

Limitation of Expenditure on Commission

Section 40A : (l) No person shall pay or contract to pay to an insurance agent, and no insurance agent shall receive or contract to receive by way of commission or remuneration in any form in respect of any policy of life insurance issued in India by an insurer after the 31st day of December, 1950, and effected through an insurance agent, an amount exceeding:

(*a*) where the policy grants an *immediate annuity or a deferred* annuity in consideration of a single premium, or where only one premium is payable on the policy, two per cent of that premium,

(*b*) where the policy grants a deferred annuity in consideration or more than one premium, seven and a half per cent of the first year's premium, and two per cent of each renewal premium payable on the policy, and

(*c*) in any other case, thirty five per cent of the first year's premium, seven and a half per cent of the second and third year's renewal premium, and thereafter five per cent of each renewal premium payable on the policy:

Provided that in a case referred to in clause (c), an insurer, during the first ten years of his business may pay to an insurance agent and an insurance agent may receive from such an insurer, forty per cent of the first year's premium payable on the policy:

Provided further that in case referred to in clause (c) where the rate of commission payable on the first year's premium is equal to or less than twenty-one per cent thereof, and the rate on the fourth and fifth year's premiums does not exceeds is per cent thereof, the Life Insurance Corporation of India may pay to an insurance agent, and the insurance agent may receive from it, commission on the sixth and subsequent year's renewal premiums payable on the policy at a rate not exceeding six per cent of each renewal premium.

(2) No person shall pay or contract to pay to a special agent, and no special agent, shall receive or contract to receive, by way of commission or as remuneration in any form, in respect of any policy of life insurance issued in India by an insurer after the 31st day of December, 1950, and effected through a special agent, an amount exceeding—

(*a*) in a case referred to in clause (a) of sub section (1), one half per cent of the premium,

(*b*) in a case referred to in clause (b) of sub section (1), two per cent of the first year's premium payable on the policy and

(*c*) in a case referred to in clause (c) of sub section (1), fifteen per cent of the first year's premium payable on the policy:

Provided that in a case referred to in clause (c), an insurer, during the first ten years of his business, may pay to a special agent, and a special agent may receive from such an insurer, seventeen and a half per cent of the first year's premium payable on the policy:

Provided further that in a case referred to in clause (c), where the rate of commission payable on the first year's premium is equal to or less than twenty-one per cent thereof, and the rate on the fourth and fifty year's premiums does not exceed six per cent thereof, the Life Insurance Corporation of India may pay to an insurance agent, and the insurance agent may receive from it, commission on the sixth and subsequent year's renewal premiums payable on the policy at a rate not exceeding six per cent of each renewal premium.

(3) No person shall pay or contract to pay to a special agent, and no special agent, shall receive or contract to receive, by way of commission or remuneration in any form in respect of any policy of general insurance issued in India by an insurer after the commencement of Insurance (Amendment Act), 1968, and effected through an insurance agent, an amount not exceeding fifteen per cent of the premium payable on the policy where the policy relates to fire or marine insurance or miscellaneous insurance.

(4) No person shall pay or contract to pay to a principal agent, and no principal agent shall receive or contract to receive, by way of commission or remuneration in any form, in respect of any policy of general insurance issued in India by an insurer after the commencement of the Insurance (Amendment) Act, 1950, and effected through a principal agent, an amount exceeding-

(*a*) in the case referred to in clause (*a*) of sub section (3), twenty per cent of the premium payable on the policy, and

(*b*) in the case referred to in clause (*b*) of that sub section, fifteen per cent of the policy, less any commission payable to any insurance agent in respect of the said policy:

Provided that the Authority may, in such circumstances and to such extent and for such period as may be specified, authorise the payment of commission or remuneration exceeding the limits specified in this sub section to a principal agent of an insurer incorporated or domiciled elsewhere than in India, if such agent carries out and has continuously carried out in his own office duties on behalf of the insurer which would otherwise have been performed by the insurer.

(5) Without prejudice to the provisions of section 102 in respect of a contravention of any of the provisions of the preceding sub sections by an insurer, any insurance agent who contravenes the provisions of sub section (1) or sub-section (3) shall be punishable with fine which may extend to one hundred rupees.

Limitation of Expenses of Management in Life Insurance Business

Section 40B : (l) Every insurer transacting life insurance business in India shall furnish to the Controller, within such time as may be prescribed, statements in the prescribed form certified by an actuary on the basis of premiums currently used by him in regard to new business in respect of mortality, rate of interest, expenses and bonus loading.

(2) After the 31st day of December, 1950, no insurer shall, in respect of life insurance business transacted by him in India, spend as expenses of management in any calendar year an amount in excess of the prescribed limits and in prescribing any such limits regard shall be had to the size and age of the insurer and the provision generally Made for expenses of management in the premium rates of insurers:

Provided that where an insurer has spent as such expenses in any year an amount in excess of the amount permissible under this sub section, he shall not be deemed to have contravened the provisions of this section, if the excess amount so spent is within such limits as may be fixed in respect of the year by the Authority after consultation with the Executive Committee of the Life Insurance Council constituted under section 64 F, by which the actual expenses incurred may exceed the expenses permissible under this sub-section.

(3) In respect of any statement mentioned in subsection (1), the Authority may require that it shall be submitted to another actuary, appointed by the insurer for the purpose and approved by the Authority, for certification by him, whether with or without modifications.

(4) Every insurer transacting life insurance business in India shall incorporate in the revenue account :

(*a*) a certificate signed by the chairman and two directors and by the principal officer of the insurer, and an auditor's certificate, certifying that all expenses of management in respect of life insurance business transacted by the insurer in India have been fully debited in the revenue account as expenses, and

(*b*) if the insurer in carrying on any other class of insurance business in addition to life insurance business an auditor's certificate certifying that all charges incurred in respect of his life insurance business and in respect of his business other than life insurance business have been fully debited in the respective revenue accounts.

Explanation : in this section.

(*a*) "calendar year" or "year" means, in relation to an insurer who is required to furnish returns in accordance with sub section (2) of section 16, the period covered by the revenue account furnished by such insurer under clause (b) of that sub section;

(*b*) "expenses of management" means all charges wherever incurred whether directly or indirectly, and includes :

(*i*) commission payments of all kinds,

(*ii*) any amount of expenses capitalized,

(*iii*) in the case of an insurer having his principal place of business outside India, a proper share of head office expenses which shall not be less than such percentage as may be prescribed of the total premiums (less re insurance) received during the year in respect of life insurance business transacted by him in India,

but does not include in the case of an insurer having his principal place of business in India any share of head office expenses in respect of life insurance business transacted by him outside India.

Limitation of Expenses of Management in General Insurance Business

Section 40C : (1) After the 31st day of December, 1949, no insurer shall, in respect of any class of general insurance business transacted by him in India, spend in any calendar year as expenses of management including commission or remuneration for procuring business an amount in excess of the prescribed limits arid in prescribing any such limits regard shall be had to the size and age of the insurer:

Provided that where an insurer has spend as such expenses in any year an amount in excess of the amount permissible under this subsection, he shall not be deemed to have contravened the provisions of this section, if the excess amount so spent is within such limits as may be fixed in respect of the year by the Authority after consultation with the Executive Committee of the General Insurance. Council constituted under section 64F, by which the actual expenses incurred may exceed the expenses permissible under this sub-section.

(2) Every insurer as aforesaid shall incorporate in the revenue account a certificate signed by the chairman and two directors and by the principal officer of the insurer, and by an auditor certifying that all expenses of management wherever incurred, whether directly or indirectly, in respect of the business referred to in this section have been fully debited in the revenue account as expenses.

Explanation : In this section.—

(*a*) "calendar year" shall have the meaning assigned to it in section 40B;

(*b*) "expenses of management" means all charges, wherever insured whether directly or indirectly, including commission payments of all kinds and, in the case of an insurer having his principal place of business outside India, a proper share of head office expenses, which shall not be less than such percentage as may be prescribed, of his gross premium income (that is to say, the premium income without taking into account premiums or re-insurance ceded or accepted) written direct in India during the year, but in computing the expenses of management in India the following, and only the following expenses may be excluded, namely :

(*i*) in the case of an insurer having his principal place of business in India, a share of head office expenses in respect of general insurance business transacted by him outside India not exceeding such percentage of his gross direct premium written outside India as may be prescribed;

(*ii*) in the case of an insurer having his principal place of business outside India, a share of the expenses of his office in India in respect of general insurance business transacted by him outside India through his office in India, not exceeding such percentage of his gross direct premium written outside India through his office in India, as may be prescribed;

(*iii*) any expenses debited to profit and loss account relating exclusively to the management of capital, and dealings with share holders and a proper share of managerial expenses calculated in such manner as may be prescribed; and

(*iv*) any expenses debited to claims in the revenue account in Form F of Part II of the Third Schedule;

(*c*) "insurance business transacted in India" includes insurance business, wherever effected relating to any property situate in India or to any vessel or aircraft registered in India.

Prohibition of Rebates

Section 41 : (1) No person shall allow or offer to allow, either directly or indirectly, as an inducement to any person to take or renew or continue an insurance in respect of any kind of risk relating to lives or property in India, any rebate of the whole or part of the commission payable or any rebate of the premium shown on the policy, nor shall any person taking out or renewing or continuing a policy accept any rebate, except such rebate as may be allowed in accordance with the published prospectuses or tables of the insurer:

Provided that acceptance by an insurance agent of commission in connection with a policy of life insurance taken out by himself on his own life shall not be deemed to be acceptance of a rebate of premium within the meaning of this sub section if at the time of such acceptance the insurance agent satisfies the prescribed conditions establishing that he is a *bona fide* insurance agent employed by the insurer.

(2) Any person making default in complying with the provisions of this section shall be punishable with fine which may extend to five hundred rupees.

Licensing of Insurance Agents

Section 42 : (1) The Authority or an officer authorised by him in this behalf shall, in the manner determined by the regulations made by it and on payment of the fee which shall not be determined by the regulations, which shall not be more than two hundred and fifty rupees, issue to any person making any application in the manner determined by the regulations, a licence to act as an insurance agent for the purpose of soliciting or procuring insurance business:

Provided that—

(i) in the case of an individual, he does not suffer from any of the disqualification mentioned in sub section (4); and

(ii) in the case of a company or firm, any of its directors or partners does not suffer from any of the said disqualifications:

Provided further that any licence issued immediately before the commencement of the Insurance Regulatory and Development Authority Act, 1999, shall be deemed to have been issued in accordance with the regulations which provide for such licence.

(2) A licence issued under this section shall entitle the holder to act as an insurance agent for any insurer.

(3) A licence issued under this section, after the commencement of the Insurance Regulatory and Development Authority Act, 1999, shall remain in force for a period of three years only from the date of issue, but shall, if the applicant being an individual does not, or being a company or firm any of its directors or partners, does not suffer from any of the disqualification mentioned in clauses (b), (c), (d), (e), (ea) and (f) of sub section (4) and the application for renewal of the licence reaches the issuing authority at least thirty days before the date on which the licence ceases to remain in force, be renewed for a period of three years at any one time on payment of the fee determined by the regulations made by the Authority which shall not be more than rupees two hundred and fifty, and an additional fee of an amount determined by the regulations not exceeding rupees one hundred by way of penalty, if the application for renewal of the licence does not reach the issuing authority at least thirty days before the date on which the licence ceases to remain in force.

(3A) No application for the renewal of a licence under this section shall be entertained if the application does not reach the issuing authority before the licence ceases to remain in force:

Provided that the Authority may, if satisfied that undue hardship would be caused otherwise, accept any application in contravention of this subsection on payment by the applicant of a penalty of seven hundred and fifty rupees.

(4) The disqualifications above referred to shall be the following:

(*a*) that the person is a minor;

(*b*) that he is found to be of unsound mind by a Court of competent jurisdiction;

(*c*) that he has been found guilty of criminal misappropriation or criminal breach of trust or cheating or forgery or an abetment of or attempt to commit any such offence by a Court of competent jurisdiction:

Provided that where at least five years have elapsed since the completion of the sentence imposed on any person in respect of any such offence, the Authority shall ordinarily declare in respect of such person that his conviction shall cease to operate as a disqualification under this clause;

(*d*) that in the course of any judicial proceeding relating to any policy of insurance of the winding up of an insurance company or in the course of an investigation of the affairs of all insurer it has then found that he has been guilty off or has knowingly participated in or connived at any fraud, dishonestly fir misrepresentation against an insurer or an insured.

(*e*) that in the case of an individual, he does not possess the requisite qualifications and practical training for a period not exceeding twelve months, as may be specified by the regulations made by the Authority in this behalf;

(*ea*) that in the case of a company or firm making an application under sub-section (1) or sub-section (3), a director or a partner or one or more of its officers or other employees so designated by it and in the case of any other person, the chief executive, by whatever name called, or one or more of his employees designated by him, do not possess the requisite qualifications and practical training and have not passed such an examination as required under clauses (e) and (f);

(*g*) that he violates the code of conduct as may be specified by the regulations made by the Authority.

(5) if it be found that an insurance agent being an individual is, or being a company or firm contains a director or partner who is suffering from any of the disqualifications mentioned in sub section (4), then, without prejudice to any other penalty to which he may be liable, the Authority shall, and if the insurance agent has knowingly contravened any of the provisions of this Act may, cancel the licence issued to the agent under this section.

(6) The Authority may issue a duplicate licence to replace a licence lost, destroyed or mutilated on payment of such fee not exceeding rupees fifty as may be determined by the regulations.

(7) Any person who acts as an insurance agent without holding a licence issued under this section to act as such shall be punishable with fine which may extend to five hundred rupees., and any insurer or any person acting on behalf of an

insurer, who appoints as an insurance agent any person not licensed to act as such or transacts any insurance business in India through any such person shall be punishable with fine which may extend to one thousand rupees.

(8) Where the person contravening sub section (7) is a company or a firm, then, without prejudice to any other proceedings which may be taken against the company, or firm, every director, manager, secretary or other officer of the company, and every partner of the firm who is knowingly a party to such contravention shall be punishable with fine which may extend to five thousand rupees.

Registration of Principal Agents, Chief Agents and Special Agents

Section 42A : (1) The Authority or an officer authorised by it in this behalf shall in the prescribed manner and on payment of the prescribed fee, which shall not be more than twenty five rupees for a principal agent or a chief agent and ten rupees for a special agent, register any person who makes an application to him in the prescribed manner if,—

(*a*) in the case of an individual, he does not suffer from any of the disqualifications mentioned in sub section (4) of Section 42, or

(*b*) in the case of a company or firm, any of its directors or partners does not suffer from any of the said disqualifications,

and a certificate to Act as a principal agent, chief agent or special agent, as the case may be, for the purpose of procuring insurance business shall be issued to him.

(2) A certificate issued under this section shall entitle the holder thereof to act as a principal agent, chief agent, or special agent, as the case may be, for any insurer.

(3) A certificate issued under this section shall remain in force for a period of twelve months only from the date of issue, but shall, on application made on this behalf, be renewed from year to year on production of a certificate from the insurer concerned that the provisions of clauses (2) and (3) of Part A of the Sixth Schedule in the case of a principal agent, the provisions of clauses (2) and (4) of Part B of the said Schedule in the case of a chief agent, and the provisions of clauses (2) and (3) of Part C of the said Schedule in the case of a special agent, have been complied with, and on payment of the prescribed fee, which shall not be more than twenty five rupees, in the case of a principal agent or a chief agent, and ten rupees in the case of a special agent, and an additional fee of the prescribed amount not exceeding five rupees by way of penalty, in cases where the application for renewal of the certificate does not reach the issuing authority before the date on which the certificate ceases to remain in force:

Provided that, where the applicant is an individual, he does not suffer from any of the disqualifications mentioned in clauses (b) to (d) of sub section (4) of section 42 and where the applicant is a company or a firm, any of its directors or partners does not suffer from any of the said disqualifications.

(4) Where it is found that the principal agent, chief agent or special agent being an individual is, or being a company or firm contains a director or partner who is suffering from any of the disqualifications mentioned in sub-section (4) of section 42, without prejudice to any other penalty to which he may be liable, the Authority shall, and where a principal agent, chief agent or special agent has contravened any of the provisions of this Act may cancel the certificate issued under this section to such principal agent, chief agent or special agent.

(5) The authority which issued any certificate under this section may issue a duplicate certificate to replace a certificate lost, destroyed or mutilated on payment of the prescribed fee, which shall not be more than two rupees.

(6) Any person who acts as a principal agent, chief agent or special agent, without holding a certificate issued under this section to act as such, shall be punishable with fine which may extend to five hundred rupees, and any insurer or any person acting on behalf of an insurer, who appoints as a principal agent, chief agent or special agent any person not entitled to act as such or transacts any insurance business in India through any such person, shall be punishable with fine which may extend to one thousand rupees.

(7) Where the person contravening sub section (6) is a company or a firm, then, without prejudice to any other proceedings which may be taken against the company or firm, every director, manager, secretary or any other officer of the company, and every partner of the firm who is knowingly a party to such contravention shall be punishable with fine which may extend to five hundred rupees.

(8) The provisions of sub sections (6) and (7) shall not take effect until the expiry of six months from the commencement of the Insurance (Amendment) Act, 1950.

(9) No insurer shall, on or after the commencement of the Insurance (Amendment) Act, 2002, appointment or transact any insurance business in India through any principal agent, chief agent or special agent.

Regulation of Employment of Principal Agents

Section 42B : (1) No insurer shall, after the expiration of seven years from the commencement of the Insurance (Amendment) Act, 1950, appoint, or transact any insurance business in India, through a principal agent.

(2) Every contract between an insurer and a principal agent shall be in writing and the terms contained in Part A of the Sixth Schedule shall be deemed to be incorporated in, and form part of, every such contract.

(3) No insurer shall, after the commencement of the Insurance (Amendment) Act, 1950 (47 of 1950), appoint any person as a principal agent except in a presidency town unless the appointment is by way of renewal of any contract subsisting at such commencement.

(4) Within sixty days of the commencement of the Insurance (Amendment) Act, 1950 (47 of 1950), every principal agent shall file with the insurer concerned a full list of insurance agents employed by him indicating the terms of the contract between the principal agent and each of such insurance agents, and, if any principal agent fails to file such a list within the period specified, any commission payable to such principal agent on premiums received from the date of expiry of the said period of sixty days until the date of the filing of the said list shall, notwithstanding anything in any contract to the contrary, cease to be so payable.

(5) A certified copy of every contract as is referred to in sub section (2) shall be furnished by the insurer to the Authority within thirty days of his entering into such contract, and intimation of any change in any such contract shall be furnished by the insurer with full particulars thereof to the Authority within thirty days of the making of any such change.

(6) If the commission due to any insurance agent in respect of any general insurance business procured by such agent is not paid by the principal agent for any reason, the insurer may pay the insurance agent the commission so due and recover the amount so paid from the principal agent concerned.

(7) Every contract as is referred to in sub section (2), subsisting at the commencement of the Insurance (Amendment) Act, 1950 (47 of 1950), shall, with respect to terms regarding remuneration, be deemed to have been so altered as to be in accordance with the provisions of sub section (4) of section 40A.

(8) If any dispute arises as to whether a person is or was a principal agent the matter shall be referred to the Authority, whose decision shall be final.

(9) Every insurer shall maintain a register in which the name and address of every principal agent appointed by him, the date of such appointment and the date, if any, on which the appointment ceased shall be entered.

Regulation of Employment of Chief and Special Agents

Section 42C : (1) Every contract between art insurer carrying on life insurance business and a chief agent shall be in writing, and shall specify the area (not being less in extent than a district or the equivalent thereof) for which the chief agent is appointed, and the terms contained in Part B of the Sixth Schedule shall be deemed to be incorporated in, and form part of, every such contract.

(2) No chief agent shall, either directly or through insurance agents or special agents employed by or through him procure life insurance business for the insurer or any area outside the area for which he has been appointed or In any area for which another chief agent has been appointed or in any area in which the head office or any branch office of the insurer is operating, and neither the head office nor any branch office of the insurer shall operate in any area for which a chief agent has been appointed:

Provided that nothing in this sub section shall be deemed to prohibit the head office of an insurer which had been operating at the commencement of the

Insurance (Amendment) Act, 1950; for a period of not less than ten years before such commencement within the municipal limits of any town where the head office is situate, and a chief agent who, in pursuance of an agreement in writing, had been operating for a similar period within such limits, from continuing to operate within the said limits:

Provided further that nothing in this sub section shall be deemed to prohibit an insurance agent from procuring life insurance business in or from any area and submitting the proposals direct to the principal office of the insurer in India.

(3) Within sixty days of the commencement of the Insurance (Amendment) Act, 1950, every chief agent shall file with the insurer concerned a full list of the insurance agents employed by him, indicating the terms of the contract between the chief agent and each of such insurance agents and the business secured by each of such agents, and if any chief agent fails to file such a list within the period specified, any commission payable to such chief agent on premiums received from the date of the expiry of the said period of sixty days until the date of the filing of the said list shall, notwithstanding anything in any contract to the contrary, cease to be so payable.

(4) Every contract between an insurer carrying on life insurance business and a special agent, or between a chief agent of such insurer and a special agent, shall be in writing and the terms contained in Part C of the Sixth Schedule shall be deemed to be incorporated in, and form part of, every such contract:

Provided that the Authority may, in the case of a contract between a co-operative life insurance society as defined in clause (b) of sub section (1) of section 95 and a co-operative society registered under the Indian Co-operative Societies Act, 1912 (2 of 1912), or under any other law for the time being in force and acting as a special agent, alter, to such extent as he thinks fit, all or any of the said terms.

(5) A certified copy of every contract as is referred to in sub section (1) or sub section (4) shall be furnished by the insurer or the chief agent to the Authority within thirty days of his entering into such contract, and intimation of any change in any such contract shall be furnished by the insurer or the chief agent with full particulars thereof to the Authority within thirty days of the making of any such change.

(6) No such contract as is referred to in sub section (1) or sub section (4) shall be entered into or renewed for a period exceeding ten years at any one time and notwithstanding the terms of any contract to the contrary, no option to renew any such contract given to any of the parties shall be enforceable without the consent of the other.

(7) Every contract between an insurer and a person acting on behalf of such insurer who, before the commencement of the Insurance (Amendment) Act, 1950), has been employing insurance agents for the purpose of life insurance business, which is subsisting on such commencement, shall terminate after the expiration of ten years from such commencement, if it does not terminate earlier:

Provided that every such contract shall be modified by the parties before the 1st day of January, 1951, to bring it into conformity with this act, and ant, such modification shall :

(*i*) as respects remuneration, whether in respect of business already procured or in respect of business to be procured thereafter, be such as may be mutually agreed upon between the parties, subject in the case of remuneration payable on business procured before such commencement, to a maximum of an overriding commission of two and a half per cent plus a further commission not exceeding three and three quarter per cent on premiums in respect of which no commission is payable to any insurance agent;

(*ii*) be deemed to include all the terms specified in Part B or Part C of the Sixth Schedule, as the case may be:

Provided further that, in the event of any dispute as to the terms of any fresh contract, the matter shall be referred to arbitration

(8) Any such contract as is referred to in sub section (7) which was subsisting on the 1st day of January, 1949, but has terminated or has been terminated before the commencement of the Insurance (Amendment) Act, 1950, shall be subject to the maximum limits specified in clause (i) of the proviso to sub-section (7) as respects remuneration, if any, payable on business procured before the termination of the contract.

(9) Nothing in this section shall be deemed to prevent any special agent from receiving any renewal commission on policies effected through him as an insurance agent at any time before his appointment as such special agent.

(10) If any dispute arises as to whether a person is or was a chief agent or a special agent for the purposes of this Act, the matter shall be referred to the Authority whose decision shall be final.

(11) Every insurer shall maintain a register in which the name and address of every chief agent appointed by him, the date on which the appointment was made and the date, if any, on which the appointment ceased shall be entered, and a separate register in which similar particulars relating to every special agent shall be entered, and every chief agent shall maintain a register in which similar particulars relating to every special agent appointed by him shall be entered.

Issue of Licence to Intermediary or Insurance Intermediary

Section 42D : (1) The Authority or an officer authorized by it in this behalf shall, in the manner determined by the regulations made by the Authority and on payment of the fees determined by the regulations made by the Authority, issue to any person making an application in the manner determined by the regulations, and not suffering from any of the disqualifications herein mentioned, a licence to act as an intermediary or an insurance intermediary under this Act:

Provided that, :

(*a*) in the case of an individual, he does not suffer from any of the disqualifications mentioned in sub-section (4) of section 42, or

(*b*) in the case of a company or firm, any of its directors or partners does not suffer from any of the said disqualifications.

(2) A licence issued under this section shall entitle the holder thereof to act as an intermediary or insurance intermediary.

(3) A licence issued under this section shall remain in force for a period of three years only from the date of issue, but shall, if the applicant, being an individual does not, or being a company or firm any of its directors or partners does not suffer from any of the disqualifications mentioned in clauses (*b*), (*c*), (*d*), (*e*) and (*f*) of sub-section (4) of section 42 and the application for renewal of licence reaches the issuing authority at least thirty days before the date on which the licence ceases to remain in force, be renewed for a period of three years at any one time on payment of the fee, determined by the regulations made by the Authority and additional fee for an amount determined by the regulations, not exceeding one hundred rupees by way of penalty, if the application for renewal of the licence does not reach the issuing authority at least thirty days before the date on which the licence ceases to remain in force.

(4) No application for the renewal of a licence under this section shall be entertained if the application does not reach the issuing authority before the licence ceases to remain in force:

Provided that the Authority may, if satisfied that undue hardship would be caused otherwise, accept any application in contravention of this sub-section on payment by the application of the penalty of seven hundred and fifty rupees.

(5) The disqualifications above referred to shall be the following :

(*a*) that the person is a minor;

(*b*) that he is found to be a unsound mind by a court of competent jurisdiction;

(*c*) that he has been found guilty of criminal misappropriation or criminal breach of trust or cheating or forgery or an abetment of or attempt to commit any such offence by a court of competent jurisdiction:

Provided that, where at least five years have elapsed since the completion of the sentence imposed on any person in respect of any such offence, the Authority shall ordinarily declare in respect of such person that his conviction shall cease to operate as a disqualification under this clause;

(*d*) that in the course of any judicial proceedings relating to any policy of insurance of the winding up of an insurance company or in the course of an investigation of the affairs of an insurer it has been found that he has been guilty of or has knowingly participated in or connived at any fraud dishonestly or misrepresentation against an insurer or an insured;

(e) that he does not possess the requisite qualifications and practical training for a period not exceeding twelve months, as may be specified by the regulations made by the Authority in this behalf;

(f) that he has not passed such examinations as may be specified by the regulations made by the Authority in this behalf;

(g) that he violates the code of conduct as may be specified by the regulations made by the Authority.

(6) If it be found that an intermediary or an insurance intermediary suffers from any of the foregoing disqualifications, without prejudice to any other penalty to which he may be liable, the Authority shall, and if the intermediary or an insurance intermediary has knowingly contravened any provisions of this Act may cancel the licence issued to the intermediary or insurance intermediary under this section.

(7) The Authority may issue a duplicate licence to replace a licence lost, destroyed or mutilated, on payment of such fee, as may be determined by the regulations made by the Authority.

(8) Any person who acts as an intermediary or an insurance intermediary without holding a licence issued under this section to act as such, shall be punishable with fine, and any insurer or any person who appoints as an intermediary or an insurance intermediary or any person not licensed to act as such or transacts any insurance business in India through any such person, shall be punishable with fine.

(9) Where the person contravening sub-section (8) is a company or a firm, then, without prejudice to any other proceedings which may be taken against the company or firm, every director, manager, secretary or other officer of the company, and every partner of the firm who is knowingly a party to such contravention shall be punishable with fine.

Commission, Brokerage or Fee Payable to Intermediary or Insurance Intermediary

Section 42E : (1) No intermediary or insurance intermediary shall be paid or contract to be paid by way of commission, fee or as remuneration in any form, an amount exceeding thirty per cent of the premium payable as may be specified by the regulations made by the Authority, in respect of any policy or policies effected through him:

Provided that the Authority may specify different amounts payable by way of commission, fee or as remuneration to an intermediary or insurance intermediary or different classes of business of insurance.

(2) Without prejudice to the provisions contained in this Act, the Authority may, by the regulations made in this behalf, specify the requirements of capital, form of business and other conditions to act as an intermediary or insurance intermediary.

Register of Insurance Agents

Section 43 : (l) Every insurer and every person who acting on behalf of an insurer employs insurance agents shall maintain a register showing the name and address of every insurance agent appointed by him and the date on which his appointment began and the date, if any, on which his appointment ceased.

2.6 DEPOSITS AND INVESTMENTS

Section 7, 8 and 9 of the Insurance Act, 1938 deals with the deposits which are required to be made by the insurer for obtaining the license to undertake the insurance and registration of the insurer with IRD Authority.

Deposits

Section 7 : (1) Every insurer shall, in respect of the insurance business carried on by him in India, deposit and keep deposited with the Reserve Bank of India in one of the offices in India of the Bank for and on behalf of the Central Government the amount hereafter specified, either in cash or in approved securities estimated at the market value of the securities on the day of deposit, or partly in cash and partly in approved securities so estimated :

(*a*) in the case of life insurance business, a sum equivalent to one per cent of his total gross premium written direct in India in any financial year commencing after the 31st day of March, 2000, not exceeding rupees ten crores;

(*b*) in the case of general insurance business, a sum equivalent to three per cent of his total gross premium written in India, in any financial year commencing after the 31st day of March, 2000, not exceeding rupees ten crores;

(*c*) in the case of re-insurance business, a sum of rupees twenty crores

Provided that, where the business done or to be done is marine insurance only and relates exclusively to country craft or its cargo or both, the amount to be deposited under this sub-section shall be one hundred thousand rupees only:

Provided further that in respect of an insurer not having a share capital and carrying on only such insurance business as in the opinion of the Central Government is not carried on ordinarily by insurers under separate policies, the Central Government may, by notification under Official Gazette, order that the provisions of this sub section shall apply to such insurer with the modification that instead of sum of rupees twenty lakhs or rupees ten lakhs, as the case may be, the deposit to be made by such insurer shall be such amount, being not less than one hundred and fifty thousand rupees, as may be specified in the said order.

(2) Where the insurer is an insurer specified in sub clause (*c*) of clause (*9*) of Section 2, he shall be deemed to have complied with the provisions of this section as to deposits, if in respect of insurance business carried on by him in India

under a standing contract of the nature referred to in sub-clause (*c*) of clause (*9*) of section 2 a deposit of an amount one-and-a half times that specified in sub-section (1) has been made in the Reserve Bank of India in one of the offices in India of the Bank for and on behalf of the Central Government in cash or approved securities estimated at the market value of the securities on the day of deposit by or on behalf of the underwriters who are members of the Society of Lloyd's with whom he has his standing contract.

(3) Where the deposit to be made by an insurer not carrying on insurance business in India immediately before the commencement of the Insurance (Amendment) Act, 1968, a deposit of rupees ten lakhs shall be made before the application for registration is made, and the provision of clause (*ii*) of sub section (1A) shall apply to such insurer after his registration as they apply to an insurer specified in clause (a) of sub-section (1).

(4) An insurer shall not be registered for any class of insurance business in addition to the class or classes for which is already registered until the full deposit required under sub-section (1) has been made.

(5) Where an insurer who intends to become a member of a group, does not carry on all the classes of insurance business carried on by the other insurers in such group, or, where out of the several insurers who desire to form themselves into a group, any insurer does not carry on all the classes of insurance business carried on by the other insurers who desire to form themselves into the group, such insurer may be registered for that class or those classes of insurance business which is or are carried on by the other insurers of the group or the proposed group, as the case may be, and where any application for registration is made by any such insurer, the Authority may, notwithstanding anything contained in sub section (2A) of Section 3 or sub section (4), register such insurer for one or more additional classes of insurance, if the following conditions are fulfilled, namely:

(*a*) the Authority is satisfied that registration for the proposed one or more additional classes of insurance business would qualify the insurer to become number of a group;

(*b*) agreements have been executed by all the insurers in the group or proposed group, as the case may be, and such agreements in the opinion of the Authority, satisfy the requirements of the *Explanation* to sub-section (1B); and

(*c*) the insurer has, after the commencement of the Insurance (Amendment) Act, 1968, made deposit of a sum not less than the total of all the instalments of deposit which he would have been required to make after such commencement till the date of his becoming a member of the group, had he been a member of the group from such commencement.

(6) The Authority shall cancel the registration made in pursuance of the provisions of sub section (5), if the insurer referred to therein fails to become, within a period of three months from the date of such registration' a member of the group or proposed group, as the case may be, and, where such registration has been

cancelled, the provisions of this Act shall apply to the insurer as if he had not been registered for the class or classes of insurance business in relation to which his registration has been cancelled.

(7) Securities already deposited with the Controller of Currency in compliance with the Indian Life Assurance Companies Act, 1912 (6 of 1912), shall be transferred by him to the Reserve Bank of India and shall, to the extent of their market value as at the date of the commencement of this Act, be deemed to be deposited under this Act, as the instalment or as part of this instalment to be made under the foregoing provisions of this section before the application for registration is made whether any such application is or is not in fact made.

(8) A deposit made in cash shall be held by the Reserve Bank of India to the credit of the insurer and shall except to the extent, if any, to which the cash has been invested in securities under sub section (9A), be returnable to the insurer in cash in any case in which under the provisions of this Act a deposit is to be returned; and any interest accruing due and collected on securities deposited under sub section (1) or sub section (2) shall be paid to the insurer, subject only to deduction of the normal commission chargeable for the realization of interest.

(9) The insurer may at any time replace any securities deposited by him under this section with the Reserve Bank of India either by cash or by other approved securities or partly by cash and partly by other approved securities, provided that such cash, or the value of such other approved securities estimated at the market rates prevailing at the time of replacement, or such cash together with such value, as the case may be, is not less than the value of the securities replaced estimated at the market rates prevailing when they were deposited.

(9A) The Reserve Bank of India shall, if so requested by the insurer,—

(*a*) sell any securities deposited by him with the Bank under this section and hold the cash realized by such sale as deposit, or

(*b*) invest in approved securities specified by the insurer the whole or any part of a deposit held by it in cash or the whole or any part of cash received by it on the sale of or on the maturing of securities deposited by the insurer, and hold the securities in which investment is so made as deposit.

and may charge the normal commission on such sale or on such investment.

(9B) where sub-section (9A) applies

(*a*) if the cash realized by the sale of or on the maturing of the securities (excluding in the former case the interest accrued) falls short of the market value of the securities at the date on which they were deposited with the Bank, the insurer shall make good the deficiency by a further deposit either in cash or in approved securities estimated at the market value of the securities, on the day on which they are deposited, or partly in cash and partly in approved securities so estimated, within a period of two months from the date on which the securities matured or were sold or where the securities matured or were sold before the 21st day of March, 1940, within a period of four months from the commencement of the Insurance (Amendment) Act, 1940 (20 of 1940); and unless he does so the insurer shall be deemed to have failed to comply with the requirements of this section as to deposits; and

(*b*) if the cash realized by the sale of or on the maturing of the securities (excluding in the former case the interest accrued) exceeds the market value of the securities at the date on which they were deposited with the Bank, the Central Government may, if satisfied that the full amount required to be deposited under sub section (1) is in deposit, direct the Reserve Bank to return the excess.

(10) If any part of a deposit made under this section is used in the discharge of any liability of the insurer, the insurer shall deposit such additional sum in cash or approved securities estimated at the market value of the securities on the day of deposit, or partly in cash and partly in such securities, as will make up the amount so used. The insurer shall be deemed to have failed to comply with the requirements of sub section (1), unless the deficiency is supplied within a period of two months from the date when the deposit or any part thereof is so used for discharge of liabilities.

Reservation of Deposits

Section 8 : (1) Any deposit made under section 7 or section 98 shall be deemed to be part of the assets of the insurer but shall not be susceptible of any assignment or charge; nor shall it be available for the discharge of any liability of the insurer other than liabilities arising out of policies of insurance issued by the insurer so long as any such liabilities remain undischarged; nor shall it be liable to attachment in execution of any decree except a decree obtained by a policy holder of the insurer in respect of a debt due upon a policy which debt the policy holder has failed to realise in any other way.

(2) Where a deposit is made in respect of life insurance business the deposit made in respect thereof shall not be available for discharge of any liability of the insurer other than liabilities arising out of policies of life insurance issued by the insurer.

Refund of Deposit

Section 9 : Where an insurer has ceased to carry on in India all classes of insurance business, and his liabilities in India in respect of all classes of insurance business have been satisfied or are otherwise provided for, the court may, on the application of the insurer, order the return to the insurer of the deposit made by him under this Act.

Section 27 and 28 deals with investments by insurance companies. Following provisions have been made :

For Life Insurance

(*a*) 25% of the sum stated above in the Government Securities.

(*b*) Not less than 25% of the sum in the Government securities or other Approved securities.

[(*a*) and (*b*) put together should not be more than 50%.]

(*c*) Not less than 15% of the sum in infrastructure and social sector

(*d*) Not less than 20% in other securities as stated in Schedule I of IRDA Regulations 2000.

(*e*) Not less than 15% in other approved investments to be governed by the prudential norms specified in the above referred Regulation.

[(*d*) and (*e*) put together should not be more than 25%.]

For Pension

(*a*) Not less than 20% in Government securities.

(*b*) And annuity business not less than 20% in Government securities or in approved Securities.

(*c*) Balance 60% in the approved investments specified in the Schedule I of IRDA Regulations 2000.

General Insurance Business

(*a*) 20% in the Central Government Securities.

(*b*) Not less than 10% State Government Securities.

[(*a*) and (*b*) class should not be more than 30%].

(*c*) 5% housing and loans to the state Government.

(*d*) Not less than 10% in infrastructure and social sector.

(*e*) Not exceeding 55% in other approved investments governed by the prudential norms including the securities specified by IRDA.

2.7 MANAGEMENT AND ADMINISTRATION

Power to Appoint Staff

Section 33A : The Authority may appoint such staff, and at such places as it or he may consider necessary, for the scrutiny of the returns, statements and information furnished by insurers under this Act and generally to ensure the efficient performance of the functions of the Authority under this Act.

Power of Authority to Issue Directions

Section 34 : (1) where the Authority is satisfied that-

(*a*) in the public interest; or

(*b*) to prevent the affairs of any insurer being conducted in a marina detrimental to the interests of the policy holders or in a manner prejudicial to the interests of the insurer; or

(*c*) generally to secure the proper management of any insurer, it is necessary to issue directions to insurers generally or to any insurer In particular, he may, from time to time, issue such directions as he deems fit, and the insurers or the insurer, as the case may be, shall be bound to comply with such directions:

Provided that no such directions shall be issued to any insurer in particular unless such insurer has been given a reasonable opportunity of being heard

(2) The Authority may, on representation made to him or on his own motion, modify or cancel any direction issued under sub section (1), and in so modifying or canceling any directions, may impose such conditions as he thinks fit, subject to which the modification or cancellation shall have effect.

Appointing of Managing Directors etc.

Section 34A to 34D provides the IRDA to appoint, reappoint remove the managerial and other staff and decide the renumeration payable to them.

Amendment of provisions relating to appointments of managing directors, etc., to be subject to previous approval of the Authority

Section 34A : (1) In the case of an insurer,—

(*a*) no amendment made, after the commencement of the Insurance (Amendment) Act, 1968, of any provision relating to the appointment, re appointment, termination of appointment or remuneration of a managing or whole time director, or of a manager or a chief executive officer, by whatever name called, whether that provision be contained in the insurers memorandum or articles of associations, or in an agreement entered into by him, or in any resolution passed by the insurer in general meeting or by his Board of Directors shall have effect unless approved by the Authority;

(*b*) no appointment, re appointment or termination of appointment made after the commencement of the Insurance (Amendment) Act, 1968, of a managing or whole time director, or a manager or a chief executive officer, by whatever name called, shall have effect unless such appointment, re-appointment or termination of appointment is made with the previous approval of the Authority.

Explanation : For the purposes of this sub section, any provision conferring any benefit or providing any amenity or perquisite, in whatever form, whether during or after the termination of the term of office of the manager or the chief executive officer, by whatever name called or a managing or whole time director, shall be deemed to be a provision relating to his remuneration.

(2) Nothing contained in Sections 268 and 269, the proviso to sub section (3) of Section 309, Sections 310 and 311, the proviso to Section 387 and Section 388 (in so far as Section 388 makes the provisions of Sections 310 and 311 apply in relation to the manager of a company) of the Companies Act, 1956 (1 of 1956), shall apply to any matter in respect of which the approval of the Authority has to be obtained under sum section (1).

(3) No act done by a person as a managing or whole time director or a director not liable to retire by rotation or a manager or a chief executive officer, by whatever name called, shall be deemed to be invalid on the ground that it is subsequently discovered that his appointment or re appointment had not taken effect by reason of any of the provisions of this Act; but nothing in this subsection shall be construed as rendering valid any act done by such person after his appointment or re appointment has been shown to the insurer not to have had effect.

Power of Authority to Remove Managerial Persons from Office

Section 34B : (1) Where the Authority is satisfied that in the public interest or for preventing the affairs of an insurer being conducted in a manner detrimental to the interests of the policy holders or for securing the proper management of any insurer it is necessary so to do, he may, for reasons to be recorded in writing, by order, remove from office, with effect from such date as may be specified in the order, any director or the chief executive officer, by whatever name called, of the insurer.

(2) No order under sub section (1) shall be made unless the director or chief executive officer concerned has been given a reasonable opportunity of making a representation to the Authority against the proposed order:

Provided that if, in the opinion of the Controller, any delay would be detrimental to the interests of the insurer or his policy holders, he may, at the time of giving the opportunity aforesaid or at any time thereafter, by order direct that, pending the consideration of the representation aforesaid, if any, the director or, as the case may be, chief executive officer, shall not, with effect from the date of such order, :

(*a*) act as such director or chief executive officer of the insurer;

(*b*) in any way, whether directly, indirectly, be concerned with, or take part in the management of the insurer.

(3) Where any order is made in respect of a director or chief executive officer of an insurer under sub section (1), he shall cease to be a director or as the case may be chief executive officer of the insurer and shall not, in any way, whether directly or indirectly, be concerned with, or take part in, the management of any insurer for such period not exceeding five years as may be specified in the order.

(4) If any person in respect of whom an order is made by the Authority under sub section (1) or under the proviso to sub section (2) contravenes the provisions of this section, he shall be punishable with fine which may extend to two hundred and fifty rupees for each day during which such contravention continues.

(5) Where an order under sub section (1) has been made, the Authority may, by order in writing, appoint a suitable person in place of the director or chief executive officer who has been removed from his office under that sub-section, with effect from such date as may be specified in the order.

(6) Any person appointed as director or chief executive officer under this section shall :

(*a*) hold office during the pleasure of the Controller and subject thereto for a period not exceeding three years or such further periods not exceeding three years at a time as the Authority may specify;

(b) not incur any obligation or liability by reason only of his being a director or chief executive officer or for anything done or omitted to be done in good faith in the execution of the duties of his office or in relation thereto.

(7) Notwithstanding anything contained in any law or in any contract, memorandum or articles of association, on the removal of a person from office under this section, that person shall not be entitled to claim any compensation for the loss or termination of office.

Power of Controller to Appoint Additional Directors

Section 34C : (1) If the Authority is of opinion that in the public interest or in the interests of an insurer or his policy holders it is necessary so to do, he may, from time to time, by order in writing, appoint, with effect from such date as may be specified in the order, one or more persons to hold office as additional directors of the insurer:

Provided that the number of additional directors so appointed shall not, at any time, exceed five or one third of the maximum strength fixed for the Board by the articles of association of the insurer, whichever is less.

(2) Any person appointed as additional director in pursuance of this section,—

(*a*) shall hold office during the pleasure of the Authority, and subject thereto for a period not exceeding three years or such further periods not exceeding three years at a time as the Authority may specify;

(*b*) shall not incur any obligation or liability by reason only of his being a director or for anything done or omitted to be done in good faith in the execution of the duties of his office or in relation thereto; and

(*c*) shall not be required to hold qualification shares of the insurer.

(3) For the purpose of reckoning any preparation of the total number of directors of the insurer, any additional director appointed under this section shall not be taken into account.

Sections 34B and 34C to Override Other Laws

Section 34 D : Any appointment or removal of a director or chief executive officer in pursuance of Section 34B or Section 34C shall have effect notwithstanding anything to the contrary contained in the Companies Act, 1956 (1 of 1956), or any other law for the time being in force or in any contract or any other instrument.

Powers of Tariff Advisory Committee (TAC)

Section 64UC read together with the Insurance Rules 1939 defines the role and powers of TAC.

Power of the Advisory Committee to Regulate Rates, Advantages, etc.

Section 64UC : (1) The Advisory Committee may, from time to time and to the extent it deems expedient, control and regulate the rates, advantages, terms and conditions that may be offered by insurers in respect of any risk or any class or category of risks, the rates, advantages, terms and conditions of which, in its opinion, it is proper to control and regulate, and any such rate, advantages, terms and conditions shall be binding on all insurers:

Provided that the Authority may, permit any insurer to offer, during such period (being not more than two years but which may be extended by periods of not more than two years at a time) and subject to such conditions as may be specified by him, rates, advantages, terms or conditions different from those fixed by the Advisory Committee in respect of any particular category of risks, if he is satisfied that such insurer generally issues policies only to a restricted class of the public or under a restricted category of risks.

(2) In fixing, amending or modifying any rates, advantages, terms or conditions, relating to any risk, the Advisory Committee shall try to ensure, as far as possible, that there is no unfair discrimination between risk of essentially the same hazard, and also that consideration is given to past and prospective loss experience:

Provided that the Advisory Committee may, at its discretion, make suitable allowances for the degree of credibility to be assigned to the past experience including allowances for random fluctuations and may also, at its discretion, make suitable allowances for future fluctuations and unforeseen future contingencies including hazards of conflagration or catastrophe or both.

(3) Every decision of the Advisory Committee shall be valid only after and to the extent it is ratified by the Authority, and every such decision shall take effect from the date on which it is so ratified by the Authority, or if the Authority so orders in any case, from such earlier date as he may specify in the order.

(4) The decisions of the Advisory Committee in pursuance of the provisions of this section shall be final.

(5) Where an insurer is guilty of breach of any rate, advantage, term or condition fixed by the Advisory Committee, he shall be deemed to have contravened the provisions of this Act.

Provided that instead of proceeding against the insurer for such contravention, the Authority may, if the insurer removes the contravention by recovering the deficiency in the premium, or where it is not practicable to do so, modifies suitably or cancels the contract of insurance, compound the offence on payment to the Advisory Committee of such fine, not exceeding rupees one thousand, as he may decide in consultation with the Advisory Committee.

Transitional Provisions

Section 64UD : (1) Notwithstanding anything contained in this Part, until the names of the members of the Advisory Committee elected for the first time after the commencement of the Insurance (Amendment) Act, 1968, are notified, the Tariff Committee of the General Insurance Council appointed under regulations made under sub section (2) of Section 64-0 as it was in force immediately before the commencement of the Insurance (Amendment) Act, 1968, and in existence on such commencement (hereafter in this Part referred to as the Tariff Committee) shall continue to function and shall be deemed to be the Advisory Committee duly elected under this Part and the Authority of Insurance shall become the Chairman of that Committee with effect from the commencement of the Insurance (Amendment) Act, 1968, and function as such, and any chairman of the Tariff Committee holding office immediately before such commencement shall cease to be the Chairman thereof from the date of such commencement but shall continue to be an ordinary member of the Advisory Committee.

Provided that the Chairperson of the Authority shall become the Chairman of the Advisory committee with effect from the commencement of the Insurance Regulatory and Development Authority Act, 1999 and function as such, and any chairman of the Tariff Committee holding office immediately before such commencement shall cease to be the Chairman.

(2) Notwithstanding anything contained in this Part, the constitution of the Regional Councils established under Section 64 P, as in force immediately before the commencement of the Insurance (Amendment) Act, 1968 (hereafter referred to as the Regional Councils), and of the Sectional Committees formed there under, existing immediately before such commencement, shall continue to be in full force and be of full effect until the regulations made by the Advisory Committee for the first time under Section 64UB come into effect and as soon as such regulations have come into effect such constitutions shall cease to have effect.

(3) Notwithstanding anything contained in this Part, until the Secretary to the Advisory Committee is nominated under sub section (2) of Section 64UA, the Secretary to the Tariff Committee holding office immediately before the commencement of the Insurance (Amendment) Act, 1968, shall function as the Secretary and shall be deemed to have been duly nominated under this Part.

(4) All rates, advantages, terms and conditions fixed by the Tariff Committee or the Regional Councils prior to the commencement of the Insurance (Amendment) Act, 1968, and in force immediately before such commencement shall continue,

except to such extent as they may be altered, replaced or abolished by the Advisory Committee, to be valid and fully in force as if they were rates, advantages, terms and conditions fixed by the Advisory Committee.

Power of the Advisory Committee to Require Information, etc.

Section 64UE : (1) The Advisory Committee may require, by notice in writing, any insurer to supply to it such information or statements, periodical or *ad hoc, as* it may consider necessary to enable it to discharge its functions under this Part and every insurer shall comply with such requirements within such period as may be specified by the Advisory Committee in this behalf, failing which the insurer shall be deemed to have contravened the provisions of this Act.

(2) Any information supplied under this section shall be certified by a principal officer of the insurer or where the Advisory Committee has agreed in advance, by such other officer or officers of the insurer as the principal officer of the insurer may nominate for the purpose and if the notice so requires, also by an auditor.

(3) The Authority may, at any time, in writing, depute any subordinate of his, to make a personal inspection of the books of account, ledgers, policy registers and other books or documents of any insurer to verify the accuracy of any return or statement furnished by him under sub section (1), or to verify that full particulars have been supplied by him in respect of all policies issued by him and the insurer shall provide all facilities for such inspection, and make available to such person all the books of account, ledgers, policy registers and other books or documents of the insurer which might be needed by him for such verification and the person deputed may himself extract from out of the books and records of the insurer such information as may be needed to fill up or complete the returns required to be submitted to the Advisory Committee under this section.

(4) The Advisory Committee may, at any time, on the application of an insurer, make arrangements for the inspection of an organization which is concerned with the inspection of risks, adjustment of losses or fire fighting appliances, and may, whenever necessary, advise insurers about the adequacy of the arrangements for the inspection of risks and adjustment of losses or the suitability of such appliances:

Provided that no such inspection shall be made without the written permission of the concerned organization

Insurance Association of India

All the existing insurers, provident societies and also new entrants to join the Insurance Association of India and the Central Government, by an official notification in the Gazette will declare that all the existing insurers and provident societies are the members of the Insurance Association of India. This association is a separate entity with a common seal and perpetual succession and will have the power to acquire, hold, to sell the movable and immovable property of the association. The Insurance Association shall maintain a register of the membership and register of associate members of the Insurance Association of India. And, the names of the insurer or provident society will be removed from the register on ceasing its business of insurance. The Insurance Association of India is having two councils – Life Insurance Council and General Insurance Council.

2.8 ACCOUNTS AND RETURNS (Section 10-26)

An insurer is required to keep a separate account of all receipts and payments in respect of each class of insurance viz., Fire, Marine and miscellaneous Insurance. Every insurer is required to prepare, at the expiration of each financial year, in the prescribed forms,

(*a*) a balance sheet

(*b*) a profit and loss account

(*c*) a revenue account for each class of insurance business

These accounts are required to be audited annually by an auditor and printed and four copies to be furnished as returns to the IRDA within 6 months from the close of the financial year. Every Insurer is required to furnish to the authority a certified copy of the minutes of the proceedings of every General Meeting, within 30 days from the holding of the meeting. The Insurance Rules framed under the Act provide that the following items of information shall be maintained in respect of each class of business :

- A record of cover notes specifying the identification number, name of party, dates of commencement and expiry, type of cover granted, the amount of premium and cross- reference to the policy.
- A record of policies, which should be serially numbered, listing all policies issued, entered in chronological order, stating the number of policy, date of commencement and expiry of risk, name/s of the insured, premium received, cross reference to the relevant bank Guarantee or deposit and the nature of risk granted, cross reference to any cover-note issued prior to the issue to the policy and cross-reference to any endorsement passed subsequent to the issue of the policy.
- A record of premiums showing, according to chronological order or receipt of premiums, date of receipt, the amount, and name of party from whom received and with cross- reference to policy number.
- A record of endorsements mentioning the policy number to which attached, dates of commencement and expiry of the endorsement, the type of endorsement and the additional premium charged or refund due and cross reference to the premium register.
- A record of bank guarantees and deposits giving particulars of the party, amount and conditions of guarantee or deposits and cross-reference to the relevant policy or policies.

- A record of claims intimate mentioning name of claimant, giving reference to policy number, date of intimation of claim, interest covered, nature and cause of the loss or damage, provisional estimate of loss, amount at which settled, date of settlement of claim, recoveries from salvage or otherwise and whether surveyed. Two separate records, one relating to claims intimated and the other relating to claims paid, may be maintained if there is adequate cross referring of information between them and if the information required under this clause is readily available from them taken together.

The rules framed under the Insurance Act, 1938 also provide that the following items of information shall be maintained for the business of the insurer as a whole.

(*i*) A register of agents.

(*ii*) A record of business procured by each agent and the amount of commission paid thereon.

(*iii*) Records of employees including field workers.

(*iv*) Cash book and disbursement book.

(*v*) A record of investments and assets.

(*vi*) Records of insurance companies with which common and facultative reinsurance arrangements of reinsurance treaties are entered into.

(*vii*) Record of facultative reinsurance ceded and accepted.

Further, the Rules provide that receipts for payments received shall be maintained in a systematic manner and documents used for assuming risk are serially numbered and field accordingly. The documents relating to claims settled, including copies of any survey of loss assessment reports, shall be maintained as follows :

(*i*) in respect of every loss or damage on which a claim of less than Rs. 5,000 has been made, for a period of three years;

(*ii*) in respect of every loss or damage on which a claim of Rs. 5,000 or more but less than rupees Rs. 20,000 has been made, for a period of five years;

(*iii*) in respect of every loss or damage on which a claim of Rs. 20,000 or more but less than rupees one lakh has been made, for a period of seven years;

(*iv*) in respect of every loss or damage on which a claim of rupees one lakh or more has been made, for a period of twelve years;

such period being counted from the date on which the claim is settled.

2.9 WINDING UP OF INSURANCE COMPANIES

All the existing insurers, provident societies and also new entrants to join the Insurance Association of India and the Central Government, by an official notification in the Gazette will declare that all the existing insurers and provident societies are the members of the Insurance Association of India. This association is a separate entity with a common seal and perpetual succession and will have the power to acquire, hold, to sell the movable and immovable property of the association. The Insurance Association shall maintain a register of the membership and register of associate members of the Insurance Association of India. And, the names of the insurer of provident society will be removed from the register on ceasing its business of insurance. The Insurance Association of India is having two councils – Life Insurance Council and General Insurance Council.

Power of Central Government to Acquire Undertakings of Insurers in Certain Cases

Section 52H : (1) If, upon receipt of a report from the Authority, the Central Government is satisfied that an insurer,-

(*a*) has persistently failed to comply with—

(*i*) any direction given to him under Section 34, Section 34 F or Section 34G, or

(*ii*) any order made under Sec. 34 E; or

(*b*) is being managed in a manner detrimental to the public interest or to the interests of his policy holders, or share holders,

and that-

I. in the public interest, or

II. in the interest of the policy holders or share holders of such insurer,

it is necessary to acquire the undertaking of such insurer, the Central Government may, by notified order, acquire the undertaking of such insurer (hereafter in this section and in Sections 52 I, 52 J and 52 N and in the Eighth Schedule referred to as the acquired insurer) with effect from such date as maybe specified in the order (hereinafter in this section and in Sections 52 1 and 52J and in the Eighth Schedule referred to as the appointed day):

Provided that no undertaking off an insurer shall be so acquired unless such insurer has been given a reasonable opportunity of showing cause against the proposed action.

Explanation : For the purposes of this section and of Sections 52 I to 52N—

(*a*) "notified order" means an order published in the official Gazette;

(*b*) "undertaking", in relation to an insurer incorporated outside India, means the undertaking of the insurer in India,

(2) Subject to the other provisions contained in this section and in Sections 52-I to 52M, on the appointed day, all the assets and liabilities of the undertaking of the acquired insurer shall stand transferred to, and vest in, the Central Government.

(3) The assets and liabilities of the undertaking of the acquired insurer shall be deemed to include all rights, powers, authorities and privileges and all property, whether movable or immovable, including, in particular, cash balances, reserve funds, investments, deposits and all other interests and rights in, or arising out of, such property' as may be in the possession of or held by, the acquired insurer immediately before the appointed day and all books, accounts and documents relating thereto, and shall also be deemed to include all debts, liabilities and obligations of whatever kind, then existing of the acquired insurer.

(4) Notwithstanding anything contained in sub section (2), the Central Government may, if it is satisfied that all the assets and liabilities of the undertaking of the acquired insurer should, instead of vesting in the Central Government, or continuing to so vest, vest in a corporation or company, whether established under the scheme made under Sec. 52 I or not (hereafter In this section and in Section 52 1 to 52 N and in the Eighth Schedule referred to as the acquired insurer), by order, direct that the assets and liabilities of the said undertaking, shall vest in the acquiring insurer, either on the publication of the notified order or no such other date as may be specified in this behalf in the direction.

(5) Where the undertaking of the acquired insurer vests in an acquiring insurer under sub section (4), the acquiring insurer shall, on and from the date of such vesting, be deemed to have become the transferee of the acquired insurer and all the rights and liabilities in relation to the acquired insurer shall, on and from the date of such vesting, be deemed to have been the rights and liabilities of such acquiring insurer.

(6) Unless otherwise expressly provided by or under this section or Sections 52 I to 52M, all contracts, deeds, bonds, agreements, powers of attorney, grants of legal representation and other instruments of whatever nature subsisting, having effect immediately before the appointed day and to which the acquired insurer is a party or which are in favour of the acquired insurer shall be of as full force and effect against or in favour, of the Central Government or, as the case may be, the acquiring insurer, and may be enforced or acted upon as fully and effectually as of in the place of the acquired insurer the Central Government or the acquiring insurer had been a party thereto or as if they had been issued in favour of the Central Government or the acquiring insurer, as the case may be.

(7) If, on the appointed day, any suit, appeal or other proceeding, of whatever nature, is pending by or against the acquired insurer the same shall not abate, be discontinued or be, in any way, prejudicially affected by reason of the transfer of the undertaking of the acquired insurer or of anything contained in this section or in Sections 52 I to 52M, but the suit, appeal or other proceeding may be continued, prosecuted and enforced by or against the Central Government or the acquiring insurer, as the case may be.

Winding up by the Court

Section 53 : (1) The Court may order the winding up in accordance with the

Indian Companies Act, 1913 (7 of 1913), of any insurance company and the provisions of that Act shall, subject to the provisions of this Act apply accordingly.

(2) In additional to the grounds on which such an order may be based, the Court may order the winding up of an insurance company

(*a*) if with the sanction of the Court previously obtained a petition in this behalf is presented by shareholders not less in number than one tenth of the whole body of shareholders and holding not less than one tenth of the whole share capital or by not less than fifty policy holders holding policies of life insurance that have been in force for not less than three years and are of the total value of not less than fifty thousand rupees; or

(*b*) if the Authority, who is hereby authorised to do so, applies in this behalf to the Court on any of the following grounds, namely-

(*i*) that the company has failed to deposit or to keep deposited with the Reserve Bank of India the amounts required by Section 7 or Section 98;

(*ii*) that the company having failed to comply with any requirement of this Act has continued such failure Nor having contravened any provision of this Act has continued such contravention for a period of three months after notice of such failure Nor contravention has been conveyed to the company by the Authority.

(*iii*) that it appears from Many returns or statements furnished under the provisions of this Act or from the results of any investigation made there under that the company is, or is deemed to be, insolvent, or

(*iv*) that the continuance of the company is prejudicial to the interest if the policy holders or to the public interest generally

Voluntary Winding Up

Section 54 : Notwithstanding anything contained in the Indian Companies Act, 1913 (7 of 1913), an insurance company shall not be wound up voluntarily except for the purpose of effecting an amalgamation or a re construction of the company, or on the ground that by reason of its liabilities it cannot continue its business.

Valuation of Liabilities

Section 55 : (1) In the winding up of an insurance company or in the insolvency of any other insurer the value of the assets and the liabilities of the insurer shall be ascertained in such manner and upon such basis as the liquidator or receiver in insolvency thinks fit, subject, so far as applicable, to the rule contained in the Seventh Schedule and to any directions which may be given by the Court.

(2) For the purposes of any reduction by the Court of the amount of the contracts of any insurance company the value of the assets and liabilities of the company and all claims in respect of policies issued by it shall be ascertained in such

manner and upon such basis as the Court thinks proper having regard to the rule aforesaid.

(3) The rule in the Seventh Schedule shall be of the same force and may be repealed, altered or amended as if it were a rule made in pursuance of section 246 of the Indian Companies Act, 1913 (7 of 1913) and rules may be made under that section for the purpose of carrying into effect the provisions of this Act with respect to the winding up of insurance companies.

Application of Surplus Assets of Life Insurance Fund in Liquidation or Insolvency

Section 56 : (1) In the winding up of an insurance company and in the insolvency of any other insurer the value of the assets and the liabilities of the insurer in respect of life insurance business shall be ascertained separately from the value of any other assets or any other liabilities of the insurer and no such assets shall be applied to the discharge of any liabilities other than those in respect of life insurance business except in so far as those assets exceed the liabilities in respect of life insurance business.

(2) In the winding up of an insurance company carrying on the business of life insurance or in the insolvency of any other insurer carrying on such business where any proportion of the profits of the insurer was before the commencement of the winding up or insolvency allocated to policy holders, if, when the assets and liabilities of the insurer have been ascertained, there is found to be a surplus of assets over liabilities (hereinafter referred to as a *prima facie* surplus) there shall be added to the liabilities of the insurer in respect of the life insurance business an amount equal to such proportion of the *prima facie* surplus as is equivalent to such proportion of the profits allocated to share-holders and policy holders as was allocated to policy holders during the ten years immediately preceding the commencement of the winding up and the assets of the insurer shall be deemed to exceed his liabilities only in so far as those assets exceed those liabilities after such addition:

Provided that :

(*a*) if in any case there has been no such allocation or if it appears to the Court that by reason of special circumstances it would be inequitable that the amount to be added to the liabilities of the insurer in respect of the life insurance business should be an amount equal to such proportion as aforesaid, the amount to be so added shall be such amount as the Court may direct, and

(*b*) for the purpose of the application of this sub section to any case where before the commencement of the winding up or insolvency a proportion of such profits as aforesaid of a branch only of the life insurance business in question has been allocated to policy holders, the value of the assets and liabilities of the insurer in respect of that branch shall be separately ascertained in like manner as the value of his assets and liabilities in respect to the life insurance business was ascertained, and the surplus so found, if any, of assets over liabilities shall, for the purpose of determining the amount to be added to :the liabilities of the insurer in respect of the life insurance business be deemed to be the *prima facie surplus*..-

Winding up of Secondary Companies

Section 57 : (l) Where the insurance business or any part of the insurance business of an insurance company has been transferred to another insurance company under an arrangement in pursuance of which the first mentioned company (in this section referred to as the secondary company) or the creditors thereof has or have claims against the company to which such transfer was made (in this section referred to as the principal company) then, if the principal company is being wound up by or under the supervision of the Court, the Court shall (subject as hereinafter mentioned) order the secondary company to be wound up in conjunction with the principal company and may, by the same or any subsequent order appoint the same person to be liquidator for the two companies and make provision for such other matters as may seem to the Court necessary with a view to the companies being wound up as if they were one company.

(2) The commencement of the winding up of the principal company shall, save as otherwise ordered by the Court, be the commencement of the winding up of the secondary company.

(3) In adjusting the rights and liabilities of the members of the several companies among themselves the Court shall have regard to the constitution of the companies and to the arrangements entered into between the companies in the same manner as the Court has regard to the rights and liabilities of different classes of contributories in the case of the winding up of a single company or as near thereto as circumstances admit.

(4) Where any company alleged to be secondary is not in process of being wound up at the same time as the principal company to which it is alleged to be secondary, the Court shall not direct the secondary company to be wound up, unless, after hearing all objections (if any) that may be urged by or on behalf of the company against its being wound up, the Court is of opinion that the company is secondary to the principal company and that the winding up of the company in conjunction with the principal company is just and equitable.

(5) An application may be made in relation to the winding up of any secondary company in conjunction with the principal company by any creditor of, or person interested in, the principal or secondary company.

(6) Where a company stands in the relation of a principal company to one insurance company and in the relation of a secondary company to some other insurance company or where there are several insurance companies standing in the relation of secondary companies to one principal company, the court may deal with any

number of such companies together or in separate groups as it thinks most expedient upon the principles laid down in this section.

Schemes for Partial Winding up of Insurance Companies

Section 58 : (1) If at any time it appears expedient that the affairs of an insurance company in respect of any class of business comprised in the undertaking of the Company should be wound up but that any other class of business comprised in the undertaking should continue to be carried on by the company or be transferred to another insurer, a scheme for such purposes may be prepared and submitted for confirmation of the Court in accordance with the provisions of this Act.

(2) Any scheme prepared under this section shall provide for the allocation and distribution of the assets and liabilities of the company between any classes of business affected (including the allocation of any surplus assets which may arise on the proposed winding up) for any future rights of every class of policy holders in respect of their policies and for the manner of winding up any of the affairs of the company which are proposed to be wound up and may contain provisions for altering the memorandum of the company with respect to its objects and such further provisions as may be expedient for giving effect to the scheme.

(3) The provisions of this Act relating to the valuation of liabilities of insurers in liquidation and insolvency and to the application of surplus assets of the life insurance fund in liquidation or insolvency shall apply to the winding up of any part of the affairs of a company in accordance with the scheme under this section in like manner as they apply in the winding up of an insurance company, and any scheme under this section may apply with the necessary modifications any of the provisions of the Indian Companies Act, 1913 (7 of 1913), relating to the winding up of companies.

(4) An order of the Court confirming a scheme under this section whereby the memorandum of a company is altered with respect to its objects shall as respects the alteration have effect as if it where an order confirmed under Sec. 12 of the Indian Companies Act, 1913 (7 of 1913), and the provisions of Sections 15 and 16 of that Act shall apply accordingly.

Notice of Policy Values

Section 60 : In the winding up of an insurance company for the purposes of a cash distribution of the assets and in the insolvency of any other insurer the liquidator or assignee, as the case may be, in the case of all persons appearing by the books of the company or other insurer to be entitled to or interested in the policies granted by the company or other insurer shall ascertain the value of the liability of the company or other insurer to each such person and shall give notice of such value to those persons in such manner as the Court may direct and any person to whom notice is so given shall be bound by the value so ascertained unless he gives notice of his intention to dispute such value in such manner and within such time as may be specified by a rule or order of the Court.

Power of Court to Reduce Amount of Contracts of Insurance

Section 61 : (1) where an insurance company is in liquidation or any other insurer is insolvent, the Court may make an order reducing the amount of the insurance contracts of the company or other insurer upon such terms and subject to such conditions as the Court thinks Just.

(2) Where a company carrying on the business of life insurance has been proved to be insolvent, the Court may if it thinks fit in place of making a winding up order reduce the amount of the insurance contracts of the company upon such terms and subject to such conditions as the Court thinks fit.

(3) Application for an order under this section may be made either by the liquidator or by or on behalf of the company or by a policy holder, or by the Authority and the Authority and any person whom the Court thinks likely to be affected shall be entitled to be heard on any such application.

2.10 MISCELLANEOUS PROVISIONS

Prohibition of Rebates

No person shall allow or offer to allow as an inducement to any person to take out insurance any rebate of the whole or part of commission payable or any rebate of the premium shown in the policy. Any person making default in complying with these provisions shall be punishable with fine which may extend to five hundred rupees.

Licensing of Surveyor or Loss Assessor

A surveyor or a loss assessor must hold a valid licence, which is subject to renewal after a period of 5 years. Before admitting a claim exceeding Rs. 20,000 a general insurance company needs to obtain a report on the loss that has occurred from the surveyor or loss assessor.

Penalties

The Act has laid down penalties for contravention of the following provisions :

- Failure to maintain solvency margins.
- Failure to comply with investment norms.
- Failure to carry out rural and social sector obligations.
- Making a false statement or furnishing a false document.
- Failure to comply with the directions of the Authority.
- Failure to furnish documents, statements and returns required by the Act.

Key Terms

- Licensing
- Rebate
- Registration
- Refund
- Investment
- Tariff Advisory Committee
- Assignment
- Commission
- Winding up
- Insurance Association of India
- Deposits
- Paid-up Capital
- Remuneration
- Controller
- Nomination

References

★ *www.irdaindia*

★ *Bare Act – Insurance Act, 1938*

★ *www.bimaonline.com*

★ *www.licindia.com*

Questions for Review

1. Briefly explain the licensing procedure for insurers under the Insurance Act, 1938.
2. Write short notes on :
   (*a*) Accounts and Return
   (*b*) Advance Premium
   (*c*) Appointment of Agents / in light of the Insurance Act, 1938.
3. Enumerate the manner of investments by insurer as prescribed by the Insurance Act, 1938.
4. Discuss the various modes of winding up of insurance companies.

Life Insurance Corporation Act, 1956

Life insurance business in India is regulated by the provisions of the Insurance Act, 1938, Insurance Rule, 1939 and the Life Insurance Corporation Act, 1956 and rules and regulation made thereunder.

Section 2(11) of the Insurance Act, 1938 defines the life insurance business as 'the business effecting contract of insurance upon human life, including any contract where by the payment of money is assured on death (except death by accident) or the happening of any contingency dependent on human life, and any contract which is subject to payment of premiums for a term dependent on human life and shall deemed to include (1) the granting of disability and double and triple indemnity accident benefits, if so, provided in the contract of insurance; (ii) the granting of annuities upon human life and granting of superannuation allowances and annuities payable out of any fund applicable solely to the relief and maintenance of persons engaged or who have been engaged in any particular profession, trade or employment or of the dependents of such persons.

Life Insurance Corporation of India (LIC) was formed in September, 1956 by an Act of Parliament, *viz.*, Life Insurance Corporation Act, 1956, with Capital contribution of Rs. 5 crore from the Government of India. Its main duty was to spread the message of Life Insurance in the country and mobilise peoples saving for nation-building activities. Life Insurance Corporation has also framed regulations *viz.*, Life Insurance Corporation (Staff) Regulation, 1960 and Life Insurance Corporation (Agents) Rules, 1972.

3.1 DEFINITIONS

(1) *"appointed day"* means the date on which the Corporation is established under section 3;

(2) *"composite insurer"* means an insurer carrying on in addition to controlled business any other kind of insurance business;

(3) *"controlled business"* means :

(*i*) in the case of any insurer specified in sub-clause (*a*) (*ii*) or sub-clause (*b*) of clause (9) of section 2 of the Insurance Act and carrying on life insurance business :

(*a*) all his business, if he carries on no other class of insurance business;

(*b*) all the business appertaining to his life insurance business, if he carries on any other class of insurance business also;

(*c*) all his business if his certificate of registration under the Insurance Act in respect of general insurance business stands wholly cancelled for a period of more than six months on the 19th day of January, 1956.

(*ii*) in the case of any other insurer specified in clause (9) of section 2 of the Insurance Act and carrying on life insurance business :

(*a*) all his business in India, if he carries on no other class of insurance business in India;

(*b*) all the business appertaining to his life insurance business in India, if he carries on any other class of insurance business also in India;.

(*c*) all his business in India if he certificate of registration under the Insurance Act in respect of general insurance business in India stands wholly cancelled for a period of more than six months on the 19th day of January, 1956.

Explanation : An insurer is said to carry on no class of insurance business other than life insurance business, if in addition to life insurance business, he carries on only capital redemption business or annuity certain business or both; and the expression "business appertaining to his life insurance business" in sub-clause (*i*) and (*ii*) shall be construed accordingly;

(*iii*) in the case of a provident society, as defined in section 65 of the Insurance Act, all its business;

(*iv*) in the case of the Central Government or a State Government, all life insurance business carried on by it, subject to the exceptions specified in section 44;

(4) "*Corporation*" means the Life Insurance Corporation of India established under section 3;

(5) "*Insurance Act*" means the Insurance Act, 1938 (4 of 1938);

(6) "*insurer*" means an insurer as defined in the Insurance Act who carries on life insurance business in India and includes the Government and a provident society as defined in section 65 of the Insurance Act;

(7) "*member*" means a member of the Corporation;

(8) "*prescribed*" means prescribed by rules made under this Act;

(9) "*Tribunal*" means a Tribunal constituted under section 17 and having jurisdiction in respect of any matter under the rules made under this Act;

(10) all other words and expressions used herein but not defined and defined in the Insurance Act shall have the meanings respectively assigned to them in that Act.

3.2 ESTABLISHMENT OF LIFE INSURANCE CORPORATION OF INDIA

Establishment and Incorporation of Life Insurance Corporation of India *Section 3:* (1) With effect from such date {1st September, 1956, vide Notification No.

S.R.O. 1937, dated 30-8-1956, Gazette of India, Extraordinary, Pt. II, Sec.3, p. 1799.} as the Central Government may, by notification in the Official Gazette, appoint, there shall be established a Corporation called the Life Insurance Corporation of India.

(2) The Corporation shall be a body corporate having perpetual succession and a common seal with power subject to the provisions of this Act, to acquire, hold and dispose of property, and may by its name sue and be sued.

Constitution of the Corporation

Section 4 : (1) The Corporation shall consist of such number of persons not exceeding fifteen as the Central Government may think fit to appoint thereto and one of them shall be appointed by the Central Government to be the Chairman thereof.

(2) Before appointing a person to be a member, the Central Government shall satisfy itself that that person will have no such financial or other interest as is likely to affect prejudicially the exercise or performance by him of his functions as a member, and the Central Government shall also satisfy itself from time to time with respect to every member that he has no such interest; and any person who is, or whom the Central Government proposes to appoint and who has consented to be, a member shall, whenever required by the Central Government so to do, furnish to it such information as the Central Government considers necessary for the performance of its duties under this sub-section.

(3) A member who is in any way directly or indirectly interested in a contract made or proposed to be made by the Corporation shall as soon as possible after the relevant circumstances have come to his knowledge, disclose the nature of his interest to the Corporation and the member shall not take part in any deliberation or discussion of the Corporation with respect to that contact.

Capital of the Corporation

Section 5 : (1) The original capital of the Corporation shall be five crores of rupees provided by the Central Government after due appropriation made by Parliament by law for the purpose, and the terms and conditions relating to the provision of such capital shall be such as may be determined by the Central Government.

(2) The Central Government may, on the recommendation of the Corporation, reduce the capital of the Corporation to such extent and in such manner as the Central Government may determine.

3.3 FUNCTIONS OF THE CORPORATION

Section 6 : (1) Subject, to the rules, if any, made by the Central Government in this behalf, it shall be the general duty of the Corporation to carry on life insurance business, whether in or outside India, and the Corporation shall so exercise its powers under this Act as to secure that life insurance business is developed to the best advantage of the community.

(2) Without prejudice to the generality of the provisions contained in sub-section (1) but subject to the other provisions contained in this Act, the Corporation shall have power :

(*a*) to carry on capital redemption business, annuity certain business or reinsurance business in so far as such re insurance business appertains to life insurance business;

(*b*) subject to the rules, if any, made by the Central Government in this behalf, to invest the funds of the Corporation in such manner as the Corporation may think fit and to take all such steps as may be necessary or expedient for the protection or realization of any investment; including the taking over of and administering any property offered as security for the investment until a suitable opportunity arises for its disposal;

(*c*) to acquire, hold and dispose of any property for the purpose of its business;

(*d*) to transfer the whole or any part of the life insurance business carried on outside India to any other person or persons, if in the interest of the Corporation it is expedient so to do;

(*e*) to advance or lend money upon the security of any movable property or otherwise;

(*f*) to borrow or raise any money in such manner and upon such security as the Corporation may think fit;

(*g*) to carry on either by itself or through any subsidiary any other business in any case where such other business was being carried on by a subsidiary of an insurer whose controlled business has been transferred to an vested in the Corporation under this Act;

(*h*) to carry on any other business which may seen to the Corporation to be capable of being conveniently carried on in connection with its business and calculated directly or indirectly to render profitable the business of the Corporation;

(*i*) to do all such things as may be incidental or conducive to the proper exercise of any of the powers of the Corporation.

(3) In the discharge of any of its functions the Corporation shall act so far as may be on business principles.

3.4 TRANSFER OF EXISTING LIFE INSURANCE BUSINESS TO THE CORPORATION

Assets and liabilities of existing insurers carrying on controlled business

Section 7 : (1) On the appointed day there shall be transferred to and vested in the

Corporation all the assets and liabilities appertaining to the controlled business of all insurers.

(2) The assets appertaining to the controlled business of an insurer shall be deemed to include all rights and powers, and all property, whether movable or immovable, appertaining to his controlled business, including, in particular, cash balances, reserve funds, investments, deposits and all other interests and rights in or arising out of such property as may be in the possession of the insurer and all books of account or documents relating to the controlled business of the insurer; and liabilities shall be deemed to include all debts, liabilities and obligations of whatever kind then existing and appertaining to the controlled business of the insurer.

Explanation : The expression "assets appertaining" to the controlled business of an insurer" :

(*a*) in relation to a composite insurer, includes that part of the paid-up capital of the insurer or assets representing such part which has or have been allocated to the controlled business of the insurer in accordance with the rules made in this behalf;

(*b*) in relation to a Government, means the amount lying to the credit of that business on the appointed day.

(3) Where any such assets are subject to any trust referred to in sub-section (6) of section 27 of the Insurance Act or to any other trust for the benefit of policy-holders, the assets shall be deemed to have vested in the Corporation free from any such trust.

On 01-09-1956, all the assets and liabilities of the existing insurers were transferred to the corporation.

3.5 CONDUCT OF BUSINESS

Provident, Superannuation and Other Like Funds

Section 8 : (1) Where an insurer whose controlled business is to be transferred to and vested in the Corporation under section 7, has established a provident or superannuation fund or any other like fund for the benefit of his employees and constituted a trust in respect thereof (hereinafter in this section referred to as an existing trust), the moneys standing to the credit of any such fund on the appointed day, together with any other assets belonging to such fund, shall, subject to the provisions of sub-section (2) stand transferred to and vest in the Corporation on the appointed day free from any such trust.

(2) Where all the employees of any such insurer do not become employees of the Corporation under section 11, the moneys and other assets belonging to any such fund as it referred to in sub-section (1), shall be apportioned between the trustees of the fund and the Corporation in the prescribed manner; and in case of any

dispute regarding such apportionment, the decision of the Central Government thereon shall be final.

(3) The Corporation shall, as soon as may be after the appointed day, constitute in respect of the moneys and other assets which are transferred to and vested in it under this section, one or more trusts having objects as similar to the objects of the existing trusts as in the circumstances may be practicable.

(4) Where all the moneys and other assets belonging to an existing trust are transferred to and vested in the Corporation under this section, the trustees of such trust, except as respects things done or omitted to be done before the appointed day.

General Effect of Vesting of Controlled Business

Section 9 : (1) Unless otherwise expressly provided by or under this Act, all contracts, agreements and other instruments of whatever nature subsisting or having effect immediately before the appointed day and to which an insurer whose controlled business has been transferred to and vested in the Corporation is a party or which are in favour of such insurer shall in so far as they relate to the controlled business of the insurer be of as full force and affect against or in favour of the Corporation, as the case may be, and may be enforced or acted upon as fully and effectually as if, instead of the insurer, the Corporation had been a party thereto or as if they had been entered into or issued in favour of the Corporation.

(2) If on the appointed day any suit, appeal or other legal proceeding of whatever nature is pending by or against an insurer, then, in so far as it relates to his controlled business, it shall not abate, be discontinued or be in any way prejudicially affected by reason of the transfer to the Corporation of the business of the insurer or anything done under this Act, but the suit, appeal or other proceeding may be continued prosecuted and enforced by or against the Corporation.

Provisions as to Composite Insurers

Section 10 : (1) For the removal of doubts it is hereby declared that in any case where an insurer whose controlled business has been transferred to an vested in the corporation under this Act is a composite insurer, the provisions of the preceding sections shall only apply to the extent to which any property appertains to his controlled business and to rights and powers acquired, and to debts, liabilities and obligations incurred, and to contracts, agreements and other instruments made by the insurer for the purposes of his controlled business and to legal proceedings relating to those purposes, and the provisions of those sections shall be construed accordingly.

(2) The Central Government may, by rules made in this behalf provide :

(*a*) for the determination of the question whether any property appertains to his controlled business or whether any rights, powers, debts, liabilities or obligations were acquired or incurred or any contract, agreement or other instrument was made by the insurer for the purposes of his controlled business or whether any documents relate to those purposes;

(*b*) doe the allocation of the paid-up capital or assets representing such paid-up capital, as the case may be, between the controlled business of the insurer and any other business;

(*c*) for substituting for any agreements entered into by any insurer partly for the purposes of his controlled business and partly for other purposes separate agreements in the requisite terms and for any apportionments and indemnities consequent thereon;

(*d*) for the severance of leases comprising property of which part only is transferred to And vested in the Corporation by virtue of this Act and for apportionment consequent on such severance;

(*e*) for the apportionment and the making of financial adjustments with respects to any debts, liabilities of obligations incurred by any such insurer partly for the purposes of his controlled business and partly for other purposes and for any necessary variation of mortgages and encumbrances relating to such debts, liabilities or obligations;

(*f*) for the apportionment of the moneys and other assets belonging to any provident or superannuation fund or any other like fund to which the provisions of section 8 do not apply between persons employed in connection with the controlled business of an insurer and other persons;

(*g*) for any other matters supplementary to or consequential on the matters aforesaid for which provision appears to be necessary or expedient.

(3) All rules made under this section shall be laid for not less than thirty days before both Houses of Parliament as soon as possible after they are made and shall be subject to such modifications as Parliament may make during the session in which they are so laid or the session immediately following.

(4) Where at any time before the expiration of six months from the appointed day a question has arisen under this section or under any rules made thereunder as to whether any property is or was held or used by the insurer for the purposes of his controlled business, the question shall be referred to the Tribunal for decision.

Power of Corporation to Modify Contracts of Life Insurance in Certain Cases

Section 14 : The corporation may, having regard to the financial condition on the appointed day of any insurer whose controlled business has been transferred to an vested in the Corporation, reduce the amounts of insurance under contracts of life insurance entered into by such insurer before the 19th day of January 1956, in such manner and subject to such conditions as it thinks fit:

Provided that no such reduction shall be made except in accordance with a scheme prepared by the Corporation in this behalf and approved by the Central Government.

Right of Corporation to Seek Relief in Respect of Certain Transactions of the Insurer

Section 15 : (1) Where an insurer whose controlled business has been transferred to and vested in the Corporation under this Act has, at any time within five years before the 19th day of January, 1956 :

(*a*) made any payment to any person without consideration;

(*b*) sold or disposed of any property of the insurer without consideration or for an inadequate consideration;

(*c*) acquired any property or rights for an excessive consideration:

(*d*) entered into or varied any agreement so as to require an excessive consideration to be paid or given by the insurer;

(*e*) entered into any other transaction of such an onerous nature as to cause a loss to, or impose a liability on, the insurer exceeding any benefit accruing to the insurer;

(*f*) if a composite insurer, transferred any property from his life department to his general department without consideration or for an inadequate consideration.

and the payment, sale, disposal, acquisition, agreement or variation thereof or other transaction or transfer was not reasonably necessary for the purpose of the controlled business of the insurer or was made with an unreasonable lack of prudence on the part of the insurer, regard being had in either case to the circumstances at the time, the Corporation may apply for relief to the Tribunal in respect of such transaction, and all parties to the transaction shall, unless the Tribunal otherwise directs, be made parties to the application.

(2) The Tribunal may make such order against any of the parties to the application as it thinks just having regard to the extent to which those parties were respectively responsible for the transaction or benefited from it and all the circumstances of the case.

(3) Where an application is made to the Tribunal under this section is respect of any transaction and the application is determined in favour of the Corporation, the Tribunal shall have exclusive jurisdiction to determine any claims outstanding in respect of the transaction.

Compensation for Acquisition of Controlled Business

Section 16 : (1) Where the controlled business of an insurer has been transferred to and vested in the Corporation under this Act, compensation shall be given by the Corporation to that insurer in accordance with the principles contained in the First Schedule.

(2) The amount of the compensation to be given in accordance with the aforesaid principles shall be determined by the Corporation in the first instance, and if the

amount so determined is approved by the Central Government it shall be offered to the insurer in full satisfaction of the compensation payable to him under this Act, and if, on the other hand, the amount so offered is not acceptable to the insurer he may within such time as may be prescribed for the purpose have the matter referred to the Tribunal for decision.

Constitution of Tribunals

Section 17 : (1) The Central Government may for the purposes of this Act constitute one or more Tribunals and each of the Tribunals shall consist of three members appointed by the Central Government one of whom shall be a person who is, or has been, a Judge of a High Court or has been a Judge of the Supreme Court, and he shall be the Chairman thereof.

(2) A Tribunal may choose one or more persons possessing special knowledge of any matter relating to any case under inquiry to assist the Tribunal in determining any question which has to be decided by it under this Act.

(3) Every Tribunal shall have the powers of a civil court while trying a suit under the Code of Civil Procedure, 1908 (5 of 1908), in respect of the following matters:

(*a*) summoning and enforcing the attendance of any person and examining him on oath;

(*b*) requiring the discovery and production of documents;

(*c*) receiving evidence on affidavits;

(*d*) issuing commissions for the examination of witnesses or documents.

(4) Every Tribunal shall have power to regulate its own procedure and decide all matters within its competence, and may review any of its decisions in the event of there being a mistake on the face of the record or correct any arithmetic or clerical error therein.

3.6 ORGANISATIONAL STRUCTURE

Offices, Branches and Agencies

Section 18 : (1) The central office of the Corporation shall be at such place as the Central Government may, by notification in the Official Gazette, specify.

(2) The Corporation shall establish a zonal office at each of the following places, namely, Bombay, Calcutta, Delhi, Kanpur and Madras, and, subject to the previous approval of the Central Government, may establish such other zonal offices as it thinks fit.

(3) The territorial limits of each zone shall be such as may be specified by the Corporation.

(4) There may be established as many divisional offices and branches in each zone as the Zonal Manager thinks fit.

Committees of the Corporation

Section 19 : (1) The Corporation may entrust the general superintendence and direction of its affairs and business to an Executive Committee consisting of not more than five of its members and the Executive Committee may exercise all powers and do all such acts and things as may be delegated to it by the Corporation.

(2) The Corporation may also constitute an investment Committed for the purpose of advising it in matters relating to the investment of its funds, and the Investment Committee shall consist of not more than seven members of whom not less than three shall be members of the Corporation and the remaining members shall be persons (whether members of the Corporation or not) who have special knowledge and experience in financial matters, particularly, matters relating to investment of funds.

(3) The Corporation may constitute such other Committees as it may think fir for the purpose of discharging such of its functions as may be delegated to them.

Managing Directors

Section 20 : The Corporation may appoint one or more persons to be the Managing Director or Directors of the Corporation, and every Managing Director shall be a whole-time officer of the Corporation and shall exercise such powers and perform such duties as may be entrusted or delegated to him by the Executive Committee or the Corporation.

Corporation to be Guided by the Directions of Central Government

Section 21 : In the discharge of its functions under this Act, the Corporation shall be guided by such directions in matters of policy involving public interest as the Central Government may give to it in writing; and if any question arises whether a direction relates to a matter of policy involving public interest the decision of the Central Government thereon shall be final.

3.7 OTHER IMPORTANT PROVISIONS

Exclusive privilege of carrying on life insurance in India : Section 30 of the Act gives the Corporation the exclusive privilege of carrying on life insurance business in India on and from the appointed day.

Policies guaranteed by Central Government : By virtue of Section 37, the sums assured by all policies issued by the Corporation or by any insurer the liabilities under which have vested in the Corporation and all bonuses declared in respect thereof are guaranteed as to payment in cash by the Central Government.

Rule making powers of the Central Government : Section 48 empowers the Central Government to make rules to carry out the purposes of the Act. The rules may provide, *interalia*, for :

(*i*) the terms of office and conditions of service of members;

(*ii*) the manner in which and the conditions subject to which investment may be made by the Corporation;

(*iii*) the form in which the report giving an account of the activities of the Corporation shall be prepared;

(*iv*) the conditions subject to which the Corporation may appoint employees.

Powers of the Corporation to make Regulations : Section 49 empowers the Corporation, with the previous approval of the Central Government, by notification in the Gazette of India, to make regulations for the purpose of giving effect to the provisions of the Act.

The Schedules to the Act deal with principles for determining, compensation, principles for determining the value of liabilities in certain cases and principles for determining compensation payable to chief agents.

3.8 LIFE INSURANCE CORPORATION REGULATION, 1959

These regulation have been made by the Life Insurance Corporation of India in accordance with the powers vested u/s 49 of the Act subject to previous approval of Central Government. A brief summary of these regulations is given below :

Corporation shall meet atleast once in three months at a place which the Chairman may determine. Five members personally present shall be a quorum for a meeting and in the absence of quorum at a meeting, the meeting shall be adjourned to another date within a week of such meeting. If at the adjourned meeting also, the quorum is not present within half an hour from the time appointed for the meeting, the members present shall be the quorum.l These provisions are similar to those given in the companies Act, 1956. Three high powered (management) committees have been prescribed :

1. The Executive Committee
2. Investment Committee
3. Building Advisory Committee

Chairman shall be the Chief Executive of the Corporation. The Managing Directors may, with the approval of the Chairman and with prior sanction of the Corporation or any Committee of the Corporation, delegate to officers or employees the powers, authorities and discretions necessary for efficient conduct of the business of the Corporation.

The Regulations also provide that :

(*a*) all amount received on behalf of the Corporation by any officer or employee shall be credited to the appropriate Bank account of the Corporation;

(*b*) payments on behalf of the Corporation shall be made only by duly authorised officers;

(*c*) the accounts of all the offices of the Corporation shall be regularly audited by Internal Auditors;

(*d*) every office of the Corporation shall be inspected by Inspecting Officers.

Key Terms

- Appointed Day
- Composite Insurer
- Controlled Business
- Tribunal
- Committees
- Quorum

References

★ *Bare Act* : Life Insurance Corporation Act, 1956
Life Insurance Corporation Regulations, 1959.

★ *www.licindia.com*

★ *Avtar Singh,* Law of Insurance, Eastern Book Company, 2004.

★ *Law and Economics of Insurance,* IC87, Insurance Institute of India, Mumbai, 2003.

Questions for Review

1. Briefly describe the functions of Life Insurance Corporation as enumerated in Life Insurance Corporation Act, 1956.
2. Write short notes on :
   (*a*) Controlled Business
   (*b*) LIC Regulations, 1959

General Insurance Business (Nationalisation) Act, 1972

General Insurance Business was nationalised in 1972 and company by name of General Insurance Corporation of India (GIC) was formed under Companies Act, 1956 and was entrusted with the task of supervising, controlling and carrying on the business of general insurance. On the formation of the Corporation, the shares of Indian Insurance Companies vested in the Central Government stood automatically transferred to the Corporation and all the Indian Insurance Companies became subsidiaries of the Corporation. Amalgamation schemes were also framed whereby the Indian Insurance Companies were merged in one another so that ultimately there would be only four Indian companies to promote competition and also consolidate general insurance business in India.

4.1 FORMATION OF GIC

GIC, under Section 9 of the Act has an authorised capital of Rs. 75 crores into Rs. 75 lakhs fully paid up shares of Rs. 100/- each. Of which, Rs. 5 crores is the initial subscribed capital of the Corporation. The Central Government could frame one or more schemes under Section 16 of the Act for merger of the companies. A copy of every scheme framed under Section 16 shall be laid before each House of Parliament.

By virtue of the provisions of Section 4 to 8 the Central Government is authorised to acquire the assets and liabilities including the share holdings of the existing Indian Insurers on an appointed day *i.e.* 01-01-73. Section 7 of the Act authorised the central government to acquire the services of existing employees on the service conditions formulated by the newly established company *viz.*, GIC.

Section 3 of the Act defines an "acquiring company" as any Indian Insurance Company and where a scheme has been framed involving the merger of one Indian Insurance Company in another or the amalgamation of two more such companies, it shall mean the Indian Insurance Company in which any other company has been merged or the company which has been formed as a result of the amalgamation.

Chapter VA of the Act contains the terms and conditions of service of officers and other employees. The company is authorized to make amendments or make rules, amend or add to the schemes which are already in existence or make new provisions or schemes for the staff of the company. All the schemes, which are newly framed or the existing schemes with amendments made thereto are to be placed before the houses of Parliament for their approval. These schemes will be operative notwithstanding anything contrary contained in any other law or any agreement, award or other instrument for the time being in force.

4.2 FUNCTIONS OF THE CORPORATION

Section 18 of the Act describes the various functions of the GIC as follows :

"18. Functions of Corporation : (1) The functions of the Corporation shall include:

(*a*) the carrying on of any part of the general insurance business, if it thinks it desirable to do so;

(*b*) aiding, assisting and advising the acquiring companies in the matter of setting up of standards of conduct and sound practice in general insurance business and in the matter of rendering efficient service to holders of policies of general insurance;

(*c*) advising the acquiring companies in the matter of the controlling their expenses including the payment of commission and other expenses.

(*d*) advising the acquiring companies in the matter of the investment of their funds;

(*e*) issuing directions to acquiring companies in relation to the conduct of general insurance business.

(2) In issuing any directions under sub-section (1), the Corporation shall keep in mind the desirability of encouraging competition amongst the acquiring companies as far as possible in order to render their services more efficient."

Section 19 defines the functions of acquiring companies :

"19. Functions of acquiring companies :

1. Subject to the rules, if any, made by the Central Government in this behalf and to its memorandum and articles of association, it shall be the duty of every acquiring company to carry on general insurance business.
2. Each acquiring company shall so function under this Act as to secure that general insurance business is developed to the best advantage of the community.
3. In the discharge of any of its functions, each acquiring company shall act so far as may be on business principles and where any directions have been issued by the Corporation shall be guided by such directions.
4. For the removal of doubts it is hereby declared that the Corporation and any acquiring company may, subject to the rules, if any, made by the Central Government in this behalf, enter into such contracts of reinsurance of reinsurance treaties as it may think fit for the protection of its interests."

4.3 POWERS OF CENTRAL GOVERNMENT

Section 23 of the Act empowers the Central Government is vested with the power to issue directions to the General Insurance Corporation of India and every acquiring company in the discharge of its functions and they shall be guided by such directions in regard to matters of policy involving public interest. No provision of law relating to winding up of a company shall apply to the Corporation or to an acquiring company and neither the Corporation nor any such company shall be placed in liquidation save by order of the Central Government and in such manner as it may direct.

Section 24, provides the acquiring companies, the exclusive privilege of carrying on general insurance business in India. No person shall take out or renew any policy of insurance in respect of any property in India or in shipping or vessel or aircraft registered in India with an insurer whose principal place of business is outside India save with the prior permission of the Central Government.

Under *Section 35,* the Central Government may be notification specify the application of the provisions of the Insurance Act, 1958 with such modifications as is deemed necessary to the Corporation and the acquiring companies. The Central Government is also empowered to make rules to carry out the provisions of the Act and such rules may provide for :

(*a*) manner in which the profits and other moneys received by the Corporation may be dealt with;

(*b*) the conditions subject to which the Corporation and the acquiring companies shall carry on general insurance business;

(*c*) the terms and conditions subject to which any re-insurance contract or treaties may be entered into;

(*d*) form and manner in which any notice or application may be made to the Central Government;

(*e*) the reports which may be called for by the Central Government from the Corporation and acquiring companies; and

(*f*) any other matter which is required to be or may be prescribed.

Key Terms

- Authorised Capital
- Acquiring Companies
- General Insurance Corporation of India
- Memorandum and Articles of Association
- Reinsurance

References

- *Base Act* : General Insurance Business (Nationalisation) Act, 1972.
- *P.K. Gupta,* Insurance & Risk Management, Himalaya Publishing House, Mumbai, 2004.

Questions for Review

1. Briefly describe the functions of GIC as per the provisions of General Insurance Business (Nationalisation) Act, 1972.
2. Write short notes on :

   (*a*) Powers of Central Government

   (*b*) Formation of GIC

C H A P T E R

Insurance Regulatory and Development Authority Act, 1999

The Insurance Regulatory and Development Authority Act, 1999 provides for the establishment of an Authority to protect the interests of holders of insurance policies, to regulate, promote and ensure orderly growth of the insurance industry and for matters connected therewith or incidental thereto and further to amend the Insurance Act, 1938, the Life Insurance Corporation Act, 1956 and the General Insurance Business (Nationalisation) Act, 1972.

The Statement of Objects and Reasons of the Act provides that the insurance industry requires a high degree of regulation. The Insurance Act, 1938 provided for the institution of the Controller of Insurance to act as a strong and powerful supervisory and regulatory authority with powers to direct, advise, caution, prohibit, investigate, inspect, prosecute, search, seize, amalgamate, authorise, register and liquidate insurance companies. However, after the nationalisation of Life Insurance in 1956 and the General Insurance in 1972, the role of Controller of Insurance diminished in significance over a period of time.

5.1 CONSTITUTION OF THE AUTHORITY

Section 2(b) of the IRDA Act, 1999 defines the Authority as the Insurance Regulatory and Development Authority established under Section 3 of the Act. The Section 3 lays down the procedure for establishing the Authority. It is established by a notification by the Central Government in the Official Gazettee. The date of operation of the Authority is also notified by the Central Government by a notification. The other important characteristics of the Authority are as follows:

- It is a body corporate with perpetual succession and common seal.
- It has the powers to acquire, hold and dispose the property in its name. The property may be a movable or immovable.
- It has the powers to enter into contract in its name.
- It can sue the parties and it can be sued by the parties.
- The Central Government by notification decides the principal place of office of the Authority and the Authority has the powers to open branches or other offices as required by it.
- It consists of a Chairperson, not more than five wholetime members, and not more than four part-time members. (S. 4).

- All the members are appointed by the Central Government by a notification.
- The Chairperson and members are appointed from the person of ability, integrity having the standing and experience or knowledge in life insurance or general insurance, actuarial science, finance, economics, law, accountancy, administration or any other discipline which is useful for the Authority. And preferably, the Chairperson and one of the whole time members should be experienced persons or have the knowledge in the life insurance or the general insurance or actuarial science. (S. 4).
- The term of the office of the Chairperson and the wholetime members of five years and the part-time members will hold office for a period not more than the five years from the date of joining the office.
- The Chairperson will be in the office till the attains the age of sixty five years and the wholetime member will be in the office till he attains the age of sixty two years (S. 5).
- The Chairperson or the whole time member or part-time member can relinquish the office by giving a notice of three months to the Central Government.
- The Central Government can remove the Chairperson, wholetime member or the part-time member for the reasons of they become insolvent, physically or mentally incapable of performing duties, convicted for the moral turpitude, has acquired the financial or other interest in the insurance business, or the position of the member or the Chairperson is detrimental to the interest of the insurance or public or the policyholders. (S. 6)
- The Central Government, before removing a person from the office, has to give opportunity to the member to explain the reasons and after hearing him, if not satisfied can remove a member from service giving causes of removal.
- Any defect found in the process of appointment or any irregularity of procedures or appointment of members cannot vitiate the appointment of the member. The existence of vacancy in the body of the Authority does not affect the proceedings of the meeting of the Authority.
- The Chairperson or the members should not take any employment at least for a period of two years after they leave their positions. Under special circumstances, they can hold any office with the previous approval of the Central Government (S. 8).
- The salaries, allowance and other remunerations will be paid to the Chairperson and members as per the provisions laid down by the Central Government. The allowances and other service conditions will be prescribed by a notification.

5.2 DUTIES, POWERS AND FUNCTIONS OF THE AUTHORITY

Duties

- The primary duty of the IRDA is to regulate, promote and ensure orderly growth and conduct of the insurance business and reinsurance business (S.14).
- It has to maintain proper accounts and other relevant records, prepare annual statements of accounts in such form as may be prescribed by the Central Government in consultation with the CAG.
- It has to comply with the directions of the Central Government and CAG will arrange the audit of the accounts and rectify any defects pointed by the audit conducted by it.
- The Authority has to submit the audited balance sheet and other financial statements to the Central Government and the Government will lay the reports before the houses of the Parliament.
- The Authority has to submit all the financial statements to the Central Government within nine months from the completion of the relevant financial year.
- It has the duty to scrutinise all existing and new insurance products, rates charged, terms and conditions offered and act in best interest of consumers.
- The authority is duty bound to follow the directions issued by the Central Government and report the outcome of the directions.
- Authority has the general duty to protect the interest of policyholders in matters concerning assignment, nomination, settlement of insurance claim, surrenders etc. and other terms and conditions of contract of insurance.

Powers

- The Authority has the general supervisory power of insurance industry and it has the administrative powers.
- Powers to appoint the staff and officers required to conduct the business of the Authority smoothly.
- Authority can even delegate some general or special powers by an order in writing to the Chairperson or the Members of the Authority along with conditions if it feels as necessity.
- Power to constitute committees of the members and delegate the powers to the committee.
- Power to hold and acquire movable or immovable property.
- Power to issue a certificate of registration, renew, modify, withdraw, suspend or cancel such registration to the insurer.

- Power to prepare a code of conduct to the agents, surveyors and loss assessors and other intermediaries associated with insurance business.
- Power to levy fees and other charges for carrying out the purposes of this Act.
- Power to call information from insurers inspect accounts and other documents conduct enquiries and investigate including the audit of the insurers, intermediaries' and other organizations connected with the insurance business.
- It has the power to regulate the margin of solvency and investment of funds by insurance companies.
- Power to exercise the powers sanctioned by other insurance laws of the country or by other notifications issued by the Central Government from time to time.
- It has the powers to make regulations with the consultancy of Insurance Advisory Committee in the field of finalizing the service conditions of the members regarding the meeting and transactions to be carried out by the Advisory committee in promoting the insurance business.

Functions

- Promoting and regulating the professional organizations connected with the insurance and reinsurance business.
- Promoting efficiency in the conduct of insurance business in India.
- To act as adjudicator in the settlement of disputes between the insurers, intermediaries of the insurers.
- To act as supervisory authority and regulate the functioning of Tariff Advisory Committee and various insurance companies.
- To control and regulate the rates, advantages, terms and conditions that may be offered by insurers in respect of general insurances, which are not controlled by the Tariff Advisory Committee (Non-Tariff Products).
- To formulate the regulations concerning insurance in rural and social sectors.

Other Provisions

The Central Government has the powers under the Act to direct the Authority and grant funds under the head with sanction of the Parliament. The fund so constituted is called the Insurance Regulatory and Development Fund. This fund can be used to meet the expenses of the salaries, allowances and other remuneration of the members, officers and other employees of the Authority and to meet all other expenses required to discharge the duties and functions of the Authority. Registration fees, application frees from insurers and other intermediaries are also credited to the fund. A credit is also received u/s 7 of the Insurance Act, 1938.

The Central Government under the Act has the power to give directions to the Authority on the questions of policy of insurance business. If the central government finds that the Authority is not able to discharge the functions or perform the duties prescribed under the provisions of this Act or the Authority has defaulted in complying with the directions of the Central Government or the provisions of the Act, the financial position of the Authority is under deterrent conditions and if the Central Government feels that the Authority is working against the interest of public, can supercede the Authority and exercise its powers. This it may do by giving a notice with reasons and the authority may continue to act accordingly for a period not exceeding six months. Authority has to submit report of action taken to the Parliament. The Central Government has the power to make following rules in relations the authority :

1. The format of annual statement of accounts of the authority form and manner of submission of returns and statements and particulars are to be furnished.
2. Rules concerning the fixation of remunerations and service conditions of the staff, officers, members of the Authority.
3. To fix the allowances payable to part-time members of the Authority.
4. Any matter as may be required for by Insurance Advisory Committee.

The Act empowers the IRDA to appoint a committee by notification, to provide the advice on various insurance matters to the Authority called as Insurance Advisory Committee (IAC). This committee is established by a notification by the Authority. IAC contains not more than 25 members excluding ex-officio members to represent the various interests of commerce, industry, transport, agriculture, consumer forums, surveyors, agents, intermediaries, organizations engaged in safety and loss prevention, research bodies and employees association of insurance companies and intermediaries. The chairperson and the members of the authority are the ex-officio members the Insurance Advisory Committee. The objects of the automatically IAC shall be to advise the Authority on matters relating to the framing the regulations in relation to service conditions of the staff, conducting the transactions of various meetings and deciding the powers to be delegated etc. and any other matters required by the Authority.

The Regulatory Authority is under a duty to submit all the rules framed by it for the approval of Parliament. The provisions of other insurance laws are also applicable for the Authority, which are not in contradiction with the policy of public interest. IRDA is also generally subject to various insurance and other laws in best interest of the public.

IRDA Regulations

Various regulations have been framed by IRDA since its inception. These relate to licencing of insurers, regulation of intermediaries, reporting requirements, business practices, etc.

Regulations Framed under Insurance Regulatory and Development Authority Act, 1999 and the Insurance (Amendment) Act, 2002

1. Insurance Regulatory and Development Authority (Actuarial Report and Abstract) Regulations, 2000.
2. Insurance Regulatory and Development Authority (Obligation of insure of Rural or Social Sectors) Regulation, 2000.
3. Insurance Regulatory and Development Authority (Insurance Advertisements and Disclosure) Regulations, 2000.
4. Insurance Regulatory and Development Authority (Licensing of Insurance Agents) Regulations, 2000.
5. Insurance Regulatory and Development Authority (General Insurance – Reinsurance) Regulations, 2000.
6. Insurance Regulatory and Development Authority (Appointed Actuary) Regulations, 2000.
7. Insurance Regulatory and Development Authority (Assets, Liabilities and Solvency Margin of Insurers) Regulations, 2000.
8. Insurance Regulatory and Development Authority (Meetings) Regulations, 2000.
9. Insurance Regulatory and Development Authority (Registration of Indian Insurance Companies) Regulations, 2000.
10. Insurance Advisory Committee (Meetings) Regulations, 2000.
11. Insurance Regulatory and Development Authority (Investment) Regulations, 2000.
12. Insurance Regulatory and Development Authority (Preparation of Financial Statements and Auditor's Report of Insurance Companies) Regulations, 2002.
13. Insurance Regulatory and Development Authority (Licensing, Professional Requirements and Code of Conduct) Regulations, 2000.
14. Insurance Regulatory and Development Authority (Conditions of Service of Officers and Other Employees) Regulations, 2000.
15. Insurance Regulatory and Development Authority (Life Insurance — Reinsurance) Regulations, 2000.
16. Insurance Regulatory and Development Authority (Investment) (Amendment) Regulations, 2001.
17. Insurance Regulatory and Development Authority (Third Party Administrators – Health Services) Regulations, 2001.
18. Insurance Regulatory and Development Authority (Re-insurance Advisory Committee) Regulations, 2001.

19. Insurance Regulatory and Development Authority (Protection of Policy Holders' Interest) Regulations, 2002.
20. Insurance Regulatory and Development Authority (Investment) (Amendment) Regulations, 2002.
21. Insurance Regulatory and Development Authority (Assets, Liabilities and Solvency Margin of Insurers) (Amendment) Regulations, 2002.
22. Insurance Regulatory and Development Authority (Licensing of Corporate Agents) Regulations, 2002.
23. Insurance Regulatory and Development Authority (Licensing of Insurance Agents) (Amendment) Regulations, 2002.
24. Insurance Regulatory and Development Authority (Insurance Bookers) Regulations, 2002.
25. Insurance Regulatory and Development Authority (Manner of Payment of Premium) Regulations, 2002.
26. Insurance Regulatory and Development Authority (Obligations of Insurers to Rural or Social Sectors) (Amendment) Regulations, 2002.
27. Insurance Regulatory and Development Authority (Protection of Policy-holders Interest) (Amendment) Regulations, 2002.

SCHEDULES TO THE IRDA ACT

AMENDMENTS TO THE INSURANCE ACT, 1938
(4 of 1938)

1. In the Act, except in clause (5B) of section 2 and section 2B, for "Controller" wherever it occurs, substitute "Authority" and such consequential changes as the rules of grammar may require shall also be made.

2. In sections 27, 27A, 27B, 31, 32A, 40A, 48B, 64F, 64G, 64-I, 64J, 64L, 64R, 64UC, 64UM, 113 and 115, for "Central Government" wherever they occur, substitute "Authority".

3. Section 2, :

(*a*) after clause (1), insert the following :

'(IA) "Authority" means the Insurance Regulatory and Development Authority established under sub-section (1) of section 3 of the Insurance Regulatory and Development Authority Act, 1999;';

(*b*) for clause (5B), substitute the following :

'(5B) "Controller of Insurance" means the officer appointed by the Central Government under section 2B to exercise all the powers, discharge the functions and perform the duties of the Authority under this Act or the Life Insurance Corporation Act, 1956 (31 of 1956) or the General Insurance Business (Nationalisation) Act, 1972 (57 of 1972) or the Insurance Regulatory and Development Authority Act, 1999;

(c) After clause (7), insert the following :

'(7A) "Indian insurance company" means any insurer being a company :

(*a*) which is formed and registered under the Companies Act, 1956 (1 of 1956);

(*b*) in which the aggregate holdings of equity shares by a foreign company, either by itself or through its subsidiary companies or its nominees, do not exceed twenty-six per cent paid-up equity capital of such Indian insurance company;

(*c*) whose sole purpose is to carry on life insurance business or general insurance business or re-insurance business.

Explanation : For the purposes of this clause, the expression "foreign company" shall have the meaning assigned to it under clause (23A) of section 2 of the Income-tax Act, 1961 (43 of 1961).';

(*d*) in clause (14), for "section 114", substitute "this Act".

4. After section 2, insert the following :

"2A. Interpretation of certain words and expressions : Words and expressions used and not defined in the Life Insurance Corporation Act, 1956 (31 of 1965), the General Insurance Business (Nationalisation) Act, 1972 (57 of 1972) and the Insurance Regulatory and Development Authority Act, 1999 shall have the meanings respectively assigned to them in those Acts.".

5. Section 2B, for sub-section (1), substitute the following :

"(1) If at any time, the Authority is superseded under sub-section (1) of section 19 of the Insurance Regulatory and Development Authority Act, 1999, the Central Government may, by notification in the Official Gazette, appoint a person to be the Controller of Insurance till such time the Authority is reconstituted under sub-section (3) of section 19 of that Act."

6. Section 2C, in sub-section (1), after the second proviso, insert the following :

'Provided also that no insurer other than an Indian insurance company shall begin to carry on any class of insurance business in India under this Act on or after the commencement of the Insurance Regulatory and Development Authority Act, 1999.".

7. Section 3,

(*a*) In sub-section (1), after the first proviso, insert the following :

"Provided further that a person or insurer, as the case may be, carrying on any class of insurance business in India, on or before the commencement of the Insurance Regulatory and Development Authority Act, 1999, for which no registration certificate was necessary prior to such commencement, may continue to do so for a period of three months from such commencement or, if he had made an application for such registration within the said period of three months, till the disposal of such application :

Provided also that any certificate of registration, obtained immediately before the commencement of the Insurance Regulatory and Development Authority Act, 1999, shall be deemed to have been obtained from the Authority in accordance with the provisions of this Act,";

(*b*) in sub-section (2), :

(*i*) in the opening portion, for "Every application for registration shall be accompanied by-", substitute the following :

"Every application for registration shall be made in such manner as may be determined by the regulations made by the Authority and shall be accompanied by-";

(*ii*) in clause (d), for "working capital", substitute "paid-up equity capital or working capital";

(*iii*) in clause (f), in the proviso, omit "and" occurring and the end;

(*iv*) for clause (g), substitute the following :

"(*g*) the receipt showing payment of fee as may be determined by the regulations which shall not exceed fifty thousand rupees for each class of business as may be specified by the regulations made by the Authority;

(*h*) such other documents as may be specified by the regulations made by the Authority."

(*c*) after sub-section (2A), insert :

"(2AA) The Authority shall give preference to register the applicant and grant him a certificate of registration if such applicant agrees, in the form and manner as may be specified by the regulations made by the Authority, to carry on the life insurance business or general insurance business for providing health cover to individuals or group of individuals."

(*d*) in sub-section (4), :

(*i*) in clause (f), for "of any rule or order made thereunder, or", substitute the following :

"of any rule or any regulation or order made or, any direction issued thereunder, or";

(*ii*) in clause (h), insert "or" at the end;

(*iii*) after clause (h), insert the following :

"(*i*) if the insurer makes a default in complying with any direction issued or order made, as the case may be, by the Authority under the Insurance Regulatory and Development Authority Act, 1999, or "(*j*) if the insurer makes a default in complying with, or acts in contravention of, any requirement of the Companies Act, 1956 (1 of 1956) or the Life Insurance Corporation Act, 1956 (31 of 1956) or the General Insurance Business (Nationalisation) Act, 1972 (57 of 1972) or the Foreign Exchange Regulation Act, 1973 (46 of 1973)."

(*e*) in sub-section (5C), :

(*i*) for "clause (h)", substitute "clause(h) or clause (i) or clause (j)";

(*ii*) for "any requirement of this Act or of any rule or order made thereunder", substitute the following :

"any requirement of this Act or the Insurance Regulatory and Development Authority Act, 1999 or of any rule or any regulation, or any order made thereunder or any direction issued under those Acts";

(*f*) after sub-section (5D), insert the following :

"(5E) The Authority may, by order, suspend or cancel any registration in such manner as may be determined by the regulations made by it :

Provided that no order under this sub-section shall be made unless the person concerned has been given a reasonable opportunity of being heard."

(*g*) for sub-section (7), substitute the following :

"(7) The Authority may, on payment of such fee, not exceeding five thousand rupees, as may be determined by the regulations, issue a duplicate certificate of registration to replace a certificate lost, destroyed or mutilated, or in any other case where the Authority is of opinion that the issue of duplicate certificate is necessary."

8. Section 3A, :

(*a*) in sub-section(1), for "the 31st day of December, 1941.", substitute the following :

"the 31st day of March, after the commencement of the Insurance Regulatory and Development Authority Act, 1999."

(*b*) in sub-section(2), :

(*i*) for "prescribed fee", substitute "fee as determined by the regulations made by the Authority";

(*ii*) for clause (i), substitute the following :

"(i) exceed one-fourth of one per cent of such premium income or rupees five crores, whichever is less,";

(*iii*) for clause (ii), substitute the following :

"(ii) be less, in any case, than fifty thousand rupees for each class of insurance business:";

(*c*) in sub-section (3), for "prescribed fee", substitute "fee as determined by the regulations made by the Authority";

(*d*) in sub-section (4), for "prescribed fee", substitute "fee as determined by the regulations made by the Authority, and"

9. For section 6, substitute the following :

"6. Requirement as to capital : No insurer carrying on the business of life insurance, general insurance or re-insurance in India on or after the commencement of the Insurance Regulatory and Development Authority Act, 1999, shall be registered unless he has, :

(*i*) a paid-up equity capital of rupees one hundred crores, in case of a person carrying on the business of life insurance or general insurance; or

(*ii*) a paid-up equity capital of rupees two hundred crores, in case of a person carrying on exclusively the business as a re-insurer :

Provided that in determining the paid-up equity capital specified under clause (I) or clause (ii), the deposit to be made under section 7 and any preliminary expenses incurred in the formation and registration of the company shall be excluded :

Provided further that an insurer carrying on business of life insurance, general insurance or re-insurance in India before the commencement of the Insurance Regulatory and Development Authority Act, 1999 and who is required to be registered under this Act, shall have a paid-up equity capital in accordance with clause (I) and clause (ii), as the case may be, within six months of the commencement of that Act."

10. Section 6A, :

(*a*) in sub-section (4), in clause (b), :

(*i*) in sub-clause (i), omit "and" occurring at the end;

(*ii*) in sub-clause (ii), for "sanction of the Central Government has been obtained to the transfer.", substitute "approval of the Authority has been obtained to the transfer;"

(*iii*) after sub-clause (ii), insert the following :

'(iii) where, the nominal value of the shares intended to be transferred by any individual, firm, group, constituents of a group, or body corporate under the same management, jointly or severally exceeds one per cent of the paid-up equity capital of the insurer, unless the previous approval of the Authority has been obtained for the transfer.

Explanation : For the purposes of this sub-clause, the expressions "group" and "same management" shall have the same meanings respectively assigned to them in the Monopolies and Restrictive Trade Practices Act, 1969 (54 of 1969).'

(*b*) in sub-section (11),

(*i*) for "Explanation 1.", substitute "Explanation";

(*ii*) omit Explanation 2.

11. After section 6A, insert the following :

"6AA. Manner of divesting excess shareholding by promoter in certain cases. : (1) No promoter shall at any time hold more than twenty-six per cent or such other percentage as may be prescribed, of the paid-up equity capital in an Indian insurance company.

Provided that in a case where an Indian insurance company begins the business of life insurance, general insurance or re-insurance in which the promoters hold more than twenty-six per cent of the paid-up equity capital or such other excess percentage as may be prescribed, the promoters shall divest in a phased manner the share capital in excess of the twenty-six per cent of the paid-up equity capital or such excess paid-up equity capital as may be prescribed, after a period of ten years from the date of the commencement of the said business by such Indian insurance company or within such period as may be prescribed by the Central Government.

Explanation : For the removal of doubts, it is hereby declared that nothing contained in the proviso shall apply to the promoters being foreign company, referred to in sub-clause (b) of clause (7A) of section 2.

(2) The manner and procedure for divesting the excess share capital under sub-section (1) shall be specified by the regulations made by the Authority."

12. Section 7, :

(*a*) in sub-section (1),-

(*i*) omit "not being an insurer specified in sub-clause (c) of clause (9) of section 2";

(*ii*) for clauses (a) and (b), substitute the following :

"(*a*) in the case of life insurance business, a sum equivalent to one per cent of his total gross premium written in India in any financial year commencing after the 31st day of March, 2000, not exceeding rupees ten crores;

(*b*) in the case of general insurance business, a sum equivalent to three per cent of his total gross premium written in India, in any financial year commencing after the 31st day of March, 2000, not exceeding rupees ten crores;

(*c*) in the case of re-insurance business, a sum of rupees twenty crores;";

(*d*) omit sub-sections (1A), (1B), (1C), (1D) and (1E).

13. Section 11, :

(*a*) in sub-section (1), for "calendar year", substitute "financial year";

(*b*) after sub-section (1), insert the following :

"(1A) Notwithstanding anything contained in sub-section (1), every insurer, on or after the commencement of the Insurance Regulatory and Development Authority Act, 1999, in respect of insurance business transacted by him and in respect of his shareholders' funds, shall at the expiration of each financial year, prepare with reference to that year, a balance-sheet, a profit and loss account, a separate account of receipts and payments, a revenue account in accordance with the regulations made by the Authority.

(1B) Every insurer shall keep separate accounts relating to funds of shareholders and policy-holders."

14. Section 13, :

(*a*) in sub-section (1), :

(*i*) for "once at least in every three years", substitute "every year";

(*ii*) in the first proviso, for "not later than four years" substitute "not later than two years";

(*iii*) after the second proviso, insert the following :

"Provided also that for an insurer carrying on life insurance business in India immediately before the commencement of the Insurance Regulatory and Development Authority Act, 1999, the last date as at which the first investigation after such commencement should be caused by an actuary, shall be the 31st day of March, 2001:";

(*iv*) after the third proviso, insert the following :

"Provided also that every insurer on or after the commencement of the Insurance Regulatory and Development Authority Act, 1999, shall cause an abstract of the report of actuary to be made in the manner specified by the regulations made by the Authority.";

(*b*) in sub-section (4), after the proviso, insert the following :

"Provided further that the statement referred to in sub-section (4) shall be appended in the form and in the manner specified by the regulations made by the Authority."

15. After section 27B, insert the following :

"27C. *Prohibition of investment of funds outside India :* No insurer shall directly or indirectly invest outside India the funds of the policy-holders.

27D. *Manner and conditions of investment :* (1) Without prejudice to anything contained in sections 27, 27A and 27B, the Authority may, in the interests of the policy-holders, specify by the regulations made by it, the time, manner and other conditions of investment of assets to be held by an insurer for the purposes of this Act.

(2) The Authority may give specific directions for the time, manner and other conditions subject to which the funds of policy holders shall be invested in the infrastructure and social sector as may be specified by regulations made by the Authority and such regulations shall apply uniformly to all the insurers carrying on the business of life insurance, general insurance, or re-insurance in India on or after the commencement of the Insurance Regulatory and Development Authority Act, 1999.

(3) The Authority may, after taking into account the nature of business and to protect the interests of the policy-holders, issue to an insurer the directions relating to the time, manner and other conditions of investment of assets to be held by him :

Provided that no direction under this sub-section shall be issued unless the insurer concerned has been given a reasonable opportunity of being heard."

16. Section 28A, in sub-section (1), for "31st day of December", substitute "31st day of March".

17. Section 28B, in sub-section (1), for "31st day of December", substitute "31st day of March".

18. Section 31B, :

(a) in sub-section (1), for "Central Government" at both the places where they occur, substitute "Authority";

(*b*) in sub-section (2), for "a statement in the prescribed from", substitute "a statement, in the form specified by the regulations made by the Authority,";

(*c*) after sub-section (3), insert the following :

"(4) Every direction under this section shall be issued by an order made by the Authority:

Provided that no order under this section shall be made unless the person concerned has been given an opportunity of being heard."

19. After section 32A, insert the following :

"32B. Insurance business in rural or social sector : Every insurer shall, after the commencement of the Insurance Regulatory and Development Authority Act, 1999, undertake such percentages of life insurance business and general insurance business in the rural or social sector, as may be specified, in the Official Gazette by the Authority, in this behalf.

32C. Obligations of insurer in respect of rural or unorganised sector and backward classes. : Every insurer shall, after the commencement of the Insurance Regulatory and Development Authority Act, 1999 discharge the obligations specified under section 32B to provided life insurance or general insurance policies to the persons residing in the rural sector, workers in the unorganised or informal sector or for economically vulnerable or backward classes of the society and other categories of persons as may specified by regulations made by the Authority and such insurance policies shall include insurance for crops."

20. For section 33, substitute the following :

Investigation : 33. Power of investigation and inspection by Authority : (1) The Authority may, at any time, by order in writing, direct any person (hereafter in this section referred to as "Investigating Authority") specified in the order to investigate the affairs of any insurer and to report to the Authority on any investigation made by such Investigating Authority :

Provided that the Investigating Authority may, wherever necessary, employ any auditor or actuary or both for the purpose of assisting him in any investigation under this section.

(2) Notwithstanding anything to the contrary contained in section 235 of the time, and shall, on being directed so to do by the Authority, cause an inspection to be made by one or more of his officers of any insurer and his books and account; and the Investigating Authority shall supply to the insurer a copy of this report on such inspection.

(3) It shall be the duty of every manager, managing director or other officer of the insurer to produce before the Investigating Authority directed to make the investigation under sub-section (1), or inspection under sub-section (2), all such books of account, registers and other documents in his custody or power and to furnish him with any statement and information relating to the affairs of the insurer as the said Investigating Authority may require of him within such time as the said Investigating Authority may specify.

(4) Any Investigating Authority, directed to make an investigation under sub-section (1), or inspection under sub-section (2), may examine on oath, any manager, managing director or other officer of the insurer in relation to his business and may administer oaths accordingly.

(5) The Investigating Authority shall, if he has been directed by the Authority to cause an inspection to be made, and may, in any other case, report to the Authority on any inspection made under this section.

(6) On receipt of any report under sub-section (1) or sub-section (5), the Authority may, after giving such opportunity to the insurer to make a representation in connection with the report as, in the opinion of the Authority, seems reasonable, by order in writing :

- (*a*) require the insurer, to take such action in respect of any matter arising out of the report as the Authority may think fit; or
- (*b*) cancel the registration of the insurer; or
- (*c*) direct any person to apply to the court for the winding up of the insurer,

if a company, whether the registration of the insurer has been cancelled under clause (b) or not.

(7) The Authority may, after giving reasonable notice to the insurer, publish the report submitted by the Investigating Authority under sub-section (5) or such portion thereof as may appear to it to be necessary.

(8) The Authority may by the regulations made by it specify the minimum information to be maintained by insurers in their books, the manner in which such information shall be maintained, the checks and other verifications to be adopted by insurers in that connection and all other matters incidental thereto as are, in its opinion, necessary to enable the Investigating Authority to discharge satisfactorily his functions under this section.

Explanation : For the purposes of this section, the expression "insurer" shall include in the case of an insurer incorporated in India :

- (*a*) all its subsidiaries formed for the purpose of carrying on the business of insurance exclusively outside India; and
- (*b*) all its branches whether situated in India or outside India.

(9) No order made under this section other than an order made under clause (b) of sub-section (6) shall be capable of being called in question in any court.

(10) All expenses of, and incidental to, any investigation made under this section shall be defrayed by the insurer, shall have priority over that debts due from the insurer and shall be recoverable as an arrear of land revenue.'

21. Section 33A, omit "Central Government or the" :

22. Section 34H, :

- (*a*) in sub-section (1), :
  - (*i*) for "Controller", substitute "Chairperson of the Authority";
  - (*ii*) for "an Assistant Controller of Insurance", substitute "an officer authorised by the Authority";
- (*b*) in sub-sections (5) and (7) for "Controller" wherever it occurs, substitute "Chairperson of the Authority".

23. Section 35 :

- (*a*) in sub-section (1), for "sanctioned by the Controller", substitute "approved by the Authority";
- (*b*) in sub-section (3), :
  - (*i*) in the first paragraph, for "to sanction any such scheme substitute "to approve any such scheme";
  - (*ii*) in the second paragraph for "the amalgamation or transfer if sanctioned", substitute "the amalgamation or transfer if approved".

24. Section 36,

(*a*) in sub-section (1) for "may sanction the arrangement", substitute "may approve the arrangement";

(*b*) in sub-section (2), :

(*i*) for "the insurers concerned in the amalgamation, the Controller may sanction", substitute "the insurers concerned in the amalgamation, the Authority may approve";

(*ii*) for "contracts as sanctioned by the Controller", substitute "contracts as approved by the Authority".

25. Section 37, in clause (c) for "scheme sanctioned", substitute "scheme approved".

26. In section 40A, in sub-section (3), for the portion beginning with the words "an amount exceeding" and ending with the words "ten per cent of the premium payable on the policy", substitute "an amount not exceeding fifteen per cent of the premium payable on the policy where the policy relates to fire or marine insurance or miscellaneous insurance."

27. Section 42, :

(*a*) for sub-section (1), substitute the following :

"(1) The Authority or an officer authorised by it in this behalf shall, in the manner determined by the regulations made by it and on payment of the fee determined by the regulations, which shall not be more than two hundred and fifty rupees, issue to any person making an application in the manner determined by the regulations, a licence to act as an insurance agent for the purpose of soliciting or procuring insurance business :

Provided that, :

(*i*) in the case of an individual, he does not suffer from any of the disqualifications mentioned in sub-section (4); and

(*ii*) in the case of a company or firm, any of its directors or partners does not suffer from any of the said disqualifications :

Provided further that any licence issued immediately before the commencement of the Insurance Regulatory and Development Authority Act, 1999 shall be deemed to have been issued in accordance with the regulations which provide for such licence."

(*b*) for sub-section (3) substitute the following :

"(3) A licence issued under this section, after the date of the commencement of the Insurance Regulatory and Development Authority Act, 1999, shall remain in force for a period of three years only from the date of issue, but shall, if the applicant, being an individual does not, or being a company or firm any of its directors or partners does not, suffer from any of the disqualifications mentioned in clauses (b), (c), (d), (e) and (f) of sub-section (4) and the application for renewal of licence reaches the issuing authority at least thirty days before the date in which the licence ceases to remain in force, be renewed for a period of three years at any one time on payment of the fee determined by the regulations made by the Authority which shall not be more than rupees two hundred and fifty, and additional fee of an amount determined by the regulations not exceeding rupees one hundred by way of penalty, if the application for renewal of the licence does not reach the issued authority at least thirty days before the date on which the licence ceases to remain in force.";

(*c*) in sub-section (3A), for the proviso, substitute the following :

"Provided that the Authority may, if satisfied that undue hardship would be caused otherwise, accept any application in contravention of this sub-section of payment by the applicant of a penalty of seven hundred and fifty rupees.";

(*d*) in sub-section (4), after clause (*d*) insert the following :

"(*e*) that he does not possess the requisite qualifications and practical training for a period not exceeding twelve months, as may be specified by the regulations made by the Authority in this behalf;

(*f*) that he has not passed such examination as may be specified by the regulations made by the Authority in this behalf:

Provided that a person who had been issued a licence under sub-section (1) of this section or sub-section (1) of section 64UM shall not be required to possess the requisite qualifications, practical training and pass such examination as required by clauses (*e*) and (*f*);

(*g*) that he violates the code of conduct as may be specified by the regulations made by the Authority.";

(*e*) for sub-section (6), substitute the following :

"(6) The Authority may issue a duplicate licence to replace a licence lost, destroyed or mutilated, on payment of such fee not exceeding rupees fifty as may be determined by the regulations.";

(*f*) in sub-section (7),-

(*i*) for "fifty rupees", substitute "five hundred rupees";

(*ii*) for "one hundred rupees", substitute "one thousand rupees";

(*g*) in sub-section (8), for "fifty rupees", substitute "five thousand rupees".

28. Section 42A, in sub-section (1), :

(*a*) for "Controller or an officer authorised by him" substitute" Authority or an officer authorised by it";

(*b*) for "an application to him", substitute "an application to it".

29. After section 42C, insert the following :

"42D. Issue of licence to intermediary or insurance intermediary.

(1) The Authority or an officer authorised by it in this behalf shall, in the manner determined by the regulations made by the Authority and on payment of the fees determined by the regulations made by the Authority, issue to any person making an application in the manner determined by the regulations, and not suffering from any of the disqualifications herein mentioned, a licence to act as an intermediary or an insurance intermediary under this Act :

Provided that, :

(*a*) in the case of an individual, he does not suffer from any of the disqualifications mentioned in sub-section (4) of section 42, or

(*b*) in the case of a company or firm, any of its directors or partners does not suffer from any of the said disqualifications.

(2) A licence issued under this section shall entitle the holder thereof to act as an intermediary or insurance intermediary.

(3) A licence issued under this section shall remain in force for a period of three years only from the date of issue, but shall, if the applicant, being an individual does not, or being a company or firm any of its directors or partners does not suffer from any of the disqualifications mentioned in clauses (b), (c), (d), (e) and (f) of sub-section (4) of section 42, and the application for renewal of licence reaches the issuing authority at least thirty days before the date on which the licence ceases to remain in force, be renewed for a period of three years at any one time on payment of the fee, determined by the regulations made by the Authority and additional fee for an amount determined by the regulations, not exceeding one hundred rupees by way of penalty, if the application for renewal of the licence does not reach the issuing authority at least thirty days before the date on which the licence ceases to remain in force.

(4) no application for the renewal of a licence under this section shall be entertained if the application does not reach the issuing authority before the licence ceases to remain in force:

Provided that the Authority may, if satisfied that undue hardship would be caused otherwise, accept any application in contravention of this sub-section on payment by the applicant of a penalty of seven hundred and fifty rupees.

(5) The disqualifications above referred to shall be the following :

(*a*) that the person is a minor;

(*b*) that he is found to be of unsound mind by a court of competent jurisdiction;

(*c*) that he has been found guilty of criminal misappropriation or criminal breach of trust or cheating or forgery or an abetment of or attempt to commit any such office by a court of competent jurisdiction:

Provided that, where at least five years have elapsed since the completion of the sentence imposed on any person in respect of any such offence, the Authority shall ordinarily declare in respect of such person that his conviction shall cease to operate as a disqualification under this clause;

(*d*) that in the course of any judicial proceedings relating to any policy of insurance of the winding up of an insurance company or in the course of an investigation of the affairs of an insurer it has been found that he has been guilty of or has knowingly participated in or connived at any fraud dishonestly or misrepresentation against an insurer or an insured;

(*e*) that he does not possess the requisite qualifications and practical training for a period not exceeding twelve months, as may be specified by the regulations made by the Authority in this behalf;

(*f*) that he has not passed such examinations as may be specified by the regulations made by the

Authority in this behalf;

(g) that he violates the code of conduct as may be specified by the regulations made by the Authority.

(6) If it be found that an intermediary or an insurance intermediary suffers from any of the foregoing disqualifications, without prejudice to any other penalty to which he may be liable, the Authority shall, and if the intermediary or an insurance intermediary has knowingly contravened any provision of this Act may cancel the licence issued to the intermediary or insurance intermediary under this section.

(7) The Authority may issue a duplicate licence to replace a licence lost, destroyed or mutilated, on payment of such fee, as may be determined by the regulations made by the Authority.

(8) Any person who acts as an intermediary or an insurance intermediary without holding a licence issued under this section to act as such, shall be punishable with fine, and any insurer or any person who appoints as an intermediary or an insurance intermediary or any person not licensed to act as such or transacts any insurance business in India through any such person, shall be punishable with fine.

(9) Where the person contravening sub-section (8) is a company or a firm, then, without prejudice to any other proceedings which may be taken against the company or firm, every director, manager, secretary or other officer of the company, and every partner of the firm who is knowingly a party to such contravention shall be punishable with fine.".

30. Section 64UA, in sub-section (1), in sub-clause(a), for "Controller or Insurance", substitute "Chairperson of the Authority".

31. Section 64UB,:

(*a*) for sub-section (1), substitute the following :

"(1) The Authority may, by notification in the Official Gazette, make regulations to carry out the purposes of this Part.";

(*b*) in sub-section (2), for "rules", substitute "regulations";

(*c*) in sub-section (3) for "Central Government" at both the places where it occur, substitute "Authority";

(*d*) in sub-section (5), for "Controller of Insurance", substitute "Chairperson of the Authority".

32. Section 64UC in sub-section (1), in proviso, for "the controller may, with the previous approval of the Central Government", substitute "the Authority may."

33. Section 64UD, after sub-section (1), insert the following :

"Provided that the Chairperson of the Authority shall become the Chairman of the Advisory Committee with effect from the commencement of the Insurance Regulatory and Development Authority Act, 1999 and function as such, and any Chairman of the Tariff Committee holding office immediately before such commencement shall cease to be the Chairman.".

34. Section 64UJ, in sub-section (5), for "Central Government", wherever it occurs, substitute "Authority".

35. Section 64UM, :

(*a*) in sub-section (1), :

(*i*) in paragraph (B), after "the Insurance (Amendment) Act, 1968", insert "but before the commencement of the Insurance Regulatory and Development Authority Act, 1999";

(*ii*) after paragraph (B), insert the following :

"(BA) Every person who intends to act as a surveyor or loss assessor after the expiry of a period of one year from the commencement of the Insurance Regulatory and Development Authority Act, 1999, shall make an application to the Authority within such time, in such manner and on payment of such fee as may be determined by the regulations made by the Authority:

Provided that any licence issued immediately before the commencement of the Insurance Regulatory and Development Authority Act, 1999 shall be deemed to have been issued in accordance with the regulations providing for such licence.";

(*iii*) in paragraph (C), for "as may be prescribed", substitute "as may be determined by the regulations";

(*iv*) in paragraph (D), in clause (*i*) :

(A) for item (*a*), substitute the following :

"(*a*) has been in practice as a surveyor or loss assessor on the date of commencement of the Insurance Regulatory and Development Authority Act, 1999, or";

(B) in item (*f*), for "prescribed ", substitute, "specified by the regulations made by the Authority";

(*b*) after sub-section (1), insert :

"(1A) Every surveyor and loss assessor shall comply with the code of conduct in respect of their duties, responsibilities and other professional requirements as may be specified by the regulations made by the Authority.".

36. Section 64V, :

(*a*) in sub-section (1), :

(*i*) in clause (i), after sub-clause (g), insert the following :

"(h) such other asset or assets as may be specified by the regulations made in this behalf;";

(*ii*) in clause (ii) :

(A) in sub-clause (b), in items (i) and (ii), for "40 per cent", substitute "50 per cent.";

(B) after sub-clause (f), insert the following :

"(g) such other liability which may be made in this behalf to be included for the purpose of clause (ii).";

(*b*) for sub-section (2), substitute the following :

"(2) Every insurer shall furnish to the Authority with his returns under section 15 or section 16, as the case may be, a statement certified by an auditor approved by the Authority in respect of general insurance business, or an actuary approved by the Authority in respect of life insurance business, as the case may be, of his assets and liabilities assessed in the manner required by this section as on the 31st day of March of the preceding year.

(3) Every insurer shall value his assets and liabilities in the manner required by this section and in accordance with the regulations which may be made by the Authority in this behalf.".

37. Section 64VA, :

(*a*) in sub-section (1), for "at all times", substitute "at all times before the commencement of the Insurance Regulatory and Development Authority Act, 1999";

(*b*) after sub-section (1), insert the following :

'(1A) Every insurer shall, at all times, on or after the commencement of the Insurance Regulatory and Development Authority Act, 1999, maintain an excess of the value of his assets over the amount of his liabilities of not less than the amount arrived at as follows (hereinafter referred to in this section referred to as the "required solvency margin"), namely :

(*i*) in the case of an insurer carrying on life insurance business, the required solvency margin shall be the higher of the following amounts :

(*a*) fifty crores of rupees (one hundred crores of rupees in case of re-insurers); or

(*b*) the aggregate sums of the results arrived at in items (I) and (II) stated below :

(I) the aggregate of the results arrived at by applying the calculation described in item (A) below (Step - I) and the calculation described in item (B) below (Step II) :

(A) for Step I :

(A.1) there shall be taken, a sum equal to a percentage determined by the regulations not exceeding five per cent of the mathematical reserves for direct business and re-insurance acceptances without any deduction for re-insurance cessions.

(A.2) the amount of mathematical reserves at the end of the preceding financial year after the deduction of re-insurance cessions shall be expressed as a percentage of the amount of those mathematical reserves before any such deduction; and

(A.3) the sum mentioned in item (A.1) above shall be multiplied :

(A.3.1) where the percentage arrived at under item (A.2) above is greater than eighty-five per cent (or in the case of a re-insurer carrying on exclusive re-insurance business, fifty per cent), by that greater percentage; and

(A.3.2) in any other case, by eighty-five per cent (or in the case of re-insurer carrying on exclusive re-insurance business, by fifty per cent);

(B) for Step II :

(B.1) there shall be taken, a sum equal to a percentage determined by the regulations made by the Authority not exceeding one per cent of the sum at risk for the policies on which the sum at risk is not a negative figure, and

(B.2) the amount of sum at risk at the end of the preceding financial year for policies on which the sum at risk is not a negative figure after the deduction of re-insurance cession shall be expressed as a percentage of the amount of that sum at risk before any such deduction, and

(B.3) the sum arrived at under item (B.1) above shall be multiplied:

(B.3.1) where the percentage arrived at under item (B.3.2) above is greater than fifty per cent, by that greater percentage; and

(B.3.2) in any other case, by fifty per cent,

(II) a percentage determined by the regulations made by the Authority of the value of assets determined in accordance with the provisions of section 64V;

(*ii*) in the case of an insurer carrying on general insurance business, the required solvency margin, shall be the highest of the following amounts:

(*a*) fifty crores of rupees (one hundred crores of rupees in case of re-insurer); or

(*b*) a sum equivalent to twenty per cent of net premium income; or

(*c*) a sum equivalent to thirty per cent of net incurred claims,

subject to credit for re-insurance in computing net premiums and net incurred claims being actual but a percentage, determined by the regulations not exceeding fifty per cent:

Provided that if in respect of any insurer, the Authority is satisfied that either by reason of an unfavourable claim experience or because of sharp increase in the volume of the business, or for any other reason, compliance with the provisions of this sub-section would cause undue hardship to the insurer, the Authority may direct, for such period and subject to such conditions, such solvency margin not being less than the lower of the amount mentioned in sub-clause (i) or sub-clause (ii) above, as the case may be.

Explanation : For the purposes of this sub-section, the expressions :

(*i*) "mathematical reserves" means the provision made by an insurer to cover liabilities (excluding liabilities which have fallen due and liabilities arising from the deposit back arrangement in relation to any policy whereby an amount is deposited by re-insurer with the cedant) arising under or in connection with policies or contracts for life insurance business. Mathematical reserves also include specific provision for adverse deviations of the bases, such as mortality and morbidity rates, interest rates, and expense rates, and any explicit provisions made, in the valuation of liabilities, in accordance with the regulations made by the Authority for this purpose;

(*ii*) "net incurred claims" means the average of the net incurred claims during the specified period of not exceeding three preceding financial years;

(*iii*) "sum at risk" in relation to a life insurance policy, means a sum which is :

(*a*) in any case in which an amount is payable inconsequence of death other than a case falling within sub-clause (b) below, the amount payable on death, and

(*b*) in any case in which the benefit under the policy in question consist of the making, in consequence of death, of the payments of annuity, payment of sum by instalments or any other kind of periodic payments, the present value of that benefit, less in either case the mathematical reserves in respect of the relevant policies."

(*c*) after sub-section (2), insert the following :

"(2A) If, at any time an insurer does not maintain the required solvency margin in accordance with the provisions of this section, he shall, in accordance with the provisions of this section, he shall, in accordance with the directions issued by the Authority, submit a financial plan, indicating a plan of action to correct the deficiency to the Authority within a specified period not exceeding three months.

(2B) An insurer who has submitted a plan under sub-section (2A) to the Authority shall propose modifications to the plan if the Authority considers it inadequate, and shall give effect to any plan accepted by the Authority as adequate.

(2C) An insurer who does not comply with the provisions of sub-section (2A) shall be deemed to be insolvent and may be wound up by the Court.";

(*d*) after sub-section (6); insert the following :

"(7) Every insurer shall furnish to the Authority his returns under section 15 or section 16, as the case may be, in case of life insurance business a statement certified by an actuary approved by the authority, and in case of general insurance business a statement certified by an auditor approved by the Authority, of the required solvency margin maintained by the insurer in the manner required by sub-section (1A).".

38. Section 70 in sub-section (1), for "the Controller a certificate of registration", substitute "the Authority, before the date of commencement of the Insurance Regulatory and Development Authority Act, 1999, a certificate of registration."

39. Section 95, in sub-section (1), for "In this Part -", substitute "In this part, before the date of commencement of the Insurance Regulatory and Development Act, 1999, -".

40. Section 101A, :

(*a*) in sub-section (1), for "the Central Government" substitute "the Authority, with the previous approval of the Central Government,";

(*b*) in sub-section (2), for "the Central Government" substitute "the Authority."

41. Section 101B, :

(*a*) in sub-section (1), for "the Central Government", substitute "the Authority with the previous approval of the Central Government.";

(*b*) in sub-section (2), for "prescribed", substitute determined by the regulations made by the Authority".

42. For sections 102 to 105, substitute the following :

"102. *Penalty for default in complying with, or Act in contravention of, this Act:* If any person who is required under this Act, or rules or regulations made thereunder,:

(*a*) to furnish any document, statement, account, return or report to the Authority, fails to furnish the same; or

(*b*) to comply with the directions, fails to comply with such directions;

(*c*) to maintain solvency margin, fails to maintain such solvency margin;

(*d*) to comply with the directions on the insurance treaties, fails to comply with such directions on the insurance treaties,

he shall be liable to a penalty not exceeding five lakh rupees for each such failure and punishable with fine.

103. *Penalty for carrying on insurance business in contravention of section 3,7. and 98:* If a person makes a statement, or furnishes any document, statement, account, return or report which is false and which he either knows or believes to be false or does not believe to be true,

(*a*) he shall be liable to a penalty not exceeding five lakh rupees for each such failure; and

(*b*) he shall be punishable with imprisonment which may extend to three years or with fine for each such failure.

104. *Penalty for false statement in document :* If a person fails to comply with the provisions of section 27 or section 27A or section 27B or section 27C or section 27D, he shall be liable to a penalty not exceeding five lakh rupees for each such failure.

105. *Wrongfully obtaining or withholding property :* If any director, managing director, manager or other officer or employees of an insurer wrongfully obtains possession of any property or wrongfully applies to any purpose of the Act, he shall be liable to a penalty not exceeding two lakh rupees for each such failure.

105A. *Offences by companies :* (1) Where any offence under this Act has been committed by a company, every person who, at the time the offence was committed, was in charge of, and was responsible to, the company for the conduct of the business of the company as well as the company shall be deemed to be guilty of the offence and shall be liable to be proceeded against and punished accordingly;

Provided that nothing contained in this sub-section shall render any such person liable to any punishment, if he proves that the offence was committed without his knowledge or that he had exercised all due diligence to prevent the commission of such offence.

(2) Notwithstanding anything contained in sub-section (1), where any offence under this Act has been committed by a company and it is proved that the offence has been committed with the consent or connivance of, or is attributable to any neglect on the part of, any director, manager, secretary or other officer of the company, such director, manager, secretary or other officer shall be deemed to be guilty of that offence and shall be liable to be proceeded against and punished accordingly.

Explanation : For the purposes of this section, :

(*a*) "company" means any body corporate, and includes :

  (*i*) a firm; and

  (*ii*) an association of persons or a body of individuals whether incorporated or not; and

(*b*) "director", in relation to :

  (*i*) a firm, means a partner in the firm;

  (*ii*) an association of persons or a body of individuals, means any member controlling the affairs thereof.

105B. Penalty for failure to comply with section 32B. : If an insurer fails to comply with the provisions of section 32B, he shall be liable to a penalty not exceeding five lakh rupees for each such failure and shall be punishable with imprisonment which may extend to three years or with fine for each such failure.

105C. Penalty for failure to comply with section 32C. : If an insurer fails to comply with the provisions of section 32C, he shall be liable to a penalty not exceeding twenty-five lakh rupees for each such failure and in the case of subsequent and continuing failure, the registration granted to such insurer under section 3 shall be cancelled by the Authority.".

43. In sections 110A, 110B and 110C, for "Controller" wherever it occurs, substitute "Chairperson of the Authority".

44. Section 110G, for "Controller" at both the places where it occurs, substitute "Chairperson of the Authority".

45. Section 110H, in sub-section (1), for "under sections", substitute "under section 27D,".

46. Section 114, in sub-section (2), :

(*a*) after clause (a), insert the following :

"(*aa*) such other percentage of paid-up equity capital in excess twenty-six per cent of the paid-up equity capital and the period within which such excess paid-up equity capital shall be divested under sub-section (1) of section 6AA.";

(*b*) omit clauses (g) and (ll),

47. After section 114, insert the following :

"114A. *Power of Authority to make regulations :* (1) The Authority may, by notification in the Official Gazette, make regulations consistent with this Act and the rules made thereunder, to carryout the purposes of this Act.

(2) In particular, and without prejudice to the generality of the foregoing power, such regulation may provide for all or any of the following matters, namely :

(*a*) the matters including fee relating to the registration of insurers under section 3;

(*b*) the manner of suspension or cancellation of registration under sub-section (5E) of section 3;

(*c*) such fee, not exceeding five thousand rupees, as may be determined by the regulations for issue of a duplicate certificate of registration under sub-section (7) of section 3;

(*d*) the matters relating to the renewal of registration and fee therefore under section 3A;

(*e*) the manner and procedure for divesting excess share capital under sub-section (2) of section 6AA;

(*f*) the preparation of balance-sheet, profit and loss account and a separate account of receipts and payments and revenue account under section (1A) of section 11;

(*g*) the manner in which an abstract of the report of the actuary to be specified under the fourth proviso to sub-section (1) of section 13;

(*h*) the form and manner in which the statement referred to in sub-section(4) of section 13 shall be appended;

(*i*) the time, manner and other conditions of investment of assets held by an insurer under sub-sections (1), (1A) and (2) of section 27D;

(*j*) the minimum information to be maintained by insurer in their books, the manner in which such information should be maintained, the checks and other verifications to be adopted by insurers in that connection and all other matters incidental thereto under sub-section (8) of section 33;

(*k*) the manner for making an application, the manner and the fee for issue of a licence to act as an insurance agent under sub-section (1) of section 42;

(*l*) the fee and the additional fee to be determined for renewal of licence of insurance agent under sub-section (3) of section 42;

(*m*) the requisite qualifications and practical training to act as an insurance agent under clause (e) of sub-section (4) of section 42;

(*n*) the passing of examination to act as an insurance agent under clause (f) of sub-section (4) of section 42;

(*o*) the code of conduct under clause (g) of sub-section (4) of section 42;

(*p*) the fee not exceeding rupees fifty for issue of duplicate licence under sub-section (6) of section 42;

(*q*) the manner and the fees for issue of a licence to an intermediary or an insurance intermediary under sub-section (1) of section 42D;

(*r*) the fee and the additional fee to be determined for renewal of licence of intermediaries or insurance intermediaries under sub-section (3) of section 42D;

(*s*) the requisite qualifications and practical training of intermediaries or insurance intermediaries under clause (e) of sub-section (5) of section 42D;

(*t*) the examination to be passed to acts as an intermediary or insurance intermediary under clause (f) of sub-section (5) of section 42D;

(*u*) the code of conduct under clause (g) of sub-section (5) of section 42D;

(*v*) the fee for issue of duplicate licence under sub-section (7) of section 42D;

(*w*) such matters as specified under sub-section (2) of section 64UB relating to the Tariff Advisory Committee;

(*x*) the matters relating to licensing of surveyors and loss assessors, their duties, responsibilities and other professional requirements under section 64UM;

(*y*) such other asset or assets as may be specified under clause (h) of sub-section (1) of section 64V for the purposes of ascertaining sufficiency of assets under section 64VA;

(*z*) the valuation of assets and liabilities under sub-section (3) of section 64V;

(*za*) the matters specified under sub-section (1A) of section 64VA relating to sufficiency of assets;

(*zb*) the matters relating to re-insurance under sections 101A and 101B;

(*zc*) the matters relating to redressal of grievances of policy-holders to protect their interest and to regulate, promote and ensure orderly growth of insurance industry; and

(*zd*) any other matter which is to be, or may be, specified by the regulation made by the Authority or in respect of which provision is to be made or may be made by the regulations.

(3) Every regulation made under this Act shall be laid, as soon as may be after it is made, before each House of Parliament, while it is in session, for a total period of thirty days which may be comprised in one session or in two or more successive sessions, and if, before the expiry of the session immediately following the session or the successive sessions aforesaid, both Houses agree in making any modification in the regulation or both Houses agree that the regulation should not be made, the regulation shall thereafter have effect only in such modified form or be of no effect, as the case may be; so, however, that any such modification or annulment shall be without prejudice to the validity of anything previously done under that regulation.".

48. Section 116 A, for "Central Government", at both places where they occur, substitute "Central Government, before the date of commencement of the Insurance Regulatory and Development Authority Act, 1999,".

THE SECOND SCHEDULE

(See Section 31)

AMENDMENTS TO THE LIFE INSURANCE CORPORATION ACT, 1956

(31 of 1956)

1. In the Act, for "Controller" wherever it occurs, substitute "Authority".
2. After section 30, insert the following :

   "30A. *Exclusive privilege of Corporation to cease :* Notwithstanding anything contained in this Act, the exclusive privilege of carrying on life insurance business in India by the Corporation shall cease on and from commencement of the Insurance Regulatory and Development Authority Act, 1999 and the Corporation shall, thereafter, carry on life insurance business in India in accordance with the provisions of the Insurance Act, 1938 (4 of 1938).".

THE THIRD SCHEDULE

(See Section 32)

AMENDMENT TO THE GENERAL INSURANCE BUSINESS (NATIONALISATION) ACT, 1972

(57 of 1972)

After section 24, insert the following :

"24A. *Exclusive privilege of Corporation and acquiring companies to cease.* : Notwithstanding anything contained in this Act, the exclusive privilege of the Corporation and the acquiring companies of carrying on general insurance business in India shall cease on an from the commencement of the Insurance Regulatory and Development Authority Act, 1999 and the Corporation and the acquiring companies shall, thereafter, carry on general insurance business in India in accordance with the provisions of the Insurance Act, 1938 (4 of 1938)."

Key Terms

- Insurance Regulatory and Development Authority
- Adjudicator
- Tariff Advisory Committee
- Insurance Advisory Committee

References

- Avtar Singh, Law of Insurance, Eastern Book Company, 2005.
- www.irdaonline.com
- Bara Act – IRDA Act, 1999.

Questions for Review

1. Briefly explain the constitution of IRDA.
2. Explain the duties, powers and functions of the IRDA under the IRDA Act, 1999.
3. Summarise the various ammendments made to different laws by the promulgation of the IRDA Act, 1999.

Key Terms

[illegible] Insurance Regulatory and Development Authority [illegible]

[illegible]

References

[illegible]

Review Questions

1. [illegible]
2. [illegible] IRDA [illegible]
3. [illegible]

Module 2

Motor Vehicle Act, 1939 & 1988

Motor Vehicles Act 1938 & 1988

Motor Vehicles Act, 1939 was the principle act that regulated the practice of motor insurance in India. The act was amended many times thereafter. The most important act is that of 1988 that replaced the 1939 act. Insurance under the Act is insurance of person and property. If from the use of vehicle, a person sustains injuries or the other parties (third party) suffers injuries or damages, the driver of the vehicle is liable and for his personal loss/damages, he can claim from the insurance company. The following paragraphs discuss the important provisions of the Act and simultaneously refer to the erstwhile provisions of the act of 1939, (given in brackets)

6.1 DEFINITIONS - SEC. 2

Definitions. – In this Act, unless the context otherwise requires,

(1) "area", in relation to any provision of this Act, means such area as the State Government may, having regard to the requirements of that provision, specify by notification in the Official Gazette;

(2) "articulated vehicle" means a motor vehicle to which a semi-trailer is attached; [2(2)]

(3) "axle weight" means in relation to an axle of a vehicle the total weight transmitted by the several wheels attached to that axle to the surface on which the vehicle rests; [2(1-B)]

(4) "certificate of registration" means the certificate issued by a competent authority to the effect that a motor vehicle has been duly registered in accordance with the provisions of Chapter IV; [2(2)]

(5) "conductor", in relation to a stage carriage, means a person engaged in collecting fares from passengers, regulating their entrance into, or exit from, the stage carriage and performing such other functions as may be prescribed; [2(2-B)]

(6) "conductor's licence" means the licence issued by a competent authority under Chapter III authorising the person specified therein to act as a conductor; [2(2-C)]

(7) "contract carriage" means a motor vehicle which carries a passenger or passengers for hire or reward and is engaged under a contract, whether expressed or implied, for the use of such vehicle as a whole for the carriage of passengers mentioned therein and entered into by a person with a holder of a permit in

relation to such vehicle or any person authorised by him in this behalf on a fixed or an agreed rate or sum –

(*a*) on a time basis, whether or not with reference to any route or distance; or

(*b*) from one point to another, and in either case, without stopping to pick up or set down passengers not included in the contract anywhere during the journey, and includes –

(*i*) a maxicab; and

(*ii*) a motorcab notwithstanding that separate fares are charged for its passengers; [2(3)]

(9) "driver" includes, in relation to a motor vehicle which is drawn by another motor vehicle, the person who acts as a steersman of the drawn vehicle; [2(5)]

(10) "driving licence" means the licence issued by a competent authority under Chapter II authorising the person specified therein to drive, otherwise than as a learner, a motor vehicle or a motor vehicle of any specified class or description; [2(5-A)]

(13) "goods" includes livestock, and anything (other than equipment ordinarily used with the vehicle) carried by a vehicle except living persons, but does not include luggage or personal effects carried in a motor car or in a trailer attached to a motor car or the personal luggage of passengers travelling in the vehicle; [2(7)]

(14) "goods carriage" means any motor vehicle constructed or adapted for use solely for the carriage of goods, or any motor vehicle not so constructed or adapted when used for the carriage of goods; [2(8)]

(15) "gross vehicle weight" means in respect of any vehicle the total weight of the vehicle and load certified and registered by the registering authority as permissible for that vehicle; [Newly Inserted]

(16) "heavy goods vehicle" means any goods carriage the gross vehicle weight of which, or a tractor or a road-roller the unladen weight of either of which, exceeds 12,000 kilograms; [2(9)]

(17) "heavy passenger motor vehicle" means any public service vehicle or private service vehicle or educational institution bus or omnibus the gross vehicle weight of any of which, or a motor car the unladen weight of which, exceeds 12,000 kilograms. [2(9-A)]

(18) "invalid carriage" means a motor vehicle specially designed and constructed, and not merely adapted, for the use of a person suffering from some physical defect or disability, and used solely by or for such a person; [2(10)]

(20) "licensing authority" means an authority empowered to issue licence under Chapter II or, as the case may be, chapter III; [2(12)]

(21) "light motor vehicle" means a transport vehicle or omnibus the gross vehicle weight of either of which or a motor car or tractor or road-roller the unladen weight of any of which, does not exceed 7500 kilograms; [2(13)]

(21-A) "manufacturer" means a person who is engaged in the manufacture of motor vehicles ; [Newly Inserted]

(22) "maxicab" means any motor vehicle constructed or adapted to carry more than six passengers, but not more than twelve passengers, excluding the driver, for hire or reward; [Newly Inserted]

(23) "medium goods vehicle" means any goods carriage other than a light motor vehicle or a heavy goods vehicle; [2(14)]

(24) "medium passenger motor vehicle" means any public service vehicle or private service vehicle, or educational institution bus other than a motor cycle, invalid carriage, light motor vehicle or heavy passenger motor vehicle ; [2(14-A)]

3. "motorcab" means any motor vehicle constructed or adapted to carry not more than six passengers excluding the driver for hire or reward; [2(15)]

(25) "motor car" means any motor vehicle other than a transport vehicle, omnibus, road-roller, tractor, motor cycle or invalid carriage; [2(16)]

(26) "motor cycle" means a two-wheeled motor vehicle, inclusive of any detachable side-car having an extra wheel, attached to the motor vehicle; [2(17)]

(28) "motor vehicle" or "vehicle" means any mechanically propelled vehicle adapted for use upon roads whether the power of propulsion is transmitted thereto from an external or internal source and includes a chassis to which a body has not been attached and a trailer ; but does not include a vehicle running upon fixed rails or a vehicle of a special type adapted for use only in a factory or in any other enclosed premises or a vehicle having less than four wheels fitted with engine capacity of not exceeding 25 C.C. [2(18)]

(29) "omnibus" means any motor vehicle constructed or adapted to carry more than six persons excluding the driver ; [2(18-A)]

(30) "owner" means a person in whose name a motor vehicle stands registered and where such person is a minor, the guardian of such minor, and in relation to a motor vehicle which is the subject of a hire-purchase, agreement, or an agreement of lease or an agreement of hypothecation, the person in possession of the vehicle under that agreement ; [2(19)]

(31) "permit" means a permit issued by a State or Regional Transport Authority or an authority prescribed in this behalf under this Act authorising the use of motor vehicle as a transport vehicle ; [2(20)]

(32) "prescribed" means prescribed by rules made under this Act; [2(21)]

(33) "private service vehicle" means a motor vehicle constructed or adapted to carry more than six persons excluding the driver and ordinarily used by or on

behalf of the owner of such vehicle for the purpose of carrying persons for, or in connection with, his trade or business otherwise than for hire or reward but does not include a motor vehicle used for public purposes ; [2(22)]

Corresponding Law. - Section 2 (33) corresponds to section 2 (22) of the Motor Vehicles Act, 1939.

(34) "public place" means a road, street, way or other place, whether a thoroughfare or not, to which the public have a right of access, and includes any place or stand at which passengers are picked up or set down by a stage carriage ; [2(24)]

(35) "public service vehicle" means any motor vehicle used or adapted to be used for the carriage of passengers for hire or reward, and includes a maxicab, a motorcab, contract carriage, and stage carriage ; [2(25)]

(36) "registered axle weight" means in respect of the axle of any vehicle, the axle weight certified and registered by the registering authority as permissible for that axle ; [2(26)]

(37) "registering authority" means an authority empowered to register motor vehicles under Chapter IV ; [2(28)]

(38) "route" means a line of travel which specifies the highway which may be traversed by a motor vehicle between one terminus and another ; [2(28-A)]

(39) "semi-trailer" means a vehicle not mechanically propelled (other than a trailer), which is intended to be connected to motor vehicle and which is so constructed that a portion of it is super-imposed on, and a part of whose weight is borne by, that motor vehicle ; [Newly Inserted]

(40) "stage carriage" means a motor vehicle constructed or adapted to carry more than six passengers excluding the driver for hire or reward at separate fares paid by or for individual passengers, either for the whole journey or for stages of the journey ; [2(29)]

(41) "State Government" in relation to a Union territory, means the Administrator thereof appointed under article 239 of the Constitution ; [Newly Inserted]

(42) "State transport undertaking" means any undertaking providing road transport service, where such undertaking is carried on by –

(*i*) the Central Government or a State Government ;

(*ii*) any Road Transport Corporation established under section 3 of the Road Transport Corporations Act, 1950 ;

(*iii*) any municipality or any corporation or company owned or controlled by the Central Government or one or more State Governments, or by the Central Government and one or more State Government ;

(*iv*) Zilla Parishad or any other similar local authority. [2(42)]

Explanation : For the purposes of this clause, "road transport service" means a service of motor vehicles carrying passengers or goods or both by road for hire or reward;

(43) "tourist vehicle" means a contract carriage constructed or adapted and equipped and maintained in accordance with such specifications as may be prescribed in this behalf; [2(29-A)]

(44) "tractor" means a motor vehicle which is not itself constructed to carry any load (other than equipment used for the purpose of propulsion); but excludes a road-roller ; [2(30)]

(45) "traffic signs" includes all signals, warning sign posts, direction posts, markings on the road or other devices for the information, guidance or direction of drivers of motor vehicles ; [2(31)]

(46) "trailer" means any vehicle, other than a semi-trailer and a sidecar, drawn or intended to be drawn by a motor vehicle ; [2(32)]

(47) "transport vehicle" means a public service vehicle, a goods carriage, an educational institution bus or a private service vehicle ; [2(33)]

(48) "unladen weight" means the weight of a vehicle or trailer including all equipment ordinarily used with the vehicle or trailer when working, but excluding the weight of a driver or attendant; and where alternative parts or bodies are used the unladen weight of the vehicle means the weight of the vehicle with the heaviest such alternative part or body ; [2(34)]

(49) "weight" means the total weight transmitted for the time being by the wheels of a vehicle to the surface on which the vehicle rests. [Newly Inserted]

6.2 NECESSITY FOR THIRD PARTY INSURANCE

Compulsory Insurance for Third Party Risks

Section 146 provides that : (1) No person shall use, except as a passenger, or cause or allow any other person to use, a motor vehicle in a public place, unless there is in force in relation to the use of the vehicle by that person or that other person, as the case may be, a policy of insurance complying with the requirements of this Chapter :

Provided that in the case of a vehicle carrying, or meant to carry, dangerous or hazardous goods, there shall also be a policy of insurance under the Public Liability Insurance Act, 1991 (6 of 1991).

Explanation : A person driving a motor vehicle merely as a paid employee, while there is in force in relation to the use of the vehicle no such policy as is required by this sub-section, shall not be deemed to act in contravention of the sub-section unless he knows or has reason to believe that there is no such policy in force.

(2) Sub-section (1) shall not apply to any vehicle owned by the Central Government or a State Government and used for Government purposes unconnected with any commercial enterprise.

(3) The appropriate Government may, by order, exempt from the operation of sub-section (1) any vehicle owned by any of the following authorities, namely :

(*a*) the Central Government or a State Government, if the vehicle is used for Government purposes connected with any commercial enterprise;

(*b*) any local authority;

(*c*) any State transport undertaking :

Provided that no such order shall be made in relation to any such authority unless a fund has been established and is maintained by that authority in accordance with the rules made in that behalf under this Act for meeting any liability arising out of the use of any vehicle of that authority which that authority or any person in its employment may incur to third parties.

Explanation : For the purposes of this sub-section, "appropriate Government" means the Central Government or a State Government, as the case may be, and–

(*i*) in relation to any corporation or company owned by the Central Government or any State Government, means the Central Government or that State Government;

(*ii*) in relation to any corporation or company owned by the Central Government & one or more State Governments, means the Central Government;

(*iii*) in relation to any other State transport undertaking or any local authority, means that Government which has control over that undertaking or authority. [94]

6.3 INSURANCE POLICIES

Policy of Insurance and Limits of Liability

Section 147 lays down the requirements of the policies and the limit of liability in respect of passengers and persons other than passengers in relation to passenger vehicles and goods carriages.

Section 147 : Requirement of policies and limits of liability : (1) In order to comply with the requirements of this Chapter, a policy of insurance must be a policy which:

(*a*) is issued by a person who is an authorised insurer; and

(*b*) insurers the person or classes of persons specified in the policy to the extent specified in sub-section (2) :

(*i*) against any liability which may be incurred by him in respect of the death of or bodily 90[injury to any person, including owner of the goods or his authorised representative carried in the vehicle] or damage to any property of a third party caused by or arising out of the use of the vehicle in a public place ;

(*ii*) against the death of or bodily injury to any passenger of a public service vehicle caused by or arising out of the use of the vehicle in a public place;

Provided that a policy shall not be required –

(*i*) to cover liability in respect of the death, arising out of and in the course of this employment, of the employee of a person insured by the policy or in respect of bodily injury sustained by such an employee arising out of and in the course of his employment other than a liability arising under the Workmen's Compensation Act, 1923 (8 of 1923), in respect of the death of, or bodily injury to, any such employee :

(*a*) engaged in driving the vehicle, or

(*b*) if it is a public service vehicle, engaged as a conductor of the vehicle or in examining tickets on the vehicle, or

(*c*) if it is a goods carriage, being carried in the vehicle, or

(*ii*) to cover any contractual liability.

Explanation : For the removal of doubts, it is hereby declared that the death of or bodily injury to any person or damage to any property of a third party shall be deemed to have been caused by or to have arisen out of, the use of a vehicle in a public place notwithstanding that the person who is dead or injured or the property which is damaged was not in a public place at the time of the accident, if the act or omission which led to the accident occurred in a public place.

(2) Subject to the proviso to sub-section (1), a policy of insurance referred to in sub-section (1), shall cover any liability incurred in respect of any accident, up to the following limits, namely :

(*a*) save as provided in clause (b), the amount of liability incurred.

(*b*) in respect of damage to any property of a third party, a limit of rupees six thousand :

Provided that any policy of insurance issued with any limited liability and in force, immediately before the commencement of this Act, shall continue to be effective for a period of four months after such commencement or till the date of expiry of such policy whichever is earlier.

(3) A policy shall be of no effect for the purposes of this Chapter unless and until there is issued by the insurer in favour of the person by whom the policy is effected a certificate of insurance in the prescribed form and containing the prescribed particulars of any condition subject to which the policy is issued and of any other prescribed matters; and different forms, particulars and matters may be prescribed in different cases.

(4) where a cover note issued by the insurer under the provisions of this Chapter or the rules made thereunder is not followed by a policy of insurance within the prescribed time, the insurer shall, within seven days of the expiry of the period of the validity of the cover note, notify the fact to the registering authority in whose records the vehicle to which the cover note relates has been registered or to such other authority as the State Government may prescribe.

(5) Notwithstanding anything contained in any law for the time being in force, an insurer issuing a policy of insurance under this section shall be liable to indemnify the person or classes of persons specified in the policy in respect of any liability which the policy purports to cover in the case of that person or those classes of persons.

Validity of Policies in Reciprocating Countries

Section 148 provides for the validity of policies of insurance issued in a reciprocating country in respect of motor vehicle of the reciprocating country operating on any route common to the two countries.

Section 148 : Validity of polices of insurance issued in reciprocating countries. – Where, in pursuance of an arrangement between India and any reciprocating country, the motor vehicle registered in the reciprocating country operates on any route or within any area common to the two countries and there is in force in relation to the use of the vehicle in the reciprocating country, a policy of insurance complying with the requirements of the law of insurance in force in that country, then, notwithstanding anything contained in section 147 but subject to any rules which may be made under section 164, such policy of insurance shall be effective throughout the route or area in respect of which, the arrangement has been made, as if the policy of insurance had complied with the requirements of this Chapter. [95-A]

Transfer of Certificate of Insurance

Section 156 provides that where the insurer has issued a certificate of insurance, and the policy of insurance has not been issued, then the policy to be issued be deemed to be in terms conforming in all respects to the particulars mentioned in the certificate of insurance.

Section 156 : Effect of certificate of insurance : When an insurer has issued a certificate of insurance in respect of a contract of insurance between the insurer and the insured person, then :

(*a*) if and so long as the policy described in the certificate has not been issued by the insurer to the insured, the insurer shall, as between himself and any other person except the insured, be deemed to have issued to the insured person a policy of insurance conforming in all respects with the description and particulars stated in such certificate; and (*b*) if the insurer has issued to the insured the policy described in the certificate, but the actual terms of the policy are less favourable to persons claiming under or by virtue of the policy against the insurer either directly or through the insured than the particulars of the policy as stated in the certificate, the policy shall, as between the insurer and any other person except the insured, be deemed to be in terms conforming in all respects with the particulars stated in the said certificate. [103]

Section 157 lays down that when the certificate of registration is transferred from one person to another, then the policy of insurance in respect of that vehicle is also deemed to have been transferred to that other person from the date on which the ownership of the motor vehicle stands transferred.

It provides that (1) Where a person in whose favour the certificate of insurance has been issued in accordance with the provisions of this Chapter transfer to another person the ownership of the another vehicle in respect of which such insurance was taken together with the policy of insurance relating thereto, the certificate of insurance and the policy described in the certificate shall be deemed to have been transferred in favour of the person to whom the motor vehicle is transferred with effect from the date of its transfer.

Explanation. – For the removal of doubts, it is hereby declared that such deemed transfer shall include transfer of rights and liabilities of the said certificate of insurance and policy of insurance.

(2) The transferee shall apply within fourteen days from the date of transfer in the prescribed form to the insurer for making necessary changes in regard to the fact of transfer in the certificate of insurance and the policy described in the certificate in his favour and the insurer shall make the necessary changes in the certificate and the policy of insurance in regard to the transfer of insurance. [103-A]

In many decided cases the Supreme Court has held that such deemed transfer is only in respect of third party risks.

Under *Section 103-A of the 1939 Act,* Insurance companies had choice of refusal to transfer the Certificate of Insurance and issuing new policy in the name of the new owner, if the driving history and other features of the risk become undersirable and adverse. *Section 157* shall be automatically deemed to be transferred in favour of the new owner from the date of transfer of ownership of the vehicle.

Section 157 (1), which states that such deemed transfer, shall include transfer of rights and liabilities of the said Certificate of Insurance and Policy of Insurance. That such deemed transfer of Certificate of Insurance can only be in respect of third party risks.

6.4 CLAIMS TRIBUNAL

Award of the Claim Tribunal

Section 168 states the duty and obligation of the Claims Tribunal to give prior notice of the third party's application for compensation to the Insurer as also giving opportunity to the insurer of being heard.

Procedures and Powers of the Claims Tribunal

Section 169 provides that where any Claims Tribunal has been constituted Civil Courts have no jurisdiction to entertain any question relating to claims for compensation.

Section 171 empowers the Claim Tribunal to order that simple interest at such rates as it thinks fit shall also be paid along with the award of compensation.

Appeal Against the Orders of the Tribunal

Within 90 days of an award by the Tribunal, any person who is aggrieved or not satisfied mya appeal to the High Court in the appropriate jurisdiction. However, the insurers cannot challenge the decision of Tribunal on grounds of Negligence. [Rohatgi S.C., National Insurance Co *vs.* MicoMeta 2002]

6.5 MISCELLANEOUS PROVISIONS

Duty of Insurers

Section 149 lays down that it is the duty of the insurers to satisfy judgements against persons insured in respect of third party risk.

Section 149 : Duty of insurers to satisfy judgments and awards against persons insured in respect of third party risks :

(1) if, after a certificate of insurance has been issued under sub-section (3) of section 147 in favour of the person by whom a policy has been effected, judgement or award in respect of any such liability as is requirement to be covered by a policy under clause (b) of sub-section (1) of section 147 (being a liability covered by the terms of the policy) or under the provisions of section 163 – A is obtained against any person insured by the policy, then, notwithstanding that the insurer may be entitled to avoid of cancel or may have avoided or cancelled the policy, the insurer shall, subject to the provisions of this section, pay to the person entitled to the benefit of the decree any sum not exceeding the sum assured payable thereunder, as if he were the judgement debtor, in respect of the liability, together with any amount payable in respect of costs and any sum payable in respect of interest on that sum by virtue of any enactment relating to interest on judgements.

(2) No sum shall be payable by an insurer under sub-section (1) in respect of any judgement or award unless, before the commencement of the proceedings in which the judgement or award is given the insurer had notice through the Court or, as the case may be, the Claims Tribunal of the bringing of the proceedings, or in respect of such judgement or award so long as execution is stayed thereon pending an appeal; and an insurer to whom notice of the bringing of any such

proceedings is so given shall be entitled to be made a party thereto and to defend the action on any of the following grounds, namely :

(*a*) that there has been a breach of a specified condition of the policy, being one of the following conditions, namely :

(*i*) a condition excluding the use of the vehicle :

(*a*) for hire or reward, where the vehicle is on the date of the contract of insurance a vehicle not covered by a permit to ply for hire or reward, or

(*b*) for organised racing and speed testing, or

(*c*) for a purpose not allowed by the permit under which the vehicle is used, where the vehicle is a transport vehicle, or

(*d*) without side-car being attached where the vehicle is a motor cycle; or

(*ii*) a condition excluding driving by a named person or persons or by any person who is not duly licenced, or by any person who has been disqualified for holding or obtaining a driving licence during the period of disqualification; or

(*iii*) a condition excluding liability for injury caused or contributed to by conditions of war, civil war, riot or civil commotion; or

(*b*) that the policy is void on the ground that it was obtained by the non-disclosure of a material fact or by a representation of fact which was false in some material particular.

(3) Where any such judgement as is referred to in sub-section (1) is obtained from a Court in a reciprocating country and in the case of a foreign judgement is, by virtue of the provisions of section 13 of the Code of Civil Procedure, 1908 (5 of 1908) conclusive as to any matter adjudicated upon by it, the insurer (being an insurer registered under the Insurance Act, 1938 (4 of 1938) and whether or not he is registered under the corresponding law of the reciprocating country) shall be liable to the person entitled to the benefit of the decree in the manner and to the extent specified in sub-section (1), as if the judgement were given by a Court in India :

Provided that no sum shall be payable by the insurer in respect of any such judgement unless, before the commencement of the proceedings in which the judgement is given, the insurer had notice through the Court concerned of the bringing of the proceedings and the insurer to whom notice is so given is entitled under the corresponding law of the reciprocating country, to be made a party to the proceedings and to defend the action on grounds similar to those specified in sub-section (2).

(4) Where a certificate of insurance has been issued under sub-section (3) of section 147 to the person by whom a policy has been effected, so much of the policy as purports to restrict the insurance of the persons insured thereby by reference to any conditions other than those in clause (b) of subsection (2) shall,

as respects such liabilities as are required to be covered by a policy under clause (b) of sub-section (1) of section 147, be of no effect :

Provided that any sum paid by the insurer in or towards the discharge of any liability of any person which is covered by the policy by virtue only of this sub-section shall be recoverable by the insurer from that person.

(5) If the amount which an insurer becomes liable under this section to pay in respect of a liability incurred by a person insured by a policy exceeds the amount for which the insurer would apart from the provisions of this section be liable under the policy in respect of that liability, the insurer shall be entitled to recover the excess from that person.

(6) In this section the expression "material fact" and "material particular" means, respectively, a fact or particular of such a nature as to influence the judgement of a prudent insurer in determining whether he will take the risk and, if so, at what premium and on what conditions, and the expression "liability covered by the terms of the policy" means liability which is covered by the policy or which would be so covered but for the fact that the insurer is entitled to avoid or cancel or has avoided or cancelled the policy

(7) No insurer to whom the notice referred to in sub-section (2) or sub-section (3) has been given shall be entitled to avoid his liability to any person entitled to the benefit of any such judgement or award as is referred to in sub-section (1) or in such judgement as is referred to in sub-section (3) otherwise than in the manner provided for in sub-section (2) or in the corresponding law of the reciprocating country, as the case may be. [96]

Explanation : For the purposes of this section, "Claims Tribunal" means a Claims Tribunal constituted under section 165 and "award" means an award made by that Tribunal under section 168.

Impleading Insurer in Certain Cases

Section 170 : Where in the course of any inquiry, the Claims Tribunal is satisfied that :

(*a*) there is collusion between the person making the claim and the person against whom the claim is made, or

(*b*) the persons against whom the claim is made has failed to contest the claim, it may, for reasons to be recorded in writing, direct that the insurer who may be liable in respect of such claim, shall be impleaded as a party to the proceeding and the insurer so impleaded shall thereupon have, without prejudice to the provisions contained in sub-section (2) of section 149, the right to contest the claim on all or any of the grounds that are available to the person against whom the claim has been made. [110-C(2-A)]

Rights of Third Parties

Section 150 provides that in the event of the insured becoming insolvent any liability incurred by the insured person and his rights against the insurer will be transferred to and vest in the third party to whom the liability was so incurred.

Section 150 : Rights of third parties against insurers on insolvency of the insured.– (1) Where under any contract of insurance effected in accordance with the provisions of this Chapter, a person is insured against liabilities which he may incur to third parties, then :

(*a*) in the event of the person becoming insolvent or making a composition or arrangement with his creditors, or

(*b*) where the insured person is a company, in the event of a winding-up order being made or a resolution for a voluntary winding-up being passed with respect to the company or of a receiver or manager of the company's business or undertaking being duly appointed, or of possession being taken by or on behalf of the holders of any debentures secured by a floating charge of any property comprised in or subject to the charge, if, either before or after that event, any such liability is incurred by the insured person, his rights against the insurer under the contract in respect of the liability shall, notwithstanding anything to the contrary in any provision of law, be transferred to and vest in the third party to whom the liability was so incurred.

(2) Where an order for the administration of the estate of a deceased debtor is made according to the law of insolvency, then, if any debt provable in insolvency is owing by the deceased in respect of a liability to a third party against which he was insured under a contract of insurance in accordance with the provisions of this Chapter, the deceased debtor's rights against the insurer in respect of that liability shall, notwithstanding anything to the contrary is any provision of law, be transferred to and vest in the person to whom the debt is owing.

(3) Any condition in a policy issued for the purposes of this Chapter purporting either directly or indirectly to avoid the policy or to alter the rights of the parties thereunder upon the happening to the insured person of any of the events specified in clause (a) or clause (b) of sub-section (1) or upon the making of an order for the administration of the estate of a deceased debtor according to the law of insolvency shall be of no effect.

(4) Upon a transfer under sub-section (1) or sub-section (2), the insurer shall be under the same liability to the third party as he would have been to the insured person, but :

(*a*) if the liability of the insurer to the insured person exceeds the liability of the insured person to the third party, nothing in this Chapter shall affect the rights of the insured person against the insurer in respect of the excess, and

(*b*) if the liability of the insurer to the insured person is less than the liability of the insured person to the third party, nothing in this Chapter shall affect the rights of the third party against the insured person in respect of the balance. [97]

Duty to Give Information as to Insurance

Section 151 prescribes that it is the duty of the insured to give information relating to the insurance on demand by or on behalf of the person making the claim for compensation.

Section 151 : (1) No person against whom a claim is made in respect of any liability referred to in clause (b) of sub-section (1) of section 147 shall on demand by or on behalf of the person making the claim refuse to state whether or not he was insured in respect of that liability by any policy issued under the provisions of this Chapter, or would have been so insured if the insurer had not avoided or cancelled the policy, nor shall he refuse, if he was or would have been so insured, to give such particulars with respect to that policy as were specified in the certificate of insurance issued in respect hereof.

(2) In the event of any person becoming insolvent or making a composition or arrangement with his creditors or in the event of an order being made for the administration of the estate of a deceased person according to the law of insolvency,

or in the event of a winding-up order being made or a resolution for a voluntary winding-up being passed with respect to any company or of a receiver or manager of the company's business or undertaking being duly appointed

or of possession being taken by or on behalf of the holders of any debentures secured by a floating charge on any property comprised in or subject to the charge, it shall be the duty of the insolvent debtor, personal representative of the deceased debtor or company, as the case may be,

or the official assignee or receiver in insolvency, trustee, liquidator, receiver or manager, or person in possession of the property to give at the request of any person claiming that the insolvent debtor, deceased debtor or company is under such liability to him as is covered by the provision of this Chapter, such information as may reasonably be required by him for the purpose of ascertaining whether any rights have been transferred to an vested in him by section 150,

and for the purpose of enforcing such rights, if any; and any such contract of insurance as purports whether directly or indirectly to avoid the contract or to alter the rights of the parties thereunder upon the giving of such information in the events aforesaid, or otherwise to prohibit or prevent the giving thereof in the said events, shall be of no effect.

(3) If, from the information given to any person in pursuance of subsection (2) or otherwise, he has reasonable ground for supporting that there have or may have been transferred to him under this Chapter rights against any particular insurer, that insurer shall be subject to the same duty as is imposed by the said sub-section on the persons therein mentioned.

(4) The duty to give the information imposed by this section shall include a duty to allow all contracts of insurance, receipts for premiums, and other relevant documents in the possession or power of the person on whom the duty so imposed to be inspected and copies thereof to be taken.

Settlement Between Insurers and Insured Persons

Section 152 lays down that any settlement made by the insurer in respect of any claim which may be made by the third party will not be valid unless the third party is a party to the claim.

Section 152 : (1) No settlement made by an insurer in respect of any claim which might be made by a third party in respect of any liability of the nature referred to in clause (b) of sub-section (1) of section 147 shall be valid unless such third party is a party to the settlement.

(2) Where a person who is insured under a policy issued for the purpose of this Chapter has become insolvent, or where, if such insured person is a company, a winding-up order has been made or a resolution for a voluntary winding-up has been passed with respect to the company, no agreement made between the insurer and the insured person after the liability has been incurred to a third party and after the commencement of the insolvency or winding-up, as the case may be, nor any waiver, assignment or other disposition made by or payment made to the insured person after the commencement aforesaid shall be effective to defeat the rights transferred to the third party under this Chapter, but those rights shall be the same as if no such agreement, waiver, assignment or disposition or payment has been made.

Production of Documents on Demand

Section 158 : This Section makes it compulsory on the part of the driver of the vehicle involved in accident, to produce the certificate of registration and insurance, the certificate of fitness and permit and driving licence without delay. It also provides that the police officer that makes a report of accident shall send a copy of the report to the Accident Claims Tribunal.

(1) Any person driving a motor vehicle in any public place shall, on being so required by a police officer in uniform authorised in this behalf by the State Government, produce :

(*a*) the certificate of insurance;

(*b*) the certificate of registration;

(*c*) the driving licence; and

(*d*) in the case of a transport vehicle also the certificate of fitness referred to in section 56 and the permit, relating to the use of the vehicle.

(2) If, where owing to the presence of a motor vehicle in a public place an accident occurs involving death or bodily injury to another person, the driver of

the vehicle does not at the time produce the certificate, driving licence and permit referred to in sub-section (1) to a police officer, he shall produce the said certificates, licence and permit at the police station at which he makes the report required by section 134.

(3) No person shall be liable to conviction under sub-section (1) or sub-section (2) by reason only of the failure to produce the certificate of insurance if, within seven days from the date on which its production was required under sub-section (1), or as the case may be, from the date of occurrence of the accident, he produces the certificate at such police station as may have been specified by him to the police officer who required its production or, as the case may be, to the police officer at the site of the accident or to the officer-in-charge of the police station at which he reported the accident :

Provided that except to such extent and with such modifications as may be prescribed, the provisions of this sub-section shall not apply to the driver of a transport vehicle.

(4) The owner of a motor vehicle shall give such information as he may be required by or on behalf of a police officer empowered in this behalf by the State Government to give for the purpose of determining whether the vehicle was or was not being driven in contravention of section 146 and on any occasion when the driver was required under this section to produce his certificate of insurance.

(5) In this section, the expression "produce his certificate of insurance" means produce for examination the relevant certificate of insurance or such other evidence as may be prescribed that the vehicle was not being driven in contravention of section 146.

(6) As soon as any information regarding any accident involving death or bodily injury to any person is recorded or report under this section is completed by a police officer, the officer-in-charge of the police station shall forward a copy of the same within thirty days from the date of recording of information or, as the case may be, on completion of such report to the Claims Tribunal having jurisdiction and a copy thereof to the concerned insurer, and where a copy is made available to the owner, he shall also within thirty days of receipt of such report, forward the same to such Claims Tribunal and insurer]. [106]

Production of Certificate of Insurance on Application for Authority to use Vehicle [Section 159]

Section 159 empowers the State Government to make rules to require production of certificate of insurance of a motor vehicle at the time of payment of taxes and in the case of transport vehicle to have a valid certificate of insurance before the vehicle is put on public road after obtaining a permit.

It provides that – A State Government may make rules requiring the owner of any motor vehicle when applying whether by payment of a tax or otherwise for authority to use the vehicle in a public place to produce such evidence as may be prescribed by those rules to the effect that either :

(*a*) on the date when the authority to use the vehicle comes into operation there will be in force the necessary policy of insurance in relation to the use of the vehicle by the applicant or by other persons on his order or with his permission, or

(*b*) the vehicle is a vehicle to which section 146 does not apply. [107]

Effect of Death of Insured Person

Section 155 provides that if the insured person dies after incurring third party liability, then the cause of action survives against the insured's estate, or legal heirs or against the insurer. If this provision is not made, then the third party's right of action against the negligent owner of the vehicle would die with the death of the owner.

Liability Without Fault

***Section 140** : Liability to pay compensaiton in certain cases on the principle of no fault*

1. Where death or permanent disablement of any person has resulted from an accident arising out of the use of motor vehicle or motor vehicles, the owner of the vehicle shall, or, as the case may be, the owners of the vehicles shall, jointly and severally, be liable to pay compensation in respect of such death or disablement in accordance with the provisions of this section.
2. The amount of compensation which shall be payable under sub-section (1) in respect of the death of any person shall be a fixed sum of [fifty thousand rupees] and the amount of compensation payable under that sub-section in respect of the permanent disablement of any person shall be a fixed sum of twenty-five thousand rupees.
3. In any claim for compensation under sub-section (1), the claimant shall not be required to plead and establish that the death or permanent diablement in respect of which the claim has been made was due to any wrongful act, neglect or default of the owner or owners of the vehicles concerned or of any other person.
4. A claim for compensation under sub-section (1) shall not be defeated by reason of any wrongful act, neglect or default of the person in respect of whose death or permanent disablement the claim has been made nor shall the quantum of compensation recoverable in respect of such death or permanent disablement be reduced on the basis of the share of such person in the responsibility for such death or permanent disablement.
5. Notwithstanding anyting contained in sub-section (2) regarding death or bodily injury to any person, for which the owner of the vehicle is liable to give compensation for relief, he is also liable to pay compensation under any other law for the time being in force.

Provided that the amount of compensation payable under this section or under section 163.

Section 141 : *Provisions as to other right to claim compensaiton for death or permanent disablement*

1. The right to claim compensation under section 140 in respect of death or permanent disablement of any person shall be in addition to [any other right, except the right to claim under the scheme referred to section 163A (such other right thereafter) in this section referred to as the right on the principle of fault) to claim compensation in respect thereof under any other provision of this Act or of any other law for the time being in force.
2. A claim for compensation under section 140 in respect of death or permanent disablement of any person shall be disposed of as expeditiously as possible and where compensation is claimed in respect of such death of permanent disablement under section 140 and also in pursuance of any right on the principle of fault, the claim for compensation under section 140 shall be disposed of as aforesaid in the first place.
3. Notwithstanding anything contained in sub-section (1), where in respect of the death, or permanent disablement of any person, the person liable to pay compensation under section 140 is also liable to pay compensaiton in accordance with the right on the principle of fault, the person so liable shall pay the first mentioned compensation and :

(*a*) if the amount of the first-mentioned compensation is less than the amount of the second-mentioned compensation, he shall be liable to pay (in addition to the first-mentioned compensation) only so much which it exceeds the first-mentioned compensaiton,

(*b*) if the amount of the first-mentioned compensation is equal to or more than the amount of the second-mentioned compensaiton, he shall not be liable to pay the second-mentioned compensation.

Section 142 : *Permanent disablement*

For the purpose of this Chapter, permanent disablement of a person shall be deemed to have resulted from an accident of the nature referred to in sub-section (1) of section 140 if such person has suffered by reason of the accident, any injury or injuries involving :

(*a*) permanent privation of the either eye or the hearing of either ear, or privation of any member of joint; or

(*b*) destruction or permanent impairing of the powers of any member or joint; or

(*c*) permanent disfiguration of the head or face.

Section 143 : Applicability of Chapter to certain claims under Act 8 of 1923

The provisions of this Chapter shall also apply in relation to any claim for compensation in respect of death or permanent disablement of any person under the Workmen's Compensation Act, 1923 resulting from an accident of the nature referred to in sub-section (1) of section 140 and for this purpose, the said provisions shall, will necessary modifications, be deemed to form part of that Act.

Section 144 : Overriding effect

The provisions of this Chapter shall have effect notwithstanding anything contained in any other provisions of this Act or of any other law for the time being in force.

The following therefore follows :

(*a*) In a claim for compensation, the claimant is not required to prove any wrongful act, neglect, or default/negligence on the part of the owner of the vehicle concerned or by any other person.

(*b*) The claim shall not be defeated in any way by any wrongful act, neglect or default on the part of the claimant; nor can the quantum of compensation be reduced on the basis of the claimant's share of responsibility for the accident. This implies that the legal defense of 'contributory negligence' is not available to the motorist and insurer of the vehicle.

(*c*) The compensation is available if and only if where the claimant suffers death or permanent disablement, as defined in the Act.

(*d*) The amount of compensation is Death, Rs. 50,000; Permanent Disablement, Rs. 25,000.

The theme of this section is to provide minimum statutory relief on grounds of social justice.

Hit and Run Accident

Section 161 : (1) The payment of compensation in respect of the death of, or grievous hurt to, any person under section 161 shall be subject to the condition that if any compensation (hereafter in this sub-section referred to as the other compensation) or other amount in lieu of or by way of satisfaction of a claim for compensation is awarded or paid in respect of such death or grievous hurt under any other provision of this Act or any other law or otherwise so much of the other compensation or other amount aforesaid as is equal to the compensation paid under section 161 shall be refunded to the insurer.

(2) Before awarding compensation in respect of an accident involving the death of, or bodily injury to, any person arising out of the use of a motor vehicle or

motor vehicles under any provision of this Act (other than section 161) or any other law, the Tribunal Court or other authority awarding such compensation shall verify as to whether in respect of such death or bodily injury compensation has already been paid under section 161 or an application for payment of compensation is pending under that section, and such Tribunal, Court or other authority shall, :

(*a*) if compensation has already been paid under section 161, direct the person liable to pay the compensation awarded by it to refund to the insurer, so much thereof as is required to be refunded in accordance with the provisions of sub-section (1);

(*b*) if an application for payment of compensation is pending under section 161 forward the particulars as to the compensation awarded by it to the insurer.

Explanation : For the purpose of this sub-section, an application for compensation under section 161 shall be deemed to be pending :

(*i*) if such application has been rejected, till the date of the rejection of the application, and

(*ii*) in any other case, till the date of payment of compensation in pursuance of the application. [109-B]

Section 162 seeks to provide that when compensation is awarded in a case where compensation under clause 161 has already been paid then so much of the compensation paid as per clause 161 shall be refunded to the insurer.

Scheme for payment of compensation in case of hit and run motor accidents.

Section 163 : (1) The Central Government may, by notification in the Official Gazette, make a scheme specifying, the manner in which the scheme shall be administered by the General Insurance Corporation, the form, manner and the time within which applications for compensation may be made, the officers or authorities to whom such applications may be made, the procedure to be followed by such officers or authorities for considering and passing orders on such applications, and all other matters connected with, or incidental to, the administration of the scheme and the payment of compensation.

(2) A scheme made under sub-section (1) may provide that :

(*a*) a contravention of any provision thereof shall be punishable with imprisonment for such term as may be specified but in no case exceeding three months, or with fine which may extend to such amount as may be specified but in no case exceeding five hundred rupees or with both;

(*b*) the powers, functions or duties conferred or imposed on any officer or authority by such scheme may be delegated with the prior approval in writing of the Central Government, by such officer or authority to any other officer or authority;

(*c*) any provision of such scheme may operate with retrospective effect from a date not earlier than the date of establishment of the Solatium Fund under the Motor Vehicles Act, 1939 (4 of 1939) as it stood immediately before the commencement of this Act.

Provided that no such retrospective effect shall be given so as to prejudicially affect the interests of any person who may be governed by such provision. [109-C]

Section 163 empowers the Central Government to makes scheme for payment of compensation in "hit and run" accident cases detailing the procedure for making claim, the authorities to whom the claim should be made, etc.

Section 163 : A. Special provisions as to payment of compensation on structured formulae basis. – (1) Notwithstanding anything contained in this Act or in any other law for the time being in force or instrument having the force of law, the owner of the motor vehicle of the authorised insurer shall be liable to pay in the case of death or permanent disablement due to accident arising out of the use of motor vehicle compensation, as indicated in the Second Schedule, to the legal heirs or the victim, as the case may be.

Explanation. – For the purposes of this sub-section, "permanent disability" shall have the same meaning and extent as in the Workmen's Compensation Act, 1923.

(2) In any claim for compensation under sub-section (1), the claimant shall not be required to plead or establish that the death or permanent disablement in respect of which the claim has been made was due to any wrongful act or neglect or default of the owner of the vehicle or vehicles concerned or of any other person.

(3) The Central Government may, keeping in view the cost of living by notification in the Official Gazette, from time to time amend the Second Schedule. [Newly Inserted]

Section 163-B : Option to file claim in certain cases. – Where a person is entitled to claim compensation under section 140 and section 163-A, he shall file the claim under either of the said sections and not under both. [Newly Inserted]

Application for Compensation

Section 166 provides for the form of application for compensation, the person who may claim compensation, the time within which the application should be filed, etc. It also provides that if the Claims Tribunal, think so, may treat the accident report filed by the Police Officer as per Section 158 as an application under this Act.

Section 166 : Application for compensation. – (1) An application for compensation arising out of an accident of the nature specified in sub-section (1) of section 165 may be made :

(*a*) by the person who has sustained the injury; or

(*b*) by the owner of the property; or

(*c*) where death has resulted from the accident, by all or any of the legal representatives of the deceased; or

(*d*) by any agent duly authorised by the person injured or all or any of the legal representatives of the deceased, as the case may be :

Provided that where all the legal representatives of the deceased have not joined in any such application for compensation, the application shall be made on behalf of or for the benefit of all the legal representatives of the deceased and the legal representatives who have not so joined, shall be impleaded as respondents to the application.

(2) Every application under sub - section (1) shall be made, at the option of the claimant, either to the Claims Tribunal having jurisdiction over the area in which the accident occurred or to the Claims Tribunal within the local limits of whose jurisdiction the claimant resides, or carries on business or within the local limits of whose jurisdiction the defendant resides and shall be in such form and contain such particulars as may be prescribed:

Provided that where no claim for compensation under section 140 is made in such application, the application shall contain a separate statement to that effect immediately before the signature of the applicant.

(4) The Claims Tribunal shall treat any report of accidents forwarded to it under sub-section (6) of section 158 as an application for compensation under this Act.

Key Terms

- Motor Accident Claims Tribunal
- No Fault
- Certificate of Insurance
- Hits and Run Accident
- Motor Vehicle
- Driving Licence

References

- *www.irdaindia.org*
- *www.bimaonline.com*
- *Motor Insurance*, IC72, Insurance Institute of India, Mumbai, 2003.
- *Bare Acts*

Questions for Review

1. Discuss the powers and functions of Motor Accident Claims Tribunal (MACT).
2. Write short notes on :
   (*a*) Hit and Run Accident
   (*b*) No Fault Liability
   (*c*) Certificate of Insurance.
3. Briefly describe the compensation available to third parties for loss or damages under the Motor Vehicles Act, 1939 and 1988.

CHAPTER 7

Marine Insurance Act, 1963

Marine Insurance Act was passed in 1963 and is largely based on the English Marine Insurance Act, 1906. The Insurance Act, 1938 defines the marine insurance business as the business of effecting contracts of insurance upon vessels of any description, including cargos, freights and other interest, which may be legally assured, in relation to such vessels, cargoes and freights, goods, wares, merchandize and property of whatever description assured for any transit by land or water or by both, and whether or not including warehouse risks or similar risks in addition or as incidental to, such transit, and includes any other risks customarily including among the risks assured against in marine insurance policies (Section 13A).

Maritime insurance business includes the following :

- Insurance of vessels of any description (Hull).
- Insurance of cargo in the vessel (Cargo).
- Freight paid or received by the assured (Freight).
- Other merchandize and other property assured, which is in the transit either in water or on the land to water or both.
- Insurance of third party liability (TPL).
- Insurance of the transactions which are incidental to the marine adventure of marine transport or transport of cargo from place of godown to the vessel or *vis-a-vis.*
- Insurance also includes all perils and risks incidental to money, documents, securities, other valuable goods in the ship.
- Freight, insurance premium paid by the assured, packaging and forwarding expenses.
- Any other incidental activities concerned to building, launching of ship or transport of stores concerned.

7.1 CONTRACT OF MARINE INSURANCE AND POLICY

Section 3 defines marine insurance as :

"A contract of marine insurance is an agreement whereby the insurer undertakes to indemnify the assured, in the manner and to the extent thereby agreed, against marine losses, that is to say, the losses incidental to marine adventure."

A defeasible interest is insurable, as also is a contingent interest. For example, liability for salvage expenses is insurable and also the liability for carriage of passengers.

A partial interest of any nature is insurable. (Section 10)

Reinsurance [S. 11]

The insurer under a contract of marine insurance has an insurable interest in his risk, and may reinsure in respect of it. The original assured will have no right in respect of such reinsurance, unless the policy so provides. This is so for the obvious reason that a reinsurance is taken out by an insurer for his own protection.

Bottomry and Respondentia [S. 12]

The lender of money on bottomry or respondentia has an insurable interest in respect of the loan. He can effect a policy on the ship to the extent of his interest.

Master's and Seamen's Wages [S. 13]

The master or any member of the crew of a ship has an insurable interest in respect of wages.

Advance Freight [S. 14]

The shipowner has an interest in the freight which he will earn on the successful completion of the voyage. He can insure the risk of his being not able to earn the freight by any accident. This interest arises out of ownership of the ship.

Section 24 of the Act provides the marine insurance policy may be issued as a token of a conclusion of the contract and can be executed and issued either at the time when the contract is conducted or afterwards. Also, the marine insurance policy must fulfil the requirements as to description as specified by the Act. The marine insurance policy should contain following particulars :

- Name of the assured or group of the assured.
- The subject matter of insurance and risk assured.
- Voyage details.
- Sum assured.
- The name or names of insurers.
- The signatures of authorized person of the insurer.
- Where the marine policy designates the subject matter assured in general terms, it shall be construed to apply to the interest intended by the assured to be covered. (Section 28).
- Schedule forming part of policy.

Insurable Interest

A contract of marine insurance made without insurable interest has been expressly declared by Section 6 to be by way of wagering and void. The section says that a contract of marine insurance shall be deemed to be a wager :

1. where the insured does not have an insurable interest in the subject-matter of insurance and the contract is entered into with no expectation of acquiring such an interest; or
2. where the policy is made "interest or no interest", or "without further proof of interest than the policy itself", or "without benefit of salvage to the insurer" or subject to any other like term.

Also, where there is no possibility of salvage, a policy may be effected without benefit of salvage to the insurer.

A policy of insurance which declares that the policy itself is a proof of interest is called a policy with a "PPI clause" (policy proof of interest). Such a policy becomes void by virtue of the above declaration stating that a policy shall be valid without further proof of interest.

Section 7 of the Act says that every person who is interested in a marine adventure is deemed to have insurable interest in it. In particular a person is interested in a marine adventure where he stands in any legal or equitable relation to the adventure or to any insurable property at risk in consequence of which he may be benefited by the safety or due arrival of insurable property or may be prejudiced by its loss, damage or detention or may incur liability in respect thereof.

The insurable interest should exist at the time of the loss. It is not necessary that it should exit at the time when the policy is effected. When the parties are not aware about the existence or loss of the goods, they are permitted to insure them under a clause "loss or not lost".

A defeasible interest is insurable, as also is a contingent interest. For example, liability for salvage expenses is insurable and also the liability for carriage of passengers. (Section 9).

A partial interest of any nature is insurable. (Section 10).

Principle of Indemnity and Evaluation of Loss

The marine insurance contract is a contract of indemnity where the insurer(s) are under obligation to compensate the loss suffered by the assured due to happening of risk covering the asset. If there are more than one insurers, they are liable to contribute such proportion of the measure of indemnity as the amount of the subscription bears to the value fixed by the policy in the case of a valued policy or to the insurable value in the case of an unvalued policy. (Section 67).

Subject to the terms of the policy, where there is a total loss of the subject-matter insured, in the case of valued policy, the measure of indemnity is the sum fixed by the policy and, in the case of an unvalued policy, the insurable value of the subject-matter insured. (S. 68).

Section 69(3) requires the measure of indemnity to be qualified on the basis of what it would have cost to repair if the repairs has been carried out.

In the case of partial loss of freight, the measure of indemnity is such proportion of the sum fixed by the policy in the case of a valued policy or of the insurable value in the case of an unvalued policy, as the proportion of the freight loss by the assured bears to the whole freight at the risk of the assured under the policy.

Insurable Value

If there is no express valuation of the subject-matter insured in the policy, Section 18 lays down as to how this value be ascertained :

1. In an insurance *on ship* – the insurable value is the value of the ship at the commencement of the risk, including her outfit, provisions and stores for the officers and crew, money advanced for seamen's wages, and other disbursements, if any, made to make the ship seaworthy for the voyage, plus the insurance charges on the whole. In case of steamships, the value of boilers, machinery, coal, etc., and other special requisites, if any, must also be included.

2. In an insurance *on freight,* the insurable value is the gross amount of the freight plus the charges of insurance.

3. In an insurance on goods, the insurable value in the prime cost of the goods incurred plus the expenses of shipping and insurance charges.

4. In an insurance on nay other subject matter – the insurable value includes the amount at risk plus insurance charges.

Disclosure and Representation : A contract of marine insurance, like any other contract of insurance, is a contract *uberrimae fidei, i.e.,* a contract requiring utmost good faith. If the utmost good faith is not observed by either party, the contract may be avoided by the other (Section 19).

Duty of Disclosure : Section 20 provides that the assured must disclose to insurer every material circumstances which is known to him. He is deemed to know everything which he ought to know in the ordinary course of the business. A circumstance is material if it would influence the judgement of a prudent insurer in fixing of determining whether to take the risk.

Every circumstance is material which would influence the judgement of a prudent insurer in fixing the premium, or determining whether he will take the risk. In the absence of an inquiry the following circumstances need not be disclosed :

(*a*) any circumstance which diminishes the risk;

(*b*) any circumstance which is known or presumed to be known to the insurer. The insurer is presumed to know matters of common notoriety or knowledge, and matters which an insurer in the ordinary course of business as such, ought to know;

(*c*) any circumstance as to which information is waived by the insurer;

(*d*) any circumstance which is superfluous to disclouse by reason of any express or implied warranty; [S. 20(3)].

Whether any particular circumstance, which is not disclosed, be material or not is, in each case, a question of fact. [S. 20(4)]

The term "circumstances" includes any communication made to, or information received, by the assured. [S. 20(5)].

When the policy is effected through an agent, the extent of his duty of disclosure is the same as that of the assured. He is also bound to disclose every material circumstance which the assured ought to disclose, unless it comes to his knowledge too late to communicate to his agent. (S. 21)

Representations Pending Negotiations [S. 22]

Representations made during the course of negotiations must be true otherwise the insurer may avoid the contract, whether the representation is as to a matter of fact or expectation or belief.

A representation will be regarded as true if it is substantially correct, that is, if the difference between the truth and the representation would not be considered material by a prudent insurer.

A representation as to expectation or belief is true if it is made in good faith.

A representation may be withdrawn or corrected before the contract is concluded.

A contract is deemed to be concluded when the proposal is accepted, whether the policy be then issued or not, and to know whether a proposal has been accepted or not reference may be made to any customary method of acceptance, although it be unstamped. (S. 23)

Double Insurance [S. 34]

Where more than one policies are effected by or on behalf of the assured on the same adventure or interest, and the sums insured exceed the indemnity allowed by the Act, the insured is said to be overinsured by double insurance. The consequences of such double insurance are as follows :

1. The assured can claim payment from any of the insurers in such order as he may think fit. But in no case he would be allowed to recover more than the indemnity allowed by the Act.
2. When he claims under a policy which is a valued policy, he will have to give credit as against the valuation, for any sum received by him under any other policy, without regard to the actual value of the subject-matter assured.

3. Whether the policy under which a claim is made is an unvalued policy, he must give credit, as against the full insurable value, for any sum received by him under any other policy.
4. Where the assured receives any sum in excess of the indemnity allowed by the Act, he shall hold such sum in trust for the insurers, according to their right of contribution among themselves.

Right of Contribution [S. 80]

Where the assured is over-assured by double insurance, each insurer is bound, as between himself and other insurers, to contribute rateably to the loss in proportion to the amount for which he is liable under the contract.

If any insurer pays more than his proportion of the loss, he is entitled to maintain a suit for contribution against the other insurers, and is entitled to the like remedies as a surety who has paid more than his proportion of the debt.

Effect of Under Insurance [S. 81]

Where the assured is insured for an amount less than the insurable value, or, in the case of a valued policy, for an amount less than the policy valuation, he is deemed to be his own insurer in respect of the uninsured balance.

If the goods are damaged/loss value, the insurer may dispose the goods at immediate port and indemnify the difference between the sale value and insured value to the insured.

Assignment of Policy

The assignment of the policy can be made either by on endorsement or by other method which is approved and established by the law in force. The assignee acquires all rights of the assignor upon assignment and can file suits or defend suits, file claims and receive the claims and settle any dispute concerned to the policy unless otherwise stated in the policy and assignment clause.

When and How Assignable [S. 52]

A marine policy is assignable, that is, transferable to any other person unless there is some provision in the policy itself prohibiting the transfer. Assignment may be made either before or after loss. The assignee will be entitled to sue in his own name. The insurer will be entitled to raise against the assignee any defence that would have been available to him against the insured. In other words, an assignment is subject to all the equities.

The assignee must have insurable interest in the subject-matter of the policy.

Where an assured has already lost or parted with his interest in the subject-matter insured, and this without any assignment at the time, any subsequent assignment will be inoperative.

The Premium [S. 54]

Unless otherwise agreed, payment of the premium and issue of the policy are concurrent conditions. The insurer is not bound to issue the policy until payment or tender of the premium.

The Voyage and Insurance

In a voyage policy it is not necessary that the ship shall be at the place mentioned in the contract as the place of sailing, but there is an implied condition that the adventure shall be commenced within a reasonable time. If the adventure is not so commenced, the insurer can avoid the contract. This implied condition of reasonable dispatch may, however, be negatived by showing that the delay was caused by circumstances known to the insurer before the contract was concluded or by showing that he waived the condition. If the ship sails to different destinations than which are mentioned in the policy the insurance contract is invalid and the risk is not covered.

The deviation of the voyage in voyage policy can be excused in the following events cases.

1. when it is authorised by the special terms of the policy;
2. where caused by circumstances beyond the control of the master, and his employer;
3. where reasonably necessary in order to comply with an express or implied warranty;
4. where reasonably necessary for the safety of the ship or subject-matter insured;
5. for the purpose of saving human life or aiding a ship in distress where human life may be in danger;
6. where reasonably necessary for the purpose of obtaining medical or surgical aid for any person on board the ship;
7. where caused by the barratrous conduct of the master or crew, if barratry be one of the perils insured against.

Sub-section (2) provides that once the cause excusing the deviation or delay ceases to operate, the ship must resume her course, and prosecute her voyage, with reasonable dispatch.

7.2 WARRANTIES AND DISCLOSURES

Warranties and Disclosures

A warranty, as defined in the Act, means a promissory warranty. A warranty becomes a condition logically in a marine insurance contract.

- A warranty stated in the marine insurance is promissory warranty. The promissory warranty is the undertaking of the assured stating the intention to do or not to do some work in a particular way.
- An insurer may waive the compliance of warranty as per the provisionary of Section 36.
- Warranty of neutrality implies that the goods or ship which is insured is of neutral character at the commencement of risk and will continue to be a neutral during the coverage of risk (Section 38).
- In a time policy there is no implied warranty that the ship shall be seaworthy at any stage of the adventure and insurer is not liable for any loss attributable to unseaworthiness.
- In a policy on goods or other movables there is no implied warranty that the goods or movables are seaworthy (Section 42).
- There is an implied warranty that the adventure is lawful and is carried on in a lawful manner.

Non-compliance with a warranty is excused in the following cases :

1. When, on account of change of circumstances, the warranty ceases to be applicable to the circumstances of the contract.
2. When compliance with the warranty is rendered unlawful by any subsequent law.
3. A breach of warranty may be waived by the insurer.
4. Express warranty must be written upon the policy or upon some document incorporated by reference into the policy and an express warranty will not exclude an implied warranty unless it is inconsistent therewith.

No Implied Warranty of Nationality [*S.* 39]

There is no implied warranty as to the nationality of a ship or that her nationality shall not be changed during the risk.

Warranty of Good Safety [*S.* 40]

When the subject-matter insured is warranted "well" or "in good safety" on a particular day, it is sufficient if it is safe at any time during that day.

Warranty of Seaworthiness [*S.* 41]

In a voyage policy there is an implied warranty that at the commencement of the voyage the ship shall be seaworthy for the purpose of the particular venture insured. There is also the implied warranty that, at the commencement of the risk, the ship shall be reasonably fit to encounter the ordinary perils of the sea.

In a voyage policy it is not necessary that the ship shall be at the place mentioned in the contract as the place of sailing, but there is an implied condition that the adventure shall be commenced within a reasonable time. If the adventure is not so commenced, the insurer can avoid the contract. This implied condition of reasonable dispatch may, however, be negatived by showing that the delay was caused by circumstances known to the insurer before the contract was concluded or by showing that he waived the condition.

Examples of Material Circumstances

(1) Concealing the nationality of the insured when such nationality is of importance [*Associated Oil Carriers Ltd.* v. *Union Ins. Society of Canton* (1917) 2 K.B. 184].

(2) The fact that the ship had developed a leak before the insurance was effected [*Russel* v. *Thorton* 1859 20 L.R. Ex. 9].

(3) The fact that the goods carried on the ship are grossly over-valued when the ship is insured. [*Ionidies* v. *Pender* (1874) L.R. 7. Q.B. 531].

7.3 PREMIUMS

Refund of Premiums

Enforcement of Refund [S. 82]

If the premium has become refundable, it can be recovered back, and if it has not been paid, it shall cease to be payable. The policy itself may provide that in the happening of an event, the premium, or any part of it, shall become refundable. This will be known as return by agreement.

Return on Failure of Consideration [S. 84]

Where the consideration for the payment of the premium totally fails, and there has been no illegality or fraud on the part of the assured, the premium becomes refundable.

When the goods are insured for damage during the transit and the goods become useless by the time the vessel arrives at the destination then the insurer faces total loss. This makes the insurer to take prudent decision of disposing the goods at an immediate port for best value before they are totally damaged. The insurer has to pay the difference of amount received by selling the goods and the amount payable to the assured. As such the insurer is saved from indemnifying the assured from the total loss.

If the goods are damaged/loss value, the insurer may dispose the goods at immediate port and indemnify the difference between the sale value and insured value to be insured.

7.4 MARINE LOSSES AND DAMAGES

Loss and Abandonment

Included and Excluded Losses : Proximate Cause [S. 55]

Unless the policy otherwise provides, the insurer is liable for any loss proximately caused by a peril insured against and is not liable for a loss not proximately caused.

This statement has been further particularised in terms of the following principles:

1. The insurer is not liable for any loss attributable to the wilful misconduct of the assured. But he is liable for a loss proximately caused by a peril insured against, even though the loss would not have happened but for the misconduct or negligence of the master or crew.
2. Unless the policy otherwise provides that insurer is not liable for the consequences of delay even if the delay is caused by a peril insured against.
3. Unless the policy otherwise provides the insurer is not liable for ordinary wear and tear, ordinary leakage and breakage, inherent vice or nature of the subject-matter insured, for any loss proximately caused by rats or vermin or for any injury to machinery not proximately caused by maritime perils.

Partial and Total Loss [S. 56]

A loss may be either total or partial. While there is no definition given of "partial loss", the section defines total loss and then says that any loss which is not total as thus defined is a partial loss. Total loss may be actual or constructive.

Actual Total Loss

1. Where the subject-matter insured is destroyed, or so damaged as to cease to be a thing of the kind insured, or where the assured is irretrievably deprived of the subject-matter, there is an actual total loss. (S. 57)
2. Where the ship concerned in the adventure is missing, and after the lapse of a reasonable time no news of her has been received, an actual total loss may be presumed. (S. 58)

Thus, there is actual total loss in three cases : (1) where the subject-matter is totally destroyed or annihilated; (2) where the subject-matter ceases to remain in its original condition; (3) though the thing is not destroyed, but the assured cannot get it, it being irretrievably lost to him.

Constructive Total Loss [S. 60]

There is constructive total loss when the cargo is abandoned on account of its actual total loss appearing to be unavoidable or when it could be saved from actual total loss only at an expense which would exceed the value of the subject-matter insured.

Sub-section (2) says that in particular there is constructive total loss in the following cases :

1. Where the assured is deprived of the possession of his ship or goods by a peril insured against and (*a*) it is unlikely that he can recover the ship or the goods; (*b*) the cost of recovering the ship or goods would exceed there value;

2. In the case of damage to a ship, where she is so damaged by a peril insured against that the cost of repairing the damage would exceed the value of the ship.

In estimating the cost of repair, general average contributions payable by others to the repair are not to be taken into account. But the cost of salvage operations and the liability of the ship to make general average contributions are to be included.

Option of the Assured [S. 61]

Section 61 which deals with the effect of constructive total loss gives this option to the assured that he may treat the constructive total loss as a partial loss or abandon the subject-matter insured to the insurer and treat the loss as if it were an actual total loss.

Notice of Abandonment [S. 62]

If he elects to treat the loss as an actual total loss he must give notice of abandonment to the insurer. If he fails to do so the loss can only be treated as a partial loss.

Notice may be in any form, *viz.,* written, oral or partily written and partly oral. All that is necessary is that is should indicate to the insurer the intention to surrender unconditionally the subject-matter of insurance.

Notice should be given with reasonable diligence after the assured reliably learns of the loss. But if the information as to loss is of doubtful nature, he is entitled to reasonable time to make an inquiry.

Where proper notice has been given but the insurer refuses to accept it, that will not prejudice the rights of the assured. The acceptance of abandonment on the part of the insurer may be express or implied, but mere silence of the insurer after notice is not an acceptance.

An unaccepted notice of abandonment can be withdrawn by the assured.

Once the notice is accepted, the abandonment becomes irrevocable. The acceptance of the notice is a conclusive admission of the liability for the loss and of the sufficiency of the notice.

When Notice not Necessary

No notice is necessary in the following cases :

1. Where at the time when the assured receives information of the loss, there would be no possibility of benefit to the insurer if notice were given to him.

2. Notice of abandonment may be waived by the insurer.

3. Where an insurer has re-insured his risk, no notice of abandonment need be given by him.

Effect of Abandonment [S. 63]

When a valid abandonment has taken place, the assured is entitled to take over the whole of the interest of the assured in the subject-matter of insurance including proprietary rights over it.

Where a ship is abandoned, the insurer will be entitled to freight which is in the course of being earned and which is earned subsequent to the casualty causing the loss, less the expenses insurred in earning it after the casualty. If the ship is carrying the owner's goods, the insurer will be entitled to a reasonable remuneration for the carriage of them subsequent to the casualty causing the loss.

Partial Losses : Salvage, General Average and Particular Charges

Particular Average Loss [S. 64]

A particular average loss is a partial loss of the subject-matter insured, and which is not a general average loss. Expenses incurred by the assured for the safety or preservation of the subject-matter insured, other than general average and salvage charges, are called particular charges. Particular charges are not included in particular average.

Salvage Charges [S. 65]

Subject to the terms of the policy, salvage charges incurred in preventing a loss by perils insured against may be recovered as a loss by those perils. "Salvage charges" means charges recoverable under maritime law by a salvor independently of contract. They do not include the expenses of services in the nature of salvage rendered by the assured or his agent, or any person employed for hire by them, for the purpose of averting a peril insured against. Such expenses where properly incurred, may be recovered as particular charges or as a general average loss, according to the circumstances under which they were incurred.

General Average Loss [S. 66]

A general average loss is a loss caused by or directly consequential on a general average act. It includes a general average expenditure as well as a general average sacrifice. Explaining the meaning of the expression "general average act", sub-section (2) says that there is a general average act where any extraordinary sacrifice or expenditure is voluntarily and reasonably made or incurred in time of peril for the purpose of preserving the property imperilled in the common adventure. It has been pointed out in *Watson (Joseph) & Son Ltd. v. Fireman's Fund Insurance Co. of San Francisco* that the peril sought to be averted should be a real one.

Where there is a general average loss, the party on whom it falls is entitled to a rateable contribution from the other parties interested, and such contribution is called a general average contribution.

Where an assured has incurred a general average of expenditure, he may recover from the insurer in respect of the proportion of the loss which falls upon him. In the case of a general average sacrifice, he may recover from the insurer in respect of the whole loss without having enforced his right of contribution from the other parties liable to contribute.

Where an assured has paid or is liable to pay, a general average contribution in respect of the interest insured, he may recover the same from the insurer.

There is no liability on the part of the insurer where the loss was not incurred for the purpose of avoiding or in connection with the avoidance of a peril against.

Where ship, freight and cargo, or any two of those interests, are owned by the same assured, the liability of the insurer in respect of general average losses or contributions is to be determined as if these interest were owned by different persons.

The right to sue for general average loss commences from the date of the loss and the period of limitation begins to run from the date and not from the date when the average adjusters publish their statements as to the liability of the parties.

Partial Loss of Goods, Merchandise, etc. [S. 71]

In the case of partial loss of goods, merchandise or other movables, the measure of indemnity, subject to the provisions of policy, is as follows :

1. In the case of a valued policy, the measure of indemnity is such proportion of the sum fixed by the policy as the insurable value of the part loss bears to the insurable value of the whole, ascertained as in the case of an unvalued policy.
2. In the case of an unvalued policy, the measure of indemnity is the insurable value of the part lost, ascertained as in the case of total loss.
3. Where the goods have been delivered damaged at their destination, the measure of indemnity is such proportion of the sum fixed by the policy in the case of a valued policy, or of the insurable value in the case of an unvalued policy, as the difference between the gross sound and damaged values at the place of arrival bears to the gross sound value.

4. "Gross value" means the whole sale price, or, if there be no such price, the estimated value, with, in either case, freight, landing charges, and duty paid before hand; provided that, in the case of goods or merchandise customarily sold in bond, the bonded price is deemed to be the gross value. "Gross proceeds" means the actual price obtained at a sale where all charges on sale are paid by the sellers.

Where the assured has paid or is liable for any general average contribution, the measure of indemnity is the full amount of such contribution if the subject-matter liable to contribution is insured for its full contributory value. But if it is not insured for its full contributory value, or if only part if it be assured, the indemnity payable by the insurer must be reduced in proportion to the underinsurance. Where there has been a particular average loss which constitutes a deduction from the contributory value, and for which the insurer is liable, that amount must be deducted from the insured value in order to ascertain what the insurer is liable to contribute.

7.5 DECIDED CASES

Conditions in a Contract; Gartsman et al. *vs.* Elite Insurance et al., 2004 ONSC 11157

The Plaintiff in this matter purchased a vessel from the Defendant marina and asked the marina about insurance. She was told that the marina could not provide insurance but was given the name of a broker who arranged insurance with the Defendant insurer. A temporary binder was issued for 30 days that was conditional on the vessel being laid up at the dock pending receipt of a completed application and survey. It was also conditional on the vessel not being used except for instructional purposes by the marina.

Although the Plaintiff alleged she was not advised of these conditions the Court did not believe her. In breach of the conditions the Plaintiff took the vessel on a cruise during which it was damaged. Predictably, the insurer denied coverage and the Court upheld the insurer's denial.

Right of Insurer on Payment; Yorkshire Insurance Co. Ltd. *vs.* Nisbet Shipping Company Ltd. (1961) 2 All ER 487

A ship became a total loss on account of a collision caused by the negligence of a Canadian government ship. The insurer paid the total loss of £ 72,000. The assured also claimed the damages from the Canadian Government and recovered £1,27,000. The insurer claimed that they were entitled to the whole amount. It was held that they are entitled only to the amount they have paid. Had there been a clause of assignment into the policy, they could have recovered whole of the amount even if it exceeds the amount indemnified.

{*Source:* Avtar Singh, Law of Insurance, Eastern Book Company, 2004}

Sue and Labour – Proportion payable when insured and uninsured property involved; North Coast Sea Products Ltd. v. ING Insurance Company of Canada, 2004 BCCA 95 affirming 2003 BCSC 592

The insured Plaintiffs incurred expenses in recovering trays and the oysters in them from the seabed when the lines of their oyster farm were vandalized. The Plaintiffs were insured for the loss of the trays but not for the oysters themselves. They claimed under the sue and labour provisions of their marine insurance policy for all the expenses incurred in recovering the trays and oysters.

Underwriters claimed that only a portion of the expenses could be claimed and that the claim should be in ratable proportion to the value of the insured trays to the uninsured oysters. The policy wording included provisions for reducing recoverable sue and labour expenses where the property was underinsured but was silent with respect to cases where there was both insured and uninsured property.

The matter was disposed of by Special Case. The underwriters relied on English case law from 1902 (Cunard Steamship Co. Ltd. v. Marten) that appeared to state that sue and labour expenses should be recoverable ratably where expenses are incurred for both insured and uninsured property. However, the trial Judge found for the insureds because the terms of the policy did not specify what would happen when expenses were incurred in respect of insured and uninsured property.

On appeal, the Court of Appeal upheld the trial Judge holding that the sue and labour clause of the policy only limited the insurer's obligation in the specific circumstances identified in that clause, none of which applied.

Insurance – Direct Action against Insurers – Interpretation of Policies – Limits of Coverage; Solway v Lloyd's Underwriters, 2005 ONSC 13407

In this case, the Plaintiffs arranged for a motor carrier to move and store their personal belongings. The truck was stolen and the Plaintiffs' belongings were never recovered. The Plaintiffs obtained a judgment against the carrier, which was not satisfied. The Plaintiffs then commenced this direct action against the carrier's primary and excess liability underwriters.

Both underwriters agreed that the Plaintiffs' loss was covered but disagreed as to how the loss should be apportioned between them. The primary underwriter argued that the limit of its policy was $500,000 as provided for in the transportation section of its policy. The excess underwriter argued that the applicable limit was that in the warehouse and storage section of the primary policy of $1,000,000. The issue was then one of interpretation of the primary policy.

The Court noted that the normal rule for construction of insurance contracts requires a search for an interpretation, which, from the whole of the contract, advances the true intent of the parties at the time the contract was entered into.

The Court further noted that the general principles of interpretation of insurance contracts include the expected performance of parties, provisions to be interpreted broadly and exclusion clauses narrowly and the desirability, at least where the policy is ambiguous, of giving effect to the reasonable expectations of the parties.

The Court finally concluded that the applicable limit depended on the proper characterization of the claim against the carrier either as breach of a transportation contract or breach of a storage contract. The Court held that since liability was imposed on the carrier at the trial for breach of a term relating to storage of the Plaintiffs' goods, the limitation of $1,000,000 for warehousing or storage was applicable.

Charters – Bailment – Waiver of Subrogation; North King Lodge Ltd. *v* Gowlland Towing Ltd. et al., 2004 BCSC 460

This matter concerned was liability for the sinking of the barge "Sea Lion VI". The owner had hired the barge to the first Defendant for use as an accommodation barge at a remote logging camp. One of the terms of the agreement was that the owner would provide a watchman. When the logging operations had ceased, the second Defendant, the towing company was retained to remove the log booms. In doing so "Sea Lion VI" went aground and sank.

The court found as a fact that the removal of the port lines caused the sinking. The Plaintiff, the owner of the barge, commenced proceedings against both the hirer and the towing company. The Plaintiff contended that the hire contract was a charter party by demise or, alternatively a bailment and that the hirer was responsible for the safekeeping of the barge. The hirer, on the other hand, argued that it did not have possession of the barge and that the contract was a time charter. The court held that it was not possible to fit the agreement between the parties into one of the traditional forms of charter party since the barge was not chartered for a voyage and had no master or crew. Also, the agreement was one of bailment but declined to imply all of the usual obligations that a contract of bailment entails.

Moreover, the owner's obligation to provide a watchman made the owner primarily responsible for the safe moorage of the barge. At the time of the sinking and for some time previous there had been no watchman on the barge and this was known to the hirer. The fact that the hirer failed to complain about the removal of the watchman by the owner was held not to be a waiver of the owner's obligation to provide a watchman.

It was also found that the hirer owed an obligation to take reasonable care of the vessel and that it breached this duty by failing to promptly advise the owner when it became apparent that the barge was in danger.

With respect to the liability of the towing company, the trial Judge found that owner of the "Sea Lion VI" committed an act of trespass in tying the barge to the log booms and that the duty owed by the towing company to a trespasser is to not intentionally harm the Plaintiff, act recklessly or without common humanity. He held that although the towing company did not act with reasonable care it did not breach the duties it in fact owed to the trespasser.

In the result, liability for the sinking was apportioned 80% to the owner and 20% to the hirer. One final issue considered in the case was whether the hirer was immune from suit by reason of clauses in the hull insurance policy including charterers as additional assured and waiving subrogation against charterers.

The court held that these clauses were not effective since the policy also contained an express clause which provided that the benefits of the insurance policy would not automatically extend to third parties but would only be extended if the option was exercised by the owner. The trial Judge found that the owner did not exercise this option.

Bad Faith – Punitive Damages – Whiten *v.* Pilot Insurance Co., 2002 SCC 18{Canada}

In this case, the Supreme Court of Canada awarded $1 Million damages to the plaintiff. The facts were that the Plaintiff's home was destroyed in a fire and the insurer (defendant) denied the claim made under the insurance policy on the grounds that the fire had been deliberately set even though the local fire chief, the Defendant's own fire investigator and the Defendant's initial expert all agreed that there was no evidence of arson. The court awarded punitive damages against the Defendant for bad faith denial of coverage and failure to act in good faith.

Key Terms

- Abandonment
- Sue and Labour Charges
- Contribution
- Subrogation
- Under Insurance
- Double Insurance
- General Average
- Particular Average
- Advance Freight
- Bottomry and Respondentia

References

- *www.bimaonline.com*
- Avtar Singh, *Law of Insurance*, Eastern Book Company, 2004.
- *Marine Clauses*, IC-63, Insurance Institute of India, Mumbai, 2000.
- *Marine Insurance Claims*, IC-66, Insurance Institute of India, Mumbai, 2005.

Questions for Review

1. Define Insurable Interest. When insurable interest should exist? Distinguish between contingent and defeasible interest with reference to Marine Insurance Act, 1963.
2. Briefly explain the various maritime losses and their computation as per the provisions of Marine Insurance, Act, 1963.
3. Write short notes on :

   (*a*) Warranties

   (*b*) Voyage Policy

Module 3

Insurance & Various Transportation Laws

The goods and passengers may be transported by land, air and sea routes. In India, various statutes have been promulgated from time to time with respect to these modes. These laws have a reference to the various *aspects* of insurance business which *inter-alia* include the subject matter of insurance, insurable interest, liability of the insurer towards insured and third parties, settlement of claims, powers of the central government etc. The said laws include:

(*a*) The Marine Insurance Act, 1963

(*b*) The Motor Vehicles Act 1939 & 1988

(*c*) The Inland Steam Vessels Act, 1917 & Amended Act of 1977

(*d*) The Carriage of Goods by Sea Act, 1925

(*e*) The Merchant Shipping Act, 1958

(*f*) The Indian Railways Act, 1890

(*g*) The Carriers Act, 1865

(*h*) The Carriage by Air Act, 1972

(*i*) The Indian Ports (Major Ports) Act, 1963

(*j*) The Bill of Lading Act, 1855

(*k*) The Indian Post Office Act, 1898

(*l*) Multi Modal Transportation Act, 1993

The act referred to in (*a*) & (*b*) above have been discussed in detail in the earlier chapters. The others are briefly discussed in the following sections.

8.1 THE INLAND STEAM VESSELS ACT, 1917 & AMMENDED ACT OF 1977

Inland Steam Vessels Act, 1917 was promulgated in 1917 and was amended several times. A major amendment was in 1977 and afterwards it was amended in 2005 recently. The act provides that the provisions of Chapter VII of the Motor Vehicles Act regarding insurance of mechanically propelled vehicles against third party risks are applicable to steam vessels. The act makes compulsory for the owners of operator of inland vessels to insure against legal liability of death, bodily injury or damage cause to third parties and passengers.

Definitions : Mechanically Propelled Vessel

Section 2 of the Act defines an inland mechanically propelled vessel :

In this Act, unless there is anything repugnant in the subject or context,

(*a*) "inland vessel" or "inland mechanically propelled vessel" means a mechanically propelled vessel, which ordinarily plies on inland water, but does not include fishing vessel and a ship registered under the Merchant Shipping Act, 1958;

(*b*) "inland water" means any canal, river, lake or other navigable water;

(*c*) "mechanically propelled vessel" means every description of vessel propelled wholly or in part by electricity, steam or other mechanical power including dumb vessel towed by the mechanically propelled vessel and vessel propelled by outboard motor

A "goods service vessel" means any mechanically propelled vessel used or adapted to be used for carriage of cargo for hire or reward (Section 145);

A "public service vessel" means any mechanically propelled vessel used or adapted to be used for the carriage of passengers for hire or reward;

Chapter VI A of the Act deals with insurance of *mechanically propelled vehicles* against third party risks. Section 54C of the Act was amended in 2005 so as to make section 134 and Chapters X, XI and XII of the Motor Vehicles Act, 1988, applicable in relation to mechanically propelled vessels with certain modifications and also to provide insurance of vessels against third party risks, compensation for accidents and Claims Tribunal, etc.

Application of the Act

Section 54C : The provisions of Chapter VIII of the Motor Vehicles Act, 1939, shall *mutatis mutandis* apply, in relation to the insurance of mechanically propelled vessels against third party risks as they apply in relation to motor vehicles, subject to the following modifications, namely :

(*a*) in section 134 and throughout in Chapters X, XI and XII, :

(*i*) references to "motor" or "motor vehicle" or "vehicle" shall be construed as references to "mechanically propelled vessel";

(*ii*) references to "public place" shall be construed as references to "inland water", and such other consequential amendments as the rules of grammar may require shall also be made;

(*iii*) references to "public service vehicle" shall be construed as references to "public service vessel";

(*iv*) references to "goods vehicle" shall be construed as references to "goods service vessel";

(*v*) references to "State Transport" shall be construed as references to "State Water Transport";

(*vi*) references to "driver" or "driver of a vehicle" shall be construed as references to "master of a vessel";

(*vii*) references to "driving licence" shall be construed as references to "a certificate granted under Chapter III of the Inland Vessels Act, 1917";

A driving licence under the act means "a certificate granted under Chapter III.

It therefore follows that an inland vessel is a mechanically propelled vessel for the purposes of Motor Vehicles Act, 1988 and all provisions of third party risks apply accordingly.

Duty of Driver in Case of Accident or Injury to a Person

Section 105A : When any person is injured or any property of third party is damaged as a result of an accident in which an inland mechanically propelled vessel is involved, the master or the driver of the vessel or other person in charge of the vessel shall :

(*a*) take all reasonable steps to secure medical attention for the injured person, and, if necessary, convey him to the nearest hospital, unless the injured person or his guardian in case he is a minor, desires otherwise;

(*b*) give on demand by a police officer any information required by him, or, if no police officer is present, report the circumstances of the occurrence at the nearest police station as soon as possible, and in any case within twenty-four hours of the occurrence."

Setting Up of a Claims Tribunal

State government is empowered to constitute tribunals in respective areas. Section 110 also defines the constitution of the tribunal.

Section 110. (1) The State Government may, by notification in the Official Gazette, constitute one or more Inland Vessels Accidents Claims Tribunals (hereinafter referred to as the Claims Tribunals) for such areas as may be specified in the notification for the purpose of adjudicating upon claims for compensation in respect of accidents involving the death of, or bodily injury to, persons arising out of the use of mechanically propelled vessels or damage to any property of a third party so arising, or both :

Provided that where such claim includes a claim for compensation in respect of damage to property exceeding rupees ten thousand the claimant may, at his option, refer the claim to a civil court for adjudication and where a reference is so made, the Claims Tribunal shall have no jurisdiction to entertain any question relating to such claim.

(2) A Claims Tribunal shall consist of such number of members, as the State Government may think fit to appoint and where it consists of two or more members, one of them shall be appointed as the Chairman thereof.

(3) A person shall not be qualified for appointment as a member of a Claims Tribunal unless he :

(*a*) is, or has been, a Judge of a High Court, or

(*b*) is, or has been, a District Judge, or

(*c*) is qualified for appointment as a Judge of the High Court.

(4) Where two or more Claims Tribunals are constituted for any area, the State Government may, by general or special order, regulate the distribution of business among them.

Application for Compensation

Section 110A : (1) An application for compensation arising out of an accident of the nature specified in sub-section (1) of section 110 may be made :

(*a*) by the person who has sustained the injury, or

(*b*) where death has resulted from the accident, by all or any of the legal representatives of the deceased, or

(*c*) by any agent duly authorised by the person injured or all or any of the legal representatives of the deceased, as the case may be :

Provided that where all the legal representatives of the deceased have not joined in any such application for compensation, the application shall be made on behalf of or for the benefit of all the legal representatives of the deceased and the legal representatives who have not so joined, shall be impleaded as respondents to the application.

(2) Every application under sub-section (1) shall be made to the Claims Tribunal having jurisdiction over the area in which the accident occurred, and shall be in such form and shall contain such particulars as may be prescribed.

(3) No application for compensation under this section shall be entertained unless it is made within six months of the occurrence of the accident:

Provided that the Claims Tribunal may entertain the application after the expiry of the said period of six months if it is satisfied that the applicant was prevented by sufficient cause from making the application in time.

Option Regarding Claim for Compensation in Certain Cases

Section 110AA : Notwithstanding anything contained in the Workmen's Compensation Act, 1923, where the death or bodily injury to any person gives rise to a claim for compensation under this Act and also under the Workmen's Compensation Act, 1923, the person entitled to compensation may claim such compensation under either of those Acts but not under both.

Award of Claim Tribunal

Section 110B : On receipt of an application for compensation made under Section 110A, the Claims Tribunal shall, after giving the parties an opportunity of being heard, hold an inquiry into the claim and may make an award determining the amount of compensation which appears to it to be just and specifying the person or persons to whom compensation shall be paid; and in making the award the Claims Tribunal shall specify the amount which shall be paid by the insurer or owner or master or driver of the vessel involved in the accident or by all or any of them, as the case may be."

Persons who carry goods or passengers, for hire or gratuitously, by land, water or air, are the carriers. In India, among the land carriers, the railways are governed under Indian Railways Act, 1890, and the road transport vehicles under the Carriers Act, 1865. The sea carriers are governed under the Carriage of Goods by Sea Act, 1925, and the international air carriers by the Carriage by Air Act, 1934. The inland air carriers are governed by the common law.

8.2 THE CARRIAGE OF GOODS BY SEA ACT, 1925

The law relating to carriage of goods by sea is contained in the Bill of Lading Act, 1856 and the Carriage of Goods by Sea Act, 1925. The contract involved in the carriage of goods by Sea Act, 1925 is popularly known as contract of affreightment. A contract of affreightment[1] may be of two forms:

(*a*) *Charter party* : where an entire ship, or a principal part of a ship is placed at the disposal of merchant (known as a charterer)

(*b*) *Bill of lading* : where the goods are to be carried in a general ship and the person consigning the goods is known as a shipper.

Definitions

The Act *inter-alia* defines the various terms as follows :

(*a*) *"carrier"* includes the owner or the charterer who enters into a contract of carriage with a shipper;

(*b*) *"contract of carriage"* applies only to contracts of carriage covered by a bill of lading or any similar document of title, in so far as such, document relates to the carriage of goods by sea including any bill of lading or any similar document as aforesaid issued under or pursuant to a charter party from the moment at which such bill of lading or similar document of title regulates the relations between a carrier and a holder of the same;

(*c*) *"goods"* includes goods, wares, merchandises, and articles of every kind whatsoever, except live animals and cargo which by the contract of carriage is stated as being carried on deck and is so carried;

---

[1] Contract of Affreightment is a contract to carry goods by sea and the consideration or charges paid for carriage is called freight.

(*d*) *"ship"* means any vessel used for the carriage of goods by sea;

(*e*) *"carriage of goods"* covers the period from the time when the goods are loaded on to the time when they are discharged from the ship.

Nature of Contract

The carrier (ship owner) undertakes the responsibility of carrying the goods of a consignor (charterer/shipper) safely and securely to the destination. In a contract of Carriage by Sea following conditions are implied:

(*a*) Warranty of seaworthiness.

(*b*) Warranty of commencement of voyage : that the ship shall be ready to commence the voyage and shall carry out the same with all reasonable dispatch and diligence.

(*c*) Non-deviation of voyage.

(*d*) Shipper not to ship dangerous goods.

Schedule to the Act contains the various rules and regulations.

Article III : Responsibilities and Liabilities

The carrier shall be bound, before and at the beginning of the voyage, to exercise due diligence to :

(*a*) make the ship seaworthy;

(*b*) properly man, equip, and supply the ship;

(*c*) make the holds, refrigerating and cool chambers, and all other parts of the ship in which goods are carried, fit and safe for their reception, carriage and preservation.

The act deals with three aspects of a shipowners liabilities towards cargo owner:

(*i*) the circumstances when the shipowner is deemed to be liable for loss or damage to cargo unless he proves otherwise;

(*ii*) the circumstance when the shipowner is exempted from liability, i.e., when loss or damage is caused by events outside his control, e.g., perils of the seas;

(*iii*) the limits of liability of a shipowner for loss of or damage to cargo calculated in monetary terms per package or unit of cargo.

Article IV : Rights and Immunities

It provides that :

1. Neither the carrier nor the ship shall be liable for loss or damage arising or resulting from unseaworthiness unless caused by want of due diligence on the

part of the carrier to make the ship seaworthy, and to secure that the ship is properly manned, equipped and supplied, and to make the holds, refrigerating and cool chambers and all other parts of the ship in which goods are carried fit and safe for their reception, carriage and preservation in accordance with the provisions of paragraph 1 of Article III.

Whenever loss or damage has resulted from unseaworthiness the burden of proving the exercise of due diligence shall be on the carrier or other person claiming exemption under this section.

2. Neither the carrier nor the ship shall be responsible for loss or damage arising or resulting from :

(*a*) act, neglect, or default of the master, mariner, pilot, or the servants of the carrier in the navigation or in the management of the ship;

(*b*) fire, unless caused by the actual fault or privity of the carrier;

(*c*) perils, dangers and accidents of the sea or other navigable waters;

(*d*) act of God;

(*e*) act of war;

(*f*) act of public enemies;

(*g*) arrest or restraint of princes, rulers of people, or seizure under legal process;

(*h*) quarantine restriction;

(*i*) act or omission of the shipper or owner of the goods, his agent, or representative;

(*j*) strikes or lock-outs or stoppage or restraint of labour from whatever cause, whether partial or general;

(*k*) riots and civil commotions;

(*l*) saving or attempting to save life or property at sea;

(*m*) wastage in bulk or weight or any other loss or damage arising from inherent defect, quality, or vice of the goods;

(*n*) insufficiency of packing;

(*o*) insufficiency or inadequacy of marks;

(*p*) latent defects not discoverable by due diligence;

(*q*) any other cause arising without the actual fault or privity of the carrier, or without the fault or neglect of the agents or servants of the carrier, but the burden of proof shall be on the person claiming the benefit of this exception to show that neither the actual fault or privity of the carrier nor the fault or neglect of the agents or servants of the carrier contributed to the loss or damage.

3. The shipper shall not be responsible for loss or damage sustained by the carrier or the ship arising or resulting from any cause without the act, fault or neglect of the shipper, his agents or his servants.

4. Any deviation in saving or attempting to save life or property at sea, or any reasonable deviation shall not be deemed to be infringement or breach of these Rules or of the contract of carriage, and the carrier shall not be liable for any loss or damage resulting therefrom.

5. Neither the carrier nor the ship shall in any event be or become liable for any loss or damage to or in connection with goods in an amount exceeding £ 100 per package or unit, or the equivalent of that sum in other currency, unless the nature and value of such goods have been declared by the shipper before shipment and inserted in the bill of lading.

This declaration is embodied in the bill of lading shall be *prima facie* evidence, but shall not be binding or conclusive on the carrier.

By agreement between the carrier, master or agent of the carrier and the shipper another maximum amount than that mentioned in this paragraph may be fixed, provided that such maximum shall not be less than the figure above named.

Neither the carrier nor the ship shall be responsible in any event for loss or damage to or in connection with goods if the nature or value thereof has been knowingly mis-stated by the shipper in the bill of lading.

6. Goods of an inflammable, explosive or dangerous nature to the shipment whereof the carrier, master or agent of the carrier, has not consented, with knowledge of their nature and character, may at any time before discharge be landed at any place or destroyed or rendered innocuous by the carrier without compensation, and the shipper of such goods shall be liable for all damages and expenses directly or indirectly arising out of or resulting from such shipment.

If any such goods shipped with such knowledge and consent shall become a danger to the ship or cargo, they may in like manner be landed at any place or destroyed or rendered innocuous by the carrier without liability on the part of the carrier except to general average, if any.

It therefore implies that :

1. A carrier of goods by sea, that is, a shipowner is liable only for loss or damage arising or resulting from his negligence, fault or failure in the duties and obligations provided in the Act, and not otherwise.
2. A shipowner cannot limit his liability arising from his negligence or failure in the duties and any clause in the contract to that effect shall be null and void and inoperative.
3. The carrier is not responsible for any loss or damage to goods exceeding £ 100 per package or unit or its equivalent unless the nature and value of such goods have been declared by the shipper and inserted in the bill of lading.

Article V : Surrender of Rights and Immunities Increase of Responsibilities and Liabilities

A carrier shall be at liberty to surrender in whole or in part all or any of his rights and immunities or to increase any of his responsibilities and liabilities under the Rules contained in any of these Articles, provided such surrender or increase shall be embodied in the bill of lading issued to the shipper.

The provisions of these Rules shall not be applicable to charter-parties, but if bills of lading are issued in the case of a ship under a charter-party, they shall comply with the terms of these Rules. Nothing in these Rules shall be held, to prevent the insertion in a bill of lading of any lawful provision regarding general average.

Average VI : Special Conditions

Notwithstanding the provisions of the preceding Articles, a carrier, master or agent of the carrier, and a shipper shall, in regard to any particular goods, be at liberty to enter into any agreement in any terms as to the responsibility and liability of the carrier for such goods, and as to the rights and immunities of the carrier in respect of such goods, or his obligation as to seaworthiness so far as the stipulation is not contrary to public policy, or the care of diligence of his servants or agents in regard to the loading, handling, stowage, carriage, custody, care, and discharge of the goods carried by sea, provided that in this case no bill of lading has been or shall be issued and that the terms agreed shall be embodied in a receipt which shall be a non-negotiable document and shall be marked as such.

Any agreement so entered into shall have full legal effect :

Provided that this Article shall not apply to ordinary commercial shipment made in the ordinary course of trade, but only to other shipments where the character or condition of the property to be carried or the circumstances, terms and conditions under which the carriage is to be performed, as such are reasonably to justify a special agreement.

Average VII : Limitations on the Application of the Rules

Nothing herein contained shall prevent a carrier or a shipper from entering into any agreement, stipulation, condition, reservation or exemption as to the responsibility and liability of the carrier or the ship for the loss or damage to or in connection with the custody and care and handling of goods prior to the loading on and subsequent to the discharge from the ship on which the goods are carried by sea.

The carrier can enter into agreements etc. relating to the responsibility and liability for loss/damage before loading of goods and also after discharge of goods.

Average VIII : Limitation of Liability

The provisions of these Rules shall not affect the right and obligation of the carrier under any Statute for the time being in force relating to the limitation of the liability of owners of sea-going vessels.

Bill of Lading : *A bill of lading is a document acknowledging the shipment of goods, signed by or on behalf of the carrier and containing the terms and conditions on which it has been agreed to carry the goods. It is a quasi-negotiable instrument. It is a document of title and can be transferred by endorsement and delivery. It is generally used for the carriage of goods on a general ship, i.e., a ship which is used for the carriage of the goods of several merchants who wish to have them conveyed by her and which is not employed for the carriage of a charterer's goods only.*

A bill of lading may be issued even where the ship is chartered. In such a case charter party will be the document evidencing the contract of affreightment, while the bill of lading would only operate as a mere acknowledgement of the receipt of the goods.

{*Source:* Website of the Indian Institute of Materials Management}

8.3 THE MERCHANT SHIPPING ACT, 1958

The Merchant Shipping Act, 1958 provides a certain protection to shipowners against carriage losses. For example- the liability of the shipowner can be limited to certain maximum sum of certain losses, provided the incident-giving rise to such claim has arisen without the actual fault or privy of the shipowner. These claims may relate to loss of life personal injury or loss or damage to property on land or water. The act also confers the obligation on the shipowner to send his ship to sea in a seaworthy and safe condition. A gist of some important sections from an insurance perspective is given below :

Liability of Owners

Section 71 : Where any person is beneficially interested otherwise than by way of mortgage in any ship or share in a ship registered in the name of some other person as owner, the person so interested shall, as well as the registered owner, be subject to all the pecuniary penalties imposed by this or any other Act on the owners of ships or shares therein, so nevertheless that proceedings for the enforcement of any such penalties may be taken against both or either of the said parties with or without joining the other of them.

This section provides that if any beneficial interest is attached in name of any person other than mortgage, that person shall be liable for all pecuniary penalties which may arise under the act.

Engagements Between Seamen and Masters of Ships other than Indian Ships

Section 114 : (1) When the master of a ship other than an Indian ship engages a seaman at any port in India to proceed to any port outside India, he shall enter into an agreement with such seaman, and the agreement shall be made before a shipping master in the manner provided by this Act for the making of agreements in the case of foreign-going Indian ships.

(2) All the provisions of this Act respecting the form of such agreements and the stipulations to be contained in them and the making and signing of the same, shall be applicable to the engagement of such seaman.

(3) The master of a ship other than an Indian ship hall give to the shipping master a bond with the security of some approved person resident in India for such amount as may be fixed by the Central Government in respect of each seaman engaged by him at any port in India and conditioned for the due performance of such agreement and stipulations, and for the repayment to the Central Government of all expenses which may be incurred by it in respect of any such seaman who is discharged or left behind at any port out of India and becomes distressed and is relieved under the provisions of this Act:

Provided that the shipping master may waive the execution of a bond under this section where the owner of the ship has an agent at any port in India and such agent accepts liability in respect of all matters for which the master of the ship would be liable if he were to execute a bond under this section or may accept from the agent such security as may be approved by the Central Governmental.

(4) The fees fixed under section 90 shall be payable in respect of weary such engagement, and deductions from the wages of seamen so engaged may be made to the extent and in the manner allowed under the said section 90.

Payment Over of Property of Deceased Seamen by Shipping Master

Section 159 : Where any property of a deceased seaman or apprentice is paid or delivered to a shipping master, the shipping master, after deducting for expenses incurred in respect of that seaman or apprentice or of his property such sums as he thinks proper to allow, may :

(*a*) pay and deliver the residue to any claimants who can prove themselves to the satisfaction of the said shipping master to be entitled thereto, and the said shipping master shall discharged from all further liability in respect of the residue so paid or delivered; or

(*b*) if he thinks fit so to do, require probate or letters of administration or a certificate under the Indian Succession Act, 1925 (39 of 1925), to be taken out, and thereupon-pay and deliver the residue to the legal representatives of the deceased.

Liability of Central Government for Costs and Damage when Ship Wrongly Detained

Section 337 : If it appears that there was not reasonable and probable cause, by reason of the condition of the ship or the at or default of the owner or the master, for the provisional detention of a ship, the Central Government shall be liable to pay to the owner of the ship his costs of and incidental to the detention and survey of the ship, and also compensation for any loss or damage sustained by him by reason of the detention or survey.

When the central government wrongly detains any ship, it shall be liable for compensation for loss or damages.

Liability of Ship Owner for Costs when Ship Rightly Detained

Section 338 : If a ship is finally detained under this Part, or if it appears that a ship provisionally detained was at the time of such detention unsafe, or if a ship is detained was at the time of such detention unsafe, or if a ship is detained in pursuance of any provision of this Part which provides for the detention of a ship until a certain event occurs, the owner of the ship shall be liable to pay to the Central Government it costs of and incidental to the detention and survey of the ship; and the ship shall not be released until such costs are paid.

Division of Loss in Case of Collision

Section 345 : (1) Whenever by the fault of two or more ships damage or loss is caused to one or more of them or to the cargo of one or more of them or to any property on board one or more of them, the liability to make good the damage or loss shall be in proportion to the degree in which each ship was at fault:

Provided that :

(*a*) if, having regard to all the circumstances of the case, it is not possible to establish different degrees of fault, the liability shall be apportioned equally;

(*b*) nothing in this section shall operate so as to render any ship liable for any loss or damage to which her fault has not contributed;

(*c*) nothing in this section shall operate so as to render any person under any contract, or shall be construed as imposing any liability upon any person from which he is exempted by any contract or by any provision of law, or as affecting the right of any person to limit his liability in the manner provided by law.

(2) For the purposes of this Part, references to damage or loss caused by the fault of a ship shall be construed as including references to any salvage or other expenses, consequent upon that fault, recoverable in law by way of damages.

Damages for Personal Injury

Section 346 : (1) Whenever loss of life or personal injuries are suffered by any person on board a ship owing to the fault of that ship and of any other ship or ships, the liability of the owners of the ships concerned shall be joint and several.

(2) Nothing in this section shall be construed as depriving any person of any right of defence on which, independently of this section, he might have relied in an action brought against him by the person injured, or any person entitled to sue in respect of such loss of life, or shall affect the right of any person to limit his liability in cases to which this section relates in the manner provided by law.

Right of Contribution

Section 347 : (1) Whenever loss of life or personal injuries are suffered by a person on board a ship owing to the fault of that ship and of any other ship or ships, and a proportion of the damages is recovered from the owner of one of the ships which exceeds the proportion in which she was in fault, the said owner may recover by way of contribution the amount of the excess from the owners of the other ship or ships to the extent to which those ships were respectively in fault:

Provided that no amount shall be so recovered which could not, by reason of any statutory or contractual limitation of, or exemption from, liability, or which could not for any the reason, have been recovered in the first instance as damages by the persons entitled to sue therefor.

(2) In addition to any other remedy provided by law, the person entitled to any contribution under sub-section (1) shall, for the purpose of recovering the contribution, have, subject to the provisions of this Act, the same rights and powers as the persons entitled to sue for damages in the first instance.

Duty of Master of Ship to Assist in Case of Collision

Section 348 : In every case of collision between two ships it shall be the duty of the master or person in charge of each ship, if and so far as be can do so without danger to his own ship, crew and passengers, if any :

(*a*) to render to the other ship, her master, crew and passengers, if any, such assistance as may be practicable and may be necessary to save them from any danger caused by the collision and to stay by the other ship until he has ascertained that she has no need of further assistance, and

(*b*) to give to the masters or persons in charge of the other ships the name of his own ship and of the port to which she belongs and also the names of the ports from which she comes and to which she is bound.

Collision to be Entered in Official Log

Section 349 : In every case of collision in which it is practicable so to do, the master of every ship concerned shall, immediately after the occurrence, cause a statement thereof and of the circumstances under which the same occurred to be entered in the official log book, if any, and the entry shall be signed by the master and also by the matte or one of the crew.

Report to Central Government of Accidents to Ships

Section 350 : When a ship has sustained or caused any accident occasioning loss of life or any serious injury to any person or has received any material damage affecting her seaworthiness or her efficiency either in her hull or is so altered in any part of her machinery as not to correspond with the particulars contained in any of the certificates issued under this Act in respect of the ship, the owner or master shall, within twenty-four hours after the happening of the accident or damage or as soon thereafter as possible, transmit to the Central Government or the nearest principal officer a report of the accident or damage and of the probable cause thereof stating the name of the ship, her official number, if any, her port of registry and the place where she is.

Notice of Loss of Indian Ship to be given to Central Government

Section 351 : If the owner or agent of any Indian ship has reason, owing to the non-appearance of the ship or to any other circumstance, to apprehend that the ship has been wholly lost, he shall, as soon as conveniently may be, send to the Central Government notice in writing of the loss and of the probable cause thereof stating the name of the ship, her official number, if any, and her port of registry.

Limitation of Liability of Owner for Damage

Section 352 : (1) The owner of a ship, whether an Indian ship or not, shall not, if any loss of life or personal injury to any person, or any loss of or damage to any property or rights of any kind, whether movable or immovable is caused without his actual fault or privity, :

(*a*) if no claim for damages in respect of loss of or damage to property or rights arises, be liable for damages in respect of loss of life or personal injury to an aggregate amount exceeding two hundred rupees for each ton of the ship's tonnage; or

(*b*) if no claim for damages in respect of loss of life or personal injury arises, be liable for damages in respect of loss of or damage to property or rights to an aggregate amount exceeding one hundred rupees for each ton of the ships tonnage; or

(*c*) if claims for damages in respect of loss of life or personal injury and also claims for damages in respect of loss of or damage to property or rights arise, be liable for damages to an aggregate amount exceeding two hundred rupees for each ton of the ship's tonnage:

Provided that in such a case claims for damages in respect of loss of life or personal injury shall, to the extent of an aggregate amount of one hundred rupees for each ton of the ship's tonnage, have priority over claims for damages in respect of loss of or damage to property or rights, and, as regards the balance or the aggregate amount of two hundred rupees for each ton of the ship's tonnage, the unsatisfied portion of the first mentioned claims shall rank pari pasu with the last-mentioned claims.

(2) The provisions of this section shall extend and apply to the owners, builders or other persons interested in any ship built at any port or place in India, from and including the launching of such ship until the registration thereof under the provisions of this Act.

(3) The provisions of this section shall apply in respect of claims for damages in respect of loss of life, personal injury and loss of or damage to property or rights arising on any single occasion, and in the application of the said provisions, claims for damages in respect of loss, injury or damage arising out of two or more distinct occasions shall not be combined.

(4) For the purposes of this section a ship's tonnage shall be determined in such manner as the Central Government may by general or special order, specify.

No Ship to Carry Passengers Without a Certificate of Survey

Section 220 : (1) No ship shall carry more than twelve passengers between ports or places in India or to or from any port or place in India from or to any port or place outside India, unless she has a certificate or survey under this Part in force and applicable to the voyage on which she is about to proceed or the service on which she is about to be employed:

Provided that nothing in this section shall apply to any ship which has been granted a certificate under section 235, unless it appears from the certificate that it is inapplicable to the voyage on which the ship is about to unless there is reason to believe that the ship has, since the grant of the certificate, sustained injury or damage or been found seaworthy or otherwise inefficient.

Survey of Ship

Section 244 : After receiving the notice required by section 238, the certifying officer may, if he thinks fit, cause the ship to be surveyed at the expense of the master or owner by a surveyor, who shall report to him whether the ship is, in his opinion, seaworthy and properly equipped, fitted and ventilated for the service on which she is to be employed:

Provided that he shall not cause a ship holding a certificate of survey or a safety certificate to be surveyed unless, by reason of the ship having met with damage or having undergone alterations, or on other reasonable grounds, he considers it likely that she may be found unseaworthy or not properly equipped fitted or ventilated for the service on which she is to be employed.

Unseaworthy Ship not to be Sent to Sea

Section 334 : (1) Every person who sends or attempts to send an Indian ship to sea from any port in India in such an unseaworthy state that the life of any person is likely to be thereby endangered shall, unless he proves that he used all reasonable means to insure her being sent to sea in a seaworthy state or that her going to sea in such unseaworthy state was under the circumstances reasonable and justifiable, be guilty of an offence under this sub-section.

(2) Every master of an Indian ship who knowingly takes such ship to sea in such unseaworthy state that the life of any person is likely to be thereby endangered shall, unless he proves that her going to sea in such unseaworthy state was,

under the circumstances, reasonable and justifiable , be guilty of an offence under this sub-section.

(3) For the purpose of giving such proof, every person charged under this section may give evidence in the same manner as any other witness.

(4) No prosecution under this section shall be instituted except by, or with the consent of, the Central Government.

(5) A ship is "unseaworthy" within the meaning of this Act where the materials of which she is made, her construction, the qualifications of the master, the number, description and qualifications of the crew including officers, the weight, description and stowage of the cargo and ballast, the condition f her hull and equipment, boilers and machinery are not such as to render her in every respect fit for the proposed voyage or service.

Obligation of Owner to Crew with Respect to Seaworthiness

Section 335 : (1) In every contract of service, express or implied between the owner of an Indian ship and the master or any seaman thereof, and in every contract of apprenticeship whereby any person is bound to serve as an apprentice on board any such ship, there shall be implied, notwithstanding any agreement to the contrary, an obligation on the owner that such owner and the master, and every agent charged with the loading of such ship or the preparing thereof for sea, or the sending thereof to sea, shall use all reasonable means to ensure the seaworthiness of such ship for the voyage at the time when such voyage commences, and to keep her in a unseaworthy state during the voyage.

(2) For the purpose of seeing that the provisions of this section have been complied with the Central Government may, either at the request of the owner or otherwise, arrange for a survey of the hull, equipment or machinery of any sea-going ship by a surveyor.

No Ship to Carry Passengers Without a Certificate of Survey

Section 220 : (1) No ship shall carry more than twelve passengers between ports or places in India or to or from any port or place in India from or to any port or place outside India, unless she has a certificate or survey under this Part in force and applicable to the voyage on which she is about to proceed or the service on which she is about to be employed:

Provided that nothing in this section shall apply to any ship which has been granted a certificate under section 235, unless it appears from the certificate that it is inapplicable to the voyage on which the ship is about to unless there is reason to believe that the ship has, since the grant of the certificate, sustained injury or damage or been found seaworthy or otherwise inefficient.

(2) No customs collector shall granted a port clearance, nor shall any pilot be assigned, to any ship for which a certificate of survey is required by this Part until after the production by the owner, agent or master thereof of a certificate

under this Part in force and applicable to the voyage on which she is about to proceed or the service on which she is about to be employed.

(3) If any ship for which a certificate of survey is required by this Part leaves or attempts to leave any port of survey without a certificate, any customs collector or any pilot on board the ship may detain her until she obtains a certificate.

8.4 THE INDIAN RAILWAYS ACT, 1890

The Indian Railways Act was passed in 1890 and was amended in 1961. Further it was substituted by the act of 1989. The Act was further amended in 2003. The Act deals with the various aspects of Railway Administration. Chapter IX and Chapter XI of the Act deals with "Carriage of Goods" and "Responsibilities of Railway Administration as Carriers"

8.4.1 Chapter IX - Carriage of Goods

Maintenance of rate-books, etc., for carriage of goods : *Section 1* : Every railway administration shall maintain, at each station and at such other places where goods are received for carriage, the rate-books or other documents which shall contain the rate authorised for the carriage of goods from one section to another and make them available for the reference of any person during all reasonable hours without payment of any fee.

Railway administration is required to maintain the rate-books or other documents containing the rate for carrying goods from one station to another,–

(*i*) at each station; and

(*ii*) at such other places where goods are received for carriage. Any person can refer to them free during all reasonable hours.

Conditions for receiving, etc., of goods : *Section 2 :* (1) A railway administration may impose conditions, not inconsistent with this Act or any rules made thereunder, with respect to the receiving, forwarding, carrying or delivering of any goods.

(2) A railway administration shall maintain, at each station and at such other places where goods are received for carriage, a copy of the conditions for the time being in force under sub-section (1) and make them available for the reference of any person during all reasonable hours without payment of any fee.

A railway administration may impose conditions with respect to the receiving, forwarding, carrying or delivering of any goods. (Section 62).

A forwarding note is a necessary condition precedent to the entrusting of any goods to a railway administration for carriage.

The consignor is responsible for the correctness of the particulars furnished in the forwarding note.

The railway administration has to be indemnified by the consignor against any damage suffered by it due to any defective particular furnished in the forwarding note. (Section 64)

Railway Receipt

Section 3 : (1) A railway administration shall, :

(*a*) in a case where the goods are to be loaded by a person entrusting such goods, on the completion of such leading; or

(*b*) in any other case, on the acceptance of the goods by it,

issue a railway receipt in such form as may be specified by the Central Government.

(2) A railway receipt shall be *prima facie* evidence of the weight and the number of packages stated therein:

Provided that in the case of a consignment in wagon-load or train-load and the weight or the number of packages is not checked by a railway servant authorised in this behalf, and a statement to that effect is recorded in such railway receipt by him, the burden of proving the weight or, as the case may be, the number of packages stated therein, shall lie on the consignor, the consignee or the endorsee.

A railway administration is bound to issue a railway receipt (RR) to the person who has entrusted any goods to it for carriage.

Carriage of Animal Suffering from Infectious or Contagious Diseases

Section 4: A railway administration shall not be bound to carry any animal suffering from such infectious or contagious disease as may be prescribed.

Passing of Property in the Goods Covered by Railway Receipt

Section 5 : The property in the consignment covered by a railway receipt shall pass to the consignee or the endorsee, as the case may be, on the delivery of such railway receipt to him and he shall have all the rights and liabilities of the consignor.

The property in the consignment covered by a railway receipt (RR) passes to the consignee or, as the case may be, to the endorse, including the consignor's rights and liabilities.

Section 74 not to Affect Right of Stoppage in Transit or Claims for Freight

Section 6 : Nothing contained in section 74 shall prejudice or affect :

(*a*) any right of the consignor for stoppage of goods in transit as an unpaid vendor [as defined under the Sale of Goods Act, 1930 (3 of 1930)] on his written request to the railway administration;

(*b*) any right of the railway to claim freight from the consignor; or

(*c*) any liability of the consignee or the endorsee, referred to in that section by reason of his being such consignee or endorsee.

Liability of Railway Administration for Wrong Delivery

Section 7 : Where a railway administration delivers the consignment to the person who produces the railway receipt, it shall not be responsible for any wrong delivery on the ground that such person is not entitled thereto or that the endorsement on the railway receipt is forged or otherwise defective.

When the consignor, or the consignee, or the endorsee, has failed to pay on demand any freight or other charges due from him in respect of any consignment, the railway administration shall have a lien on any consignment which is in, or thereafter comes into, its possession.

In order to realising a sum equal to the freight or other charges, the railway administration can sell the consignment or part thereof :

(*i*) at once, or

(*ii*) by public auction. (Section 83)

The railway administration has two rights :

(*i*) of sale under sections 83 to 85 and

(*ii*) of recovery by suit, any freight, charge, amount or other expenses due to it. (Section 86)

When the person concerned fails to remove goods within 7 days after the termination of transit thereof, the railway administration is free to sell the unremoved goods by public auction.

If the person entitled to remove the goods pays the freight and other charges, before the sale thereof, to the railway administration, then he can remove such goods. (Section 90)

8.4.2 Chapter XI : Responsibilities of Railway Administration as Carriers

The liability of a railway administration is the same as that of a common carrier. In other words, even where any loss, destruction, damage, deterioration or non-delivery is proved to have arisen from any one or more of the aforesaid nine cases, a railway administration shall not be relieved of its responsibility unless it further proves that it has used reasonable foresight and care in the carriage of the goods [Union of India *v.* Orissa Textile Mills, AIR (1979) Ori. 165]. A railway administration, like a common carrier, is bound to carry the goods of every person who is willing to pay the freight and comply with other requirements.

General Responsibility of a Railway Administration as Carrier of Goods

Section 93 : Save as otherwise provided in this Act, a railway administration shall be responsible for the loss, destruction, damage or deterioration in transit, or non-delivery of any consignment, arising from any cause except the following namely:

(*a*) act of God

(*b*) act of war

(*c*) act of public enemies

(*d*) arrest, restraint or seizure under legal process

(*e*) orders or restrictions imposed by the Central Government or a State Government or by an officer or authority subordinate to the Central Government or a State Government authorised by it in this behalf

(*f*) act or omission or negligence of the consignor or the consignee or the endorsee or the agent or servant of the consignor or the consignee or the endorsee

(*g*) natural deterioration or wastage in bulk or weight due to inherent defect, quality ore vice of the goods

(*h*) latent defects

(*i*) fire, explosion or any unforeseen risk.

Provided that even where such loss, destruction, damage, deterioration or non-delivery is proved to have arisen from any one or more of the aforesaid causes, the railway administration shall not be relieved of its responsibility for the loss, destruction, damage, deterioration or non-delivery unless the railway administration further proves that it has used reasonable foresight and care in the carriage of the goods.

A railway administration is responsible not only for the loss, destruction, damage or deterioration in transit but also for the non-delivery of any consignment unless it proves that it has used reasonable foresight and care in the carriage of the goods.

Delay or Detention in Transit

Section 95 : A railway administration shall not be responsible for the loss, destruction, damage or deterioration of any consignment proved by the owner to have been caused by the delay or detention in their carriage if the railway administration proves that the delay or detention arose for reasons beyond its control or without negligence or misconduct on its part or on the part of any of its servants.

A railway administration cannot be held responsible for the loss, destruction, damage or deterioration of any consignment due to delay or detention in their carriage.

However, the railway administration has to prove that the delay or detention arose:

(*i*) for reasons beyond its control, or

(*ii*) without negligence on its part or on the part of any its servants, or

(*iii*) without misconduct on its part or on the part of any its servants.

Traffic Passing Over Railway in India and Railways in Foreign Countries

Section 96 : Where in the course of carriage of any consignment from a place in India to a place outside India or from a place outside India to a place in India or from one place outside India to another place outside India or from one place in India to another place in India over any territory outside India, it is carried over the railways of any railway administration in India, the railway administration shall not be responsible under any of the provisions of this chapter for the loss, destruction, damage or deterioration of the goods, from whatever cause arising, unless it is proved by the owner of the goods that such loss, destruction, damage or deterioration arose over the railway of the railway administration.

The owner of goods, while claiming damages, is required to prove that the loss, destruction, damage or deterioration of goods arose over the railway of the railway administration.

Owner's Risk Rate or Railway Risk Rate

Section 97 : A consignment may be carried by a railway administration either at owner's risk rate or railway risk rate. Owner's risk rate is a special reduced rate whereas railway risk rate is an ordinary tariff rate. Owner's risk rate is lower than the railway risk rate for the simple reason that the goods in this case are carried at the owner's risk. In case of owner's risk rate, the railway administration is not responsible unless it is proved that any loss, destruction, damage or deterioration or non-delivery of goods arose from negligence or misconduct on the part of the railway administration or its servants.

Liability for Damage to Goods in Defective Condition or Defectively Packed

Section 98 : Goods tendered to a railway administration to be carried by railway may be (a) in a defective condition or (b) defectively packed. As a result of these, goods are liable to damage, deterioration, leakage or wastage. If the fact of such condition or defective or improper packing has been recorded by the sender or his agent in the forwarding note, the railway administration is not responsible for any damage, deterioration, leakage or wastage unless negligence or misconduct on the part of the railway administration or of its servants is proved.

Liability After Termination of Transit

Section 99 : Whether the goods are carried at owner's risk rate or railway risk rate, the liability of the railway administration for any loss of goods within a period of seven days after the termination of transit is that of a bailee under Sections 151, 152 and 161 of the Indian Contract Act, 1872. But where the goods are carried at owner's risk rate the railway administration is not liable for such loss, destruction, damage, deterioration or non-delivery of goods except on proof of negligence or misconduct on the part of the railway administration or any of its servants.

After seven days from the date of termination of transit the railway administration is not liable in any case for any loss of such goods. Notwithstanding this provision, the railway administration is not responsible after the termination of transit for the loss, destruction, damage, deterioration or non-delivery of articles of perishable goods, animals, explosives and other dangerous goods.

Responsibility as Carrier of Luggage

Section 100 : A railway administration shall not be responsible for the loss, destruction, damage, deterioration or non-delivery of any luggage unless a railway servant has booked the luggage and given a receipt therefor. Also it is to be proved that the loss, etc., was due to the negligence or misconduct on the part of the railway administration or on the part of any of its servants.

In the case of luggage which is carried by the passenger in his own charge, the railway administration shall not be responsible for the loss, etc., unless it is proved that the loss, etc., was due to the negligence or misconduct on the part of the railway administration or on the part of any of its servants.

Responsibility as a carrier of animals (*Section 101*). A railway administration shall not be responsible for any loss or destruction of, or injuries to, any animal carried by railway arising from fright or restiveness of the animal or from overloading of wagons by the consignor.

Exoneration from liability in certain cases (*Section 102*). A railway administration shall not be responsible for the loss, destruction, damage or deterioration or nondelivery of any consignment :

(*i*) when such loss, etc., is due to the fact that a materially false description of the consignment is given; or

(*ii*) where a fraud has been practised by the consignor or the endorsee, or by an agent of the consignor, consignee or the endorsee; or

(*iii*) where it is proved by the railway administration to have been caused by, or to have arisen from :

  (*a*) improper loading or unloading by the consignor, or the consignee or the endorsee, or by an agent of the consignor, consignee or the endorsee;

  (*b*) riot, civil commotion, strike, lock-out, stoppage or restraint of labour from whatever cause arising whether partial or general; or

(*iv*) for any indirect or consequential loss or damage or for loss of particular market.

The liability of the railway administration for the loss, destruction, damage, deterioration or non-delivery of the consignment cannot exceed

(*a*) the amount calculated with reference to the weight of the consignment as may be prescribed, or

(*b*) the amount as may be prescribed when the consignment consists of an animal, or

(*c*) the value of the consigned declared at the time of entrustment. Sub-section (3) overrides the provisions of sub-sections (1) and (2).

The Central Government can notify goods for which the value must be declared and percentage charge has to be. (*Section 103*)

The responsibility of railway administration for the destruction, damage or deterioration of any goods, with the consignor's consent, carried in open wagon, shall be ½ of the amount of liability to be determined under this Chapter. (Section 104).

A person who claims compensation against a railway administer for the loss, destruction, damage, deterioration or non-delivery of goods, must served a notice thereof, :

(*a*) to the railway administration to which the goods were entrusted for carriage; or

(*b*) to the railway administration on whose railway the destination station lies, or the loss, destruction, damage or deterioration occurred.

Such notice is required to be served upon either of the railway administration within a period of 6 months (not 180 days) from the date of entrustment of the goods.

A complaint, or any communication, in writing regarding the non-delivery or delayed delivery of the goods is deemed to be a notice of claim for compensation.

Similarly, a person who claims refund of an overcharge, should also serve a notice in the manner aforesaid. (*Section 106*)

Applications for Compensation for Loss, *etc.*, of Goods

Section 107 : An application for compensation for loss, destruction, damage, deterioration or non-delivery of goods shall be filed against the railway administration on whom a notice under section 106 has been served.

Person Entitled to Claim Compensation

Section 108 : (1) If a railway administration pays compensation for loss, destruction, damage, deterioration or non-delivery of goods entrusted to it for carriage, to the consignee or the endorsee producing the railway receipt, the railway administration shall be deemed to have discharged its liability and no application before the Claims Tribunal or any other legal proceeding shall lie against the railway administration on the ground that the consigned or the endorsee was not legally entitled to receive such compensation.

(2) Nothing in sub-section (1) shall affect the right of any person having any interest in the goods to enforce the same against the consignee or the endorsee receiving compensation under that sub-section.

An application before the Claims Tribunal for compensation for the loss of life or personal injury to a passenger lies against the railway administration, :

(*i*) from which the passenger obtained his pass or purchased his ticket; or

(*ii*) on whose railway the destination lies or the loss or personal injury occurred. (Section 102)

Burden of Proof

Section 110 : In an application before the Claims Tribunal for compensation for loss, destruction, damage, deterioration or non-delivery of any goods, the burden of proving :

(*a*) the monetary loss actually sustained; or

(*b*) where the value has been declared under sub-section (2) of section 103 in respect of any consignment that the value so declared is its true value,

shall lie on the person claiming compensation, but subject to the other provisions contained in this Act, it shall not be necessary for him to prove how the loss, destruction, damage, deterioration or non-delivery was caused.

Where a railway administration contracts to carry passengers or goods partly by railway and partly by sea, it is liable to pay compensation for any loss of life, personal injury, or loss of or damage to goods which has happened during the carriage by sea. (Section 111)

8.4.3 Railway Claims Tribunal Act, 1987

The Railway Claims Tribunal Act, 1987 provides for the formation of tribunal to deal with claims for cargo losses, personal injuries, excess freight etc. and prescribes the procedure thereunder.

Chapter III of deals with the jurisdiction, powers and authority of claims tribunal. Section 13 of the Act provides that :

Application to Claims Tribunal : (1) A person seeking any relief in respect of the matters referred to in sub-section (1) [or sub-section (1A)] of Section 13 may make an application to the Claims Tribunal.

(2) Every application under sub-section (1) shall be in such form and be accompanied by such documents or other evidence and by such fee in respect of the filing of such application and by such other fees for the service or execution of processes as may be prescribed :

Provided that no such fee shall be payable in respect of an application under sub-clause (*ii*) of clause (*a*) of sub-section (1) [or, as the case may be, sub-section (1A)] of section 13.

An application seeking relief in respect of the matters referred to in section 13(1) or (1A) is to be made in the prescribed form and manner to the Claims Tribunal.

No fee is payable to an application, if made, under section 13(1)(a)(ii) or section 13(1A) of the Act.

Limitation : (1) The Claims Tribunal shall not admit an application for any claim:

(*a*) under sub-section (*i*) of clause (*a*) of sub-section (1) of section 13 unless the application is made within three years from the date on which the goods in question were entrusted to the railway administration for carriage by railway;

(*b*) under sub-section (*ii*) of clause (*a*) of sub-section (1) [or, as the case may be, sub-section (1A)] of section 13 unless the application is made within one year of occurrence of the accident;

(*c*) under clause (*b*) of sub-section (1) of section 13 unless the application is made within three years from the date on which the fare or freight is paid to the railway administration:

Provided that no application for any claim referred to in sub-clause (1) of clause (*a*) of sub-section (1) of section 13 shall be preferred to the Claims Tribunal until the expiration of three months next after the date on which the intimation of the claim has been preferred under section 78B of the Railway Act.

(2) Notwithstanding anything contained in sub-section (1), an application may be entertained after the period specified in sub-section (1) if the applicant satisfies the Claims Tribunal that he had sufficient cause for not making the application within such period.

Procedure and Powers of Claims Tribunal : (1) The Claims Tribunal shall not be bound by the procedure laid down by the Code of Civil Procedure, 1908 (5 of 1908), but shall be guided by the principles of natural justice and, subject to the other provisions of this Act and of any rules, the Claims Tribunal shall have powers to regulate its own procedure including the fixing of places and times of its enquiry.

(2) The Claims Tribunal shall decide every application as expeditiously as possible and ordinarily every application shall be decided on a perusal of documents, written representations and affidavits and after hearing such oral arguments as may be advanced.

(3) The Claims Tribunal shall have, for the purposes of discharging its functions under this Act, the same powers as are vested in a civil court under the Code of Civil Procedure, 1908 (5 of 1908), while trying a suit, in respect of the following matters, namely :

(*a*) summoning and enforcing the attendance of any person and examining him on oath;

(*b*) requiring the discovery and production of documents;

(*c*) receiving evidence on affidavits;

(*d*) subject to the provisions of sections 123 and 124 of the Indian Evidence Act, 1872 (1 of 1872), requisitioning any public record or document or copy of such record or document from any office;

(*e*) issuing commissions for the examination of witnesses or documents;

(*f*) reviewing its decisions;

(*g*) dismissing an application for default or deciding it *ex parte;*

(*h*) setting aside any order of dismissal of any application for default or any order passed by it *ex parte;*

(*i*) any other matter which may be prescribed.

It therefore implies that the claims tribunal,

(*i*) shall not be bound by the procedure laid down in the Code of Civil Procedure, 1908;

(*ii*) shall be guided by the principles of natural justice;

(*iii*) shall have powers to regulate its own procedure.

It shall decide every application as expeditiously as possible and the powers as vested in a civil court under the 1908 Code, while trying a suit, have been conferred on the Claims Tribunal in respect of the matters referred to in sub-section (3)(*a*) to (*i*).

8.5 THE CARRIERS ACT, 1865

The Carriers Act, 1865, is framed by the legislature on the lines of the English Carriers Act, 1930.

The carriers are generally classified into common carriers and private carriers. The distinction between a common carrier and private carrier is important for the purpose of attaching liability against the loss or damage of the goods in transit.

Common Carrier vs. Private Carrier

A common carrier is insurer of the goods and he is liable to the consignor or consignee in all events save and except where the loss is occurred on account of an Act of God, State's enemies or inherent vice in the goods itself. Thus a common carrier may not be liable in respect of perishable goods if the goods are delivered in time or where the loss or damage arises on account of some supernatural act. A private carrier does not hold himself out as exercising the public employment of common carrier. He reserves the right to accept the goods or rejects it and one who carries goods casually or occasionally. Private carriers select the goods of his choice and also looks to the attractiveness of the freight he is getting. He does not accept the goods indiscriminately and when he accept the goods by entering into a regular contract his liability is governed by the terms of the contract and not under the Act.

A private carrier is not an insurer of the goods but merely a *bailee* and in case of loss or damage, the consignor or consignee must prove negligence on the part of the private to recover damages (R.R.N. Ramalinga Nadar *v.* V. Narayan Reddiar, AIR 1971 Ker. 197).

Liability under the Indian Contract Act, 1972

In Kuverji Tulsidas *v.* G. I. P. Rly. Company (ILR 3 Bom., 109), the Bombay High Court has decided that the rights and liabilities of the common carrier in India were governed under Section 151 and 152 of the Indian Contract Act, 1872. The Court had taken the view that the effect of the Indian Contract Act, 1872, was to relieve common carriers from the liability of insurers answerable for the goods entrusted to them 'at all events', except in the case of loss or damage by the act of God or the Queen's enemies, and to make them responsible only for that amount care which the Contract Act requires of all bailees a like in the absence of special contract. However, after some years, the Calcutta High Court came to the conclusion that the liability of the common carriers were not affected by the Contract Act, 1872.

A carrier of passengers in law is neither an insurer nor precluded from making a special contract with his passengers, which may either enlarge, diminish or exclude his general duty to exercise care. In Indian Airlines corporation *v.* Jothaji Maniram, AIR 1959 Mad 285, it was held that the rights and liabilities of the inland Air Carriers are not governed either by the Carriers Act, 1965 or the Carriage by Air Act, 1934, though the Airlines Corporation was a common Carrier. Its rights and liabilities were governed by the common law. At the common law, the Airlines Corporation was entitled to enter into a contract absolving its liabilities even against negligence.

A common carrier of animals is expected provide vehicle reasonably and sufficient for such animals as the professes to carry and his rights and liabilities are within the Act. He is insurer of animal's safety and he is not liable for accident if the same happens on account of inherent vice.

Carrier not Liable for Losses

Section 3 : Where the consignor has declared the value and contents of the goods to be carried, the carrier accept the same under his full common law liability as an insurer, unless such loss or damage results from an act of God, an act of the state's enemies, the fault of the consignor or inherent vice in the goods themselves. The carrier is liable in all events save and except as mentioned above even cases where he was robbed by highway men Forward v. Pittard (1785) 1 Term Re. 27(34); Goggs v. Bernard (1703) 2 Ld. Raym 909.

This sectional also authorises common carriers to charge extra rates for the risk involved in carrying articles of great value in small parcels. The risk intended to be covered is the risk of carrier who are also insures, and part of the extra charge would be in the nature of premium for insurance. The section provides for two rates, one is the ordinary rate and the other is the higher rate. In order to entitled common carrier to charge higher rate, he must exhibit a notice that effect printed or written in English and in the local (vernacular) language of the place where he carriers on his business.

Limiting Liability by Special Contract

Section 6 provides that the common law liability of the carrier as an insurer of the goods cannot be limited or taken away by the carrier by any public notice, whether such notice is exhibited in his premises or by way of advertisement in the newspaper. This safeguard is made only for the purpose of non-scheduled articles as otherwise for scheduled articles Section 3 will apply. The common carrier will not be permitted to say that he is exempted from his liability against loss or damage of non-scheduled articles as per his public notice either exhibited at his place of business or given under the form of newspaper advertisement.

A stipulation in the contract that the carrier will be liable for particular heads of damage is valid so also limitation of amount of his liability in respect of loss or damage of the goods. A stipulation that the carrier must file a suite within a particular time which is less than the statutory period will be void in law. A condition that the carrier is entitled to carry through his agent under sub-contract is valid. The provisions regarding undelivered goods, sorting of such goods, dangerous goods, and liability for indirect or consequential damage or loss of a market made in the contract are valid. A carrier can stipulate that he shall have a lien or particular lien over the goods of the consignor with power to sell the same in given circumstances will be valid. A condition that the carrier will insure the goods on behalf of the consignor and the consignor will pay the charges is valid. (Hill *v.* Scott, (1895) 2 Q.B. 371).

Territorial Jurisdiction

The Supreme Court has held in Haim Singh v. Gammon (India) Ltd., AIR 1971 S.C. 740 that where two or more courts have jurisdiction to try a suit, and agreement between the parties that the claims shall be settled by only one of such courts is valid stipulation and the parties by agreement cannot confer jurisdiction on a court where it has no such jurisdiction in regard to a court where it has no such jurisdiction in regard to a particular matter

In T.K. Nanjunda Setty and Sons, AIR 1964 Mysore 147, plaintiff has taken out two policies of insurance against the fire in respect of his shop at Bangalore. Clause 40 of the first policy provided as follows-

"It is hereby declared and agreed that in case of any claim arising in respect of the property insured under the policy, the same shall be settled and paid in

Madras and the entire cause of action shall also be deemed to arise in Madras and further that all legal proceedings in respect of any such claim shall be instituted in a competent court in the City of Madras only.

Burden of Proof in Relation to Special Contract

A common carrier is liable practically as an insurer of the goods, but the liability can be regulated by the contract entered into between the parties. A common carrier as a matter of general practice enters into a contract defining and limiting its liabilities. A consignor of goods must look into conditions in which are formed in consignment notes for his own benefit. Where a consignor or his agent has signed the declaration and expressly agreed to all the conditions in the consignment note, the burden lies upon the consignor to prove that there was no misrepresentation or that he had no notice of the condition.

Section 8 of the act provides for the liability of the common carrier for loss or damage caused by negligence or fraud or his agent.

Notwithstanding anything herein before contained, every common carrier shall be liable to the owner for loss of or to any property delivered to such carrier to be carried where such loss or damage shall have arisen from the () 1 criminal act of the carrier or any of his agents or servants. (and shall also be liable to the owner for loss or damage to any such property other than property to which the provisions of section 3 apply and in respect of which the declaration required by that section has not been made, where such loss or damage has a arisen from the negligence of the carrier or any of his agents or servants).

In some decided cases the following terms and conditions and stipulations are held reasonable by the courts without affecting the intention of Section 8 of the Carriers Act.

- 'The goods are carried at the owner's risk'. The carrier is protected against all acts, which are not negligent. (N.I. Goods Transport Co. Pvt. Ltd. V. Guru Hosiery Factory AIR 1964 Punj. 318).
- 'The carriers will not be liable if the goods are not insured through them'. This condition is acceptable however it does not extent to loss arising from the negligence or criminal act of the carrying company. (British and Foreign Marine Insurance Co. Ltd. v. I.G.N. & Rly. Co. Ltd. 15 C.W.N. 226)

Section 9 of the act holds a carrier liable whether the goods are not delivered in part or whole for the word non-delivery' covers both. Until the consignment is not placed under the dominion and control of the person who is to receive it, the delivery is not complete.

'Damage' implies loss or deterioration of the goods. If the damage is total, it is a loss to the owner of the goods. Where the goods are partly damaged, the loss is partial and the consignee or the owner of the goods. A certificate issued by the carrier or the surveyor certifying the percentage of damage to the goods shall be deemed to be the prima facie evidence of the percentage of damage suffered by the owner.

The carrier is liable per se for loss, damage or non-delivery of the consignment. Even if the carrier establishes that the goods were taken care of by him by applying ordinary prudence, he may be held liable if the loss was not occasioned by an circumstances beyond control (River Steam Navigation v. Shyam Sunder Tea Co., AIR 1955, Assam 65).

Carriers' Lien

Every common carrier has a particular lien on the property carried for the freight payable. At common law, the carrier has no lien upon the goods carried for a general balance of account due by the consignee for the carriage of other goods. If the carrier claims general lien, the burden is upon him. The right of a carrier to exercise a general or a particular lien, does not arise until the transit of the goods is completed. He therefore cannot stop the goods at the commencement of the journey.

In Prenty *v.* Midland Great Western Rly. (1866), 14 W.R. 314, it was held that where the consignor has sent several parcels for carriage, freight of which was paid on some and unpaid for the rest, the carrier had no right to exercise lien in respect of all the parcels.

Liability for Breach of Duty

Where however an action is laid against the carrier by the consignee who is not a party to the contract, the liability sought to be enforced would be independent of the contract, though proof of the contract might be necessary to show that the defendant was acting as a carrier and as such liable as an insurer. In such a case the liability for the breach of duty to deliver the goods safely would be independent of the terms of the contract entered into between the consignor and the common carrier.

In K.C. Dhar *v.* Ahmed Bux, AIR 1933 Cal. 735, it was held that a person, who had suffered loss by a common carrier's breach of his obligation, could maintain a suit independent of the contract. It was observed that "the liability of a common carrier was not under any contract of insurance; but he was only liable as an insurer". Therefore the common carrier's liability existed irrespective of any Privity of contract between himself and the plaintiff.

Section 10 : If the loss or injury occurs to the goods intended for carriage and such loss or injury may arise where the goods are not delivered to the consignee in the same condition in which it was delivered to him by the consignor for carriage , the notice of loss or injury to be given within six months. No suit shall be instituted against a common carrier for the loss of, or injury to, goods entrusted to him for carriage, unless notice in writing of the loss or injury has been given to him before the institution of the suit and within six months of the time when the loss or injury first came to the knowledge of the plaintiff.

Notice in Writing

To enable the common carrier to locate the exact location of the goods entrusted to him for carriage, the consignor or consignee is required to give notice in writing before filing of the suit. It is only if the notice is given within a period of six months from the date of knowledge that the plaintiff can file a suit within three years from the date of loss or damage of the goods. It is not necessary for the plaintiff to state the issue of notice in the plaint.

Loss of or Injury to the Goods

The notice is required to be given where there is a loss of or injury to the goods occurred. It has been held that the provisions of this section will not be applicable If the goods are not delivered to the consignee or the owner of the goods intended to be delivered for whatsoever reasons other than for loss of or injury to the goods (Union of India v. Jatmall Sukaurai (1971) 2 M.L.J. 257(262)).

Institution of the Suit

The suit against the common carrier for loss of or injury to the goods or for compensation for non-delivery of, or delay in delivering the goods to be instituted within a period of three years as per Article 11 of the Limitation Act, 1963. The limitation period commences from the date when the goods ought to have been delivered which means the reasonable time from the date of despatch of the goods to the consignee.

8.6 THE CARRIAGE BY AIR ACT, 1972

This act gives effects to the provisions of the Warsaw Convention, 1929 and the Hague Protocol, 1955 relating to the international carriage of passengers and goods by air.

The Warsaw convention was given effect to in India by the enactment of the Indian Carriage by Air Act, 1934 in regard to the international carriage and the provisions of the Act have been extended to the domestic carriage, by means of notification issued in 1964.

A diplomatic conference under the auspices of International Civil Aviation Organisation was held in Hague in September 1955 which adopted a protocol to amend the provisions of Warsaw Convention. The act of 1934 was repealed to apply the provisions based on Warsaw Convention and on 15th May 1973 the act came into force as the Carriage by Air Act, 1972. The act defines the liability of the air carrier for death of, injury, or injury to passengers and damage/loss to registered luggage and cargo.

Liability in Case of Death

(1) Notwithstanding anything contained in the Fatal Accidents Act, 1855 or any other enactment or rule of law in force in any part of India, the rules contained

in the First Schedule and in the Second Schedule shall, in all cases to which those rules apply, determine the liability of a carrier in respect of the death of a passenger.

(2) The liability shall be enforceable for the benefit of such of the members of the passenger's family as sustained damage by reason on his death.

Explanation : In this sub-section, the expression "member of a family" means wife or husband, parent, step-parent, grand parent, brother, sister, half-brother, half-sister, child, step-child and grand child:

Provided that indeducing any such relationship as aforesaid any illegitimate person and any adopted person shall be treated as being or as having been, the legitimate child of his mother and reputed father or, as the case may be, of his adopters.

(3) An action to enforce the liability may be brought by the personal representative of the passenger or by any person for whose benefit the liability is under sub-section (2) enforceable, but only one action shall be brought in India in respect of the death of any one passenger, and every such action by whomsoever brought shall be for the benefit of all such persons so entitled as aforesaid as either are domiciled in India or not being domiciled there express a desire of take the benefit of the action.

(4) Subject to the provisions of sub-section (5), the amount recovered in any such action after deducing any costs not recovered from the defendant, shall be divided between the persons entitled in such proportion as the Court may direct.

(5) The Court before which any such action is brought may, at any stage of the proceedings make any such order as appears to the Court to be just and equitable in view of the provisions, the First Schedule or of the Second Schedule, as the case may be, limiting the liability of a carrier and of any proceedings which have been or are likely to be commenced outside India in respect of the death of the passenger in question.

The liability of a carrier in respect of death of a passenger is determined by the rules contained in the first schedule and the second schedule of the Act.

The act also provides for the maximum limits of liability for death, injury damage etc. and also prescribes the time limits within which the claims have to be filed on the air carrier.

First Schedule to The Act (Rules – Chapter III]

1. The carrier is liable for damage sustained in the event of the death or wounding of a passenger or any other bodily injury suffered by a passenger, if the accident which caused the damage so sustained took place on board the aircraft or in the course of any of the operations of embarking or disembarking.

2. (1) The carrier is liable for damage sustained in the event of the destruction or loss of, or of damage to, any registered luggage or any goods, if the occurrence which caused the damage so sustained took place during the carriage by air.

(2) The carriage by air within the meaning of sub-rule (1) comprises the period during which the luggage or goods are in charge of the carrier, whether in an aerodrome or on board an aircraft, or, in the case of a landing outside an aerodrome in any place whatsoever.

(3) The period of the carriage by air does not extend to any carriage by land, by sea or by river performed outside an aerodrome. If, however, such a carriage takes place in the performance of a contract for carriage by air, for the purpose of loading, delivery or transhipment, any damage is presumed, subject to proof to the contrary, to have been the result of an event which took place during the carriage by air.

3. The carrier is liable for damage occasioned by delay in the carriage by air of passengers, luggage or goods.

4. (1) The carrier is not liable if he proves that he and his agents have taken all necessary measures to avoid the damage or that it was impossible for him or them to take such measures.

(2) In the carriage of goods and luggage the carrier is not liable if he proves that the damage was occasioned by negligent pilotage or negligence in the handling of the aircraft or in navigation and that, in all other respects, he and his agents have taken all necessary measures to avoid the damage.

5. If the carrier proves that the damage was caused by or contributed to by the negligence of the injured person the Court may exonerate the carrier wholly or partly from his liability.

6. (1) In the carriage of passengers the liability of the carrier for each passenger is limited to the sum of 1,25,000 francs. Where damages may be awarded in form of periodical payments, the equivalent capital value of the said payments shall not exceed 1,25,000 francs. Nevertheless, by special contract the carrier and the passenger may agree to a higher limit of liability.

(2) In the carriage of registered luggage and of goods, the liability of the carrier is limited to a sum of 250 fracs per kilogramme, unless the consignor has made, at the time when the package was handed over to the carrier, a special declaration of the value at delivery and has paid a supplementary sum if the case so requires. In that case the carrier will be liable to pay a sum not exceeding the declared sum, unless he proves that sum is greater than the actual value to the consignor at delivery.

(3) As regards objects of which the passenger takes charge himself the liability of the carrier is limited to 5,000 francs per passenger.

(4) The sums mentioned in this rule shall be deemed to refer to the French franc consisting of sixty-five and a half miligrammes gold of millesimal fineness nine hundred.

7. Any provision tending to relieve the carrier of liability or to fix a lower limit than that which is laid down in these rules shall be null and void, but the nullity of any such provision does not involve the nullity of the whole contract which shall remain subject to the provisions of this Schedule.

8. (1) In the cases covered by rules 18 to 19 any action for damage, however founded, can only be brought subject to the conditions and limits set out in this Schedule.

(2) In the cases covered by rule 17, the provisions of sub-rule (1) also apply, without prejudice to the questions as to who are the person who have the right to bring suit and what are their respective rights.

9. (1) The carrier shall not be entitled to avail himself of the provisions of this Schedule which exclude or limit his liability, if the damage is caused by his wilful misconduct or by such default on his part as is in the opinion of the Court equivalent to wilful misconduct.

(2) Similarly the carrier shall not be entitled to avail himself of the said provisions, if the damage is caused as aforesaid by any agent of the carrier acting within the scope of his employment.

10. (1) Receipt by the person entitled to delivery of luggage or goods without complaint is *prima facie* evidence that the same have been delivered in good condition and in accordance with the document of carriage.

(2) In the case of damage, the person entitled to delivery must complain to the carrier forthwith after the discovery of the damage, and, at the latest, within three days from the date of receipt in the case of luggage and seven days from the date of receipt in the case of goods. In the case of delay the complaint must be made at the latest within fourteen days from the date on which the luggage or goods have been placed at his disposal.

(3) Every complaint must be made in writing upon the document of carriage or by separate notice in writing despatched within the times aforesaid.

(4) Failing complaint within the times aforesaid, no action shall be against the carrier, save in the case of fraud on his part.

11. In the case of the death of the person liable, an action for damages lies in accordance with these rules against those legally representing his estate.

12. An action for damages must be brought at the option of the plaintiff either before the Court having jurisdiction whether the carrier is ordinarily resident, or has his principal place for business, or has an establishment by which the contract has been made of before the Court having jurisdiction at the place of destination.

13. The right of damages shall be extinguished if an action is not brought within two years reckoned from the date of arrival at the destination, or from the date on which the aircraft ought to have arrived, or from the date on which the carriage stopped.

14. (1) In the case of carriage to be performed by various successive carriers and falling within and definition set out in sub-rule (4) of rule 1, each carrier who accepts passenger's luggage or goods is subjected to the rules set out in this Schedule, and is deemed to be one of the contracting parties to the contract of carriage in so far as the contract deals with that part of the carriage which is performed under his supervision.

(2) In the case of carriage of this nature, the passenger or his representative can take action only against the carrier who performed the carriage during which the accident of the delay occurred, save in the case where, by express agreement, the first carrier has assumed liability for the whole journey.

(3) As regards luggage or goods, the passenger or consignor will have a right of action against the first carrier, and the passenger or consignee who is entitled to delivery will have a right of action against the last carrier, and further, each may take action against the carrier who performed the carriage during which the destruction, loss, damage or delay took place. These carriers will be jointly and severally liable to the passenger or to the consignor or consignee.

8.7 THE INDIAN PORTS(MAJOR PORTS) ACT, 1963

This Act defines the liability of Port Trust Authorities for loss of or damage to goods whilst in their custody and prescribes time limits for filing monetary claim on, or suit against, the Port Trust Authorities.

8.8. THE BILL OF LADING ACT, 1855

This Act defines the character of the Bill of Lading as an evidence of the contract of carriage of goods between the shipowner and the shipper, as an acknowledgement of the receipt of the goods on board the vessel and, as a document of title. The bill of lading is one of the various documents required in connection with settlement of marine cargo claims.

8.9 THE INDIAN POST OFFICE ACT, 1898

This Act defines the liability of the Government for loss, misdelivery, delay of or damage to any postal articles in course of transmission by post.

8.10 MULTI MODAL TRANSPORTATION ACT, 1993

The Act provides for registration of multi-modal transport operators engaged in transportation of goods under more than one mode of transport, i.e., by rail/road and sea. The Act prescribes limits of liability of the operator, contents of documents to be issued by them, notice of loss, etc.

As per Section 2 of the Act, "multimodal transportation" means carriage of goods, by atleast two different modes of transport under a multimodal transport contract, from the place of acceptance of goods in India to a place of delivery of the goods outside India;

Section 3 of the act prohibits any person from carrying on or even commencing the business of multi-modal transportation without registration under the act.

Basis of Liability of Multimodal Transport Operator

Section 13 : Section 13 of the Act provides that if any loss of, or damage to, the consignment, delay in delivery of the consignment and any consequential loss or damage arising out of such delay happens to take place then the multimodal transport operator shall be liable for such loss or damage. (1) The multimodal transport operator shall be liable for loss resulting from :

(*a*) any loss of, or damage to, the consignment;

(*b*) delay in delivery of the consignment and any consequential loss or damage arising from such delay,

where such loss, damage or delay in delivery took place which the consignment was in his charge :

Provided that the multimodal transport operator shall mot be liable if he proves that no fault or neglect on his part or that of his servants or agents had caused or contributed to such loss, damage or delay in delivery:

Provided further that the multimodal transport operator shall not be liable for loss or damage arising out of delay in delivery unless the consignor had made a declaration of interest in timely delivery which has been accepted by the multimodal transport operator.

Explanation : For the purposes of this sub-section," delay in delivery" shall be deemed to occur when the consignment has not been delivered within the time expressly agreed upon or , in the absence of such agreement, within a reasonable time required by a diligent multimodal transport operator, having regard to the circumstances of the case, to effect the delivery of the consignment.

(2) If the consignment has not been delivered within ninety consecutive days following the date of delivery expressly agreed upon or the reasonable time referred to in the *Explanation* to sub-section (1), the claimant may treat the consignment as lost.

Limits of liability when the nature and value of the consignment have not been declared and stage of transport where loss or damage occurred is not known

Section 14 : When the nature and value of consignment have not been declared and the stage of transport where loss or damage occurred is unknown, then liability of the operator to pay compensation is limited as per section 14. (1) Where a multimodal transport operator becomes liable for any loss of, or damage to, any consignment, the nature and value where of have not been declared by the consignor before such consignment has been taken in charge by the multimodal transport operator and the stage of transport at which such loss or damage occurred is not known, then the liability of the multimodal transport operator to pay compensation shall not exceed two Special Drawing Rights per kilogram of the gross weight of the consignment lost or damage or 666.67 Special Drawing Rights per package or unit lost or damaged, whichever is higher.

Explanation : For the purposes of this sub-section, where a container, pallet or similar article of transport is loaded with more than one package or unit, the package or units enumerated in the multimodal transport document, as packed in such container, pallet or similar article of transport shall be deemed as packages or units.

(2) Notwithstanding anything contained in sub-section (1), if the multimodal transportation does not, according to the multimodal transport contract , include carriage of goods by sea or by inland waterways, the liability of the multimodal transport operator shall be limited to an amount not exceeding 8.33 Special Drawing Rights per kilogram of the gross weight of the goods lost or damaged.

Limits of liability when the nature and value of the consignment have not been declared and stage of transport where loss or damage occurred is known

Section 15 : Where a multimodal transport operator becomes liable for any loss of ,or damage to, any consignment, the nature and value whereof have not been declared by the consignor before such consignment has been taken in charge by the multimodal transport operator and the stage of transport at which such loss or damage occurred is known, then the limit of the liability of the multimodal transport operator for such loss or damage shall be determined in accordance with the provisions of the relevant law applicable in relation to the mode of transport during the course of which the loss or damage occurred and any stipulation in the multimodal transport contract to the contrary shall be void and unenforceable.

Liability of the multimodal transport operator in case of delay in delivery of goods under certain circumstances

Section 16 : In case of delay in delivery, the liability of the operator is limited to freight payable for the consignment so delayed. Where delay in delivery of the consignment occurs under any of the circumstances mentioned in the Explanation to sub-section (1) of section 13, or any consequential loss or damage arises from such delay, then the liability of the multimodal transport operator shall be limited to the freight payable for the consignment so delayed.

Assessment of Compensation

Section 17 : (1) Assessment of compensation for loss of ,or damage to, the consignment shall be made with reference to the value of such consignment at the place where, and the time at which, such consignment is delivered to the consignee or at the place and time when, in accordance with the multimodal transport contract, it should have been delivered.

(2) The value of the consignment shall be determined according to the current commodity exchange price, or if there is no such price, according to the current market price, or if the current market price is not ascertainable, with reference to the normal value of a consignment of the same king and quantity.

Loss of right of multimodal transport operator to limit liability

Section 18 : The multimodal transport operator shall not be entitled to the benefit of limitation of liability under any of the provisions of the Chapter if it is proved that the loss, damage of delay in delivery of consignment resulted from an act or omission of the multimodal transport operator with intent to cause such loss damage or delay or recklessly and with knowledge that such loss, damage or delay would probably result.

Limit of liability of multimodal transport operator for total loss of goods

Section 19 : The operator shall not, in any case, be liable for an amount greater than the liability for total loss of goods for which a person will be entitled to make a claim against him under the provision of this Act. The multimodal transport operator shall not, in any case, be liable for an amount greater than the liability for total loss of goods for which a person will be entitled to make a claim against him under the provisions of this Act.

Notice of loss of or damage to goods

Section 20 : The responsibility of the multimodal transport operator starts from the time when the goods are put under his charge and ends when the delivery thereof has been made. (1) The delivery of the consignment to the consignee by the multimodal transport operator shall be treated as *prima facie* evidence of delivery of the goods as described in the multimodal transport document unless notice of the general nature of loss of, or damage to, the goods is given, in writing, by the consignee to the multimodal transport operator at the time of handing over of the goods to the consignee.

(2) Where the loss or damage is not apparent, the provisions of sub-section (1) shall apply unless notice in writing is given by the consignee of the loss of, or damage to, the goods within six consecutive days after the day when the goods were handed over to the consignee.

Key Terms

- Bill of Lading
- Charter Party
- Mechanically Propelled Vehicle
- Multimodal Transportation
- Private Carrier
- Public Carrier
- Railway Claim Tribunal
- Third Party Risks

- Warranties
- Inland Vessels Accident Claims Tribunal

References

- *www.indianlawinfor.com*
- *http:\\shipping.inc.in*
- *www.indialawinfo.com*
- *Bare Acts*
- Gulshan & Kapoor, *Business Law Including Company Law,* New Age, Delhi, 2004.
- Motor Insurance, IC72, *Insurance Institute of India,* Mumbai, 2003.
- R.C. Chawla & K.C. Garg, *Commercial Law,* Kalyani Publishers, 1998.

Questions for Review

1. Define "a mechanically propelled vessel" under the Inland Steam Vessels Act, 1977 & Amended Act of 1977. Briefly explain the liability of the owners of inland mechanically propelled vessel towards third parties.
2. List the various steps involved in claiming compensation via Claims Tribunal under the Inland Steam, 1977.
3. Distinguish Between :

   (*a*) Public Carrier and Private Carrier

   (*b*) Charter Party and Bill of Lading

   in view of the provisions of Carriage of Goods by Sea Act, 1925.
4. Write short notes on :

   (*a*) Implied Condition and Warranties

   (*b*) Rights and Immunities of Carrier

   in view of the provisions of Carriage of Goods by Sea Act, 1925.
5. List the various provisions relating to the liability of shipowners against carriage losses as per the provisions of Merchant Shipping Act, 1958.
6. Discuss the various provisions contained in Chapter IX and XI of the Indian Railway Act, 1890 relating to "Carriage of Goods" and "Responsibilities of Railway Administration as Carrier".

7. Briefly describe the jurisdiction, powers and authority of claims tribunal as per the provisions of the Railway Claims Tribunal Act, 1987.
8. List the various liabilities of common carrier under the Carriers Act, 1965.
9. Explain the liability of air carrier towards :
   (*a*) death of injury to passengers
   (*b*) damage/loss registered luggage and cargo

   under the carriage by Air Act, 1972.
10. Write short notes on :
    (*a*) Multimodel Transportation
    (*b*) Basis of Liability of Multi-model Transport Operator
    (*c*) Assessment of Compensation under the Provisions of Multi-Model Transportation Act, 1993.

Module 4

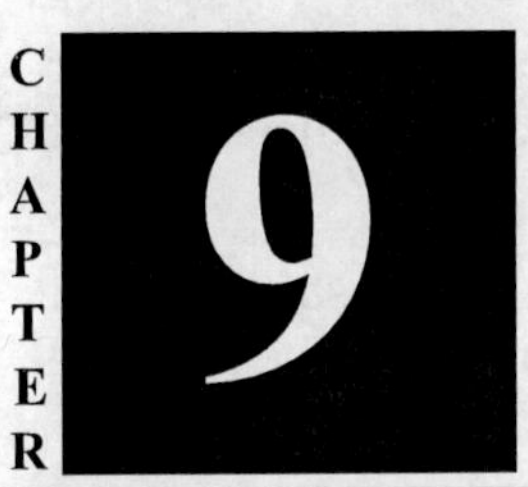

Liability Laws & Insurance

Liability insurance laws have been framed to provide indemnity to the insured against the financial consequences of legal liabilities including third party risks. These liabilities may be :

(a) *Contractual* : which arise out of a contractual relationship.

(b) *Statutory* : prescribed in the various enactments.

In this chapter the employers' liability and the public liability for industrial and non-industrial risks are discussed in light of respective enactments.

9.1 WORKMEN COMPENSATION ACT, 1923

The employer in any organisation is liable under the common law of the land to his employees for negligence or injuries or diseases arising out of and in course of employment. The Workmen Compensation Act, 1923 has been promulgated for the following object and reasons:

The Act provides for the payment by employers to their workmen of compensation for injury by accident, arising out of and in the course of employment. The object of this legislation has been stated as follows:

The growing complexity of industry in this country, with the increasing use of machinery and consequent danger to workmen, along with the comparative poverty of the workmen themselves render it advisable that they should be protected as far as possible, from hardship out of accidents. The act provides certain benefits to employees in case of accidents during employment, sickness, maternity etc.

Employer's Liability for Compensation

Section 3 : (1) If personal injury is caused to a workman by accident arising out of and in the course of his employment, his employer shall be liable to pay compensation in accordance with the provisions of this Chapter mean Provided that the employer shall not be so liable :

(a) in respect of any injury which does not result in the total or partial disablement of the workman for a period exceeding three days;

(b) in respect of any injury, not resulting in death, caused by] an accident which is directly attributable to :

(i) the workman having been at the time thereof under the influence of drink or drugs, or (*ii*) the wilful disobedience of the workman to an order expressly given, or to a rule expressly framed, for the purpose of securing the safety of workmen, or

(*iii*) the wilful removal or disregard by the workman of any safety guard or other device which he knew to have been provided for the purpose of securing the safety of workmen.

(2) The words 'in the course of employment' indicate the time when injury is caused, whereas the words 'out of employment' establishes the causal connection between the injury and the employment.

(3) If the workman dies a natural death while on duty, no liability attaches to the employer unless it is proved that the death was caused by strains and stresses peculiar to the particular employment. When the death of the workman is caused by aggravation of a pre-existing disease due to an accident it has been held that the death is deemed to have resulted from the accident.

In *Laxmibai Atmaram v. Bombay Port Trust, 1954, the Bombay High Court* held, where a workman suffers from a heart aliment dies on account of excessive strain associated with the work, the accident occurred out of employment.

In *Divisional Personnel Officer, Southern Railway v. Karthiayani (1987)* the facts were: Drinking water was provided by the railway for the workmen. The death of the workman was caused by gastro-enteritis which itself was caused by the contaminated water which the deceased had drunk a few hours before his death. Death arose out of and in the course of employment. The High Court found that the railway was liable in terms of Section 3 of the Act to pay compensation.

In *Koduri Alchayamma v. Palangi Alchamma* (High Court at Hyderabad) it was held that the act which resulted in the injury should not be foreign to the employment. The facts of the case were : Palangi was engaged to load the quarry material in the lorry and travel alongwith the lorry and to unload it at the work site. The deceased who was in the lorry saw a wild rabbit passing on the road and he attempted to hit it and in this attempt he fell down from the lorry and met with a fatal accident.

The High Court observed, it was not part of the duties of a workman to hit a wild rabbit running across the road. His act does not arise out of the employment. The principle is that if the workman was responsible for an act unconnected with his duties and that resulted in the injury, the employer is not liable.

Amount of Compensation

Section 4 : (1) Subject to the provisions of this Act, the amount of compensation shall be as follows, namely :

(*a*) Where death results an amount equal to forty per from the injury cent of the monthly wages of the deceased workman multiplied by the relevant factor; or an amount of twenty thousand rupees, whichever is more;

(*b*) Where permanent total an amount equal to fifty per disablement results from cent. of the monthly wages the injury of the injured workman multiplied by the relevant factor; or an amount of twenty-four thousand rupees, whichever is more;

Explanation I : For the purposes of clause (*a*) and clause (*b*), "relevant factor", in relation to a workman means the factor specified in the second column of Schedule IV against the entry in the first column of that Schedule specifying the number of years which are the same as the completed years of the age of the workman on his last birthday immediately preceding the date on which the compensation fell due;

Explanation II : Where the monthly wages of a workman exceed one thousand rupees, his monthly wages for the purposes of clause (*a*) and clause (*b*) shall be deemed to be one thousand rupees only,

(*c*) Where permanent partial disablement result from injury

(*i*) in the case of an injury disablement results from specified in Part II of Schedule the injury I, such percentage of the compensation which would have been payable in the case of permanent total disablement as is specified therein as being the percentage of the loss of earning capacity caused by that injury, and

(*ii*) in the case of an injury not specified in Schedule I, such percentage of the compensation payable in the case of permanent total disablement as is proportionate to the loss of earning capacity (as assessed by the qualified medical practitioner) permanently caused by the injury;

Explanation I : Where more injuries than one are caused by the same accident, the amount of compensation payable under this head shall be aggregated but not so in any case as to exceed the amount which would have been payable if permanent total disablement had resulted from the injuries;

Explanation II : In assessing the loss of earning capacity for the purposes of sub-clause (ii), the qualified medical practitioner shall have due regard to the percentages of loss of earning capacity in relation to different injuries specified in Schedule I;

(*d*) Where temporary disablement whether total or partial result from injury - a half-monthly payment of the sum equivalent to twenty-five the per cent. of monthly wages of the workman, to be paid in accordance with the provisions of sub- section 2.

(2) The half-monthly payment referred to in clause (d) of sub- section (1) shall be payable on the sixteenth day :

(*i*) from the date of disablement where such disablement lasts for a period of twenty-eight days or more, or (*ii*) after the expiry of a waiting period of three days from the date of disablement where such disablement lasts for a period of less than twenty-eight days; and thereafter half-monthly during the disablement or during a period of five years, whichever period is shorter: Provided that—(*a*) there shall be deducted from any lump sum or half- monthly payments to which the workman is entitled the amount of any payment or allowance which the workman has received from the employer by way of compensation during the period of disablement prior to the receipt of such lump sum or of the first half- monthly payment, as the case may be; and (*b*) no half-monthly payment shall in any case exceed the amount, if any, by which half the amount of the monthly wages of the workman before the accident exceeds half the amount of such wages which he is earning after the accident. *Explanation* : Any payment or allowance which the workman has received from the employer towards his medical treatment shall not be deemed to be a payment or allowance received by him by way of compensation within the meaning of clause (a) of the proviso. (3) On the ceasing of the disablement before the date on which any half-monthly payment falls due, there shall be payable in respect of that half-month a sum proportionate to the duration of the disablement in that half-month.

Section 4A : Compensation to be paid when due and penalty for default : (1) Compensation under section 4 shall be paid as soon as it falls due.

(2) In cases where the employer does not accept the liability for compensation to the extent claimed, he shall be bound to make provisional payment based on the extent of liability which he accepts, and, such payment shall be deposited with the Commissioner or made to the workman, as the case may be, without prejudice to the right of the workman to make any further claim.

(3) Where any employer is in default in paying the compensation due under this Act within one month from the date it fell due, the Commissioner may direct that, in addition to the amount of the arrears, simple interest at the rate of six per cent per annum on the amount due together with, if in the opinion of the Commissioner there is no justification for the delay, a further sum not exceeding fifty per cent of such amount, shall be recovered from the employer by way of penalty.

The amount of compensation payable for death is 50% of monthly wages multiplied by the relevant factor (minimum Rs. 50,000/-) and for permanent total disablement 60% of monthly wages multiplied by the relevant factor (minimum Rs. 60,000/-).

Notice and Claim

Section 10 : Notice and Claim : (1) [No claim for compensation shall be entertained by a Commissioner unless notice of the accident has been given in the manner hereinafter provided as soon as practicable after the happening thereof and unless the claim is preferred before him within two years of the occurrence of the accident or, in case of death, within two years from the date of death;

Provided that, where the accident is the contracting of a disease in respect of which the provisions of sub-section (2) of section 3 are applicable, the accident shall be deemed to have occurred on the first of the days during which the workman was continuously absent from work in consequence of the disablement caused by the disease;

Provided further that in case of partial disablement due to the contracting of any such disease and which does not force the workman to absent himself from work, the period of two years shall be counted from the day the workman gives notice of the disablement to his employer: Provided further that if a workman who, having been employed in an employment for a continuous period, specified under sub-section (2) of section 3 in respect of that employment, ceases to be so employed and develops symptoms of an occupational disease peculiar to that employment within two years of the cessation of employment, the accident shall be deemed to have occurred on the day on which the symptoms were first detected;

Provided further that the want of or any defect or irregularity in a notice shall not be a bar to the entertainment of a claim—

(*a*) if the claim is preferred in respect of the death of a workman resulting from an accident which occurred on the premises of the employer, or at any place where the workman at the time of the accident was working under the control of the employer or of any person employed by him, and the workman died on such premises or at such place, or on any premises belonging to the employer, or died without having left the vicinity of the premises or place where the accident occurred, or

(*b*) if the employer or any one of several employers or any person responsible to the employer for the management of any branch of the trade or business in which the injured workman was employed] had knowledge of the accident from any other source at or about the time when it occurred;

Provided further, that the Commissioner may entertain and decide any claim to compensation in any case notwithstanding that the notice has not been given, or the claim has not been preferred, in due time as provided in this sub-section, if he is satisfied that the failure so to give the notice or prefer the claim, as the case may be, was due to sufficient cause.

(2) Every such notice shall give the name and address of the person injured and shall state in ordinary language the cause of the injury and the date on which the accident happened, and shall be served on the employer or upon any one of several employers, or upon any person responsible to the employer for the management of any branch of the trade or business in which the injured workman was employed.

(3) The State Government may require that any prescribed class of employers shall maintain at their premises at which workmen are employed a notice-book, in the prescribed form, which shall be readily accessible at all reasonable times

to any injured workman employed on the premises and to any person acting bona fide on his behalf. (4) A notice under this section may be served by delivering it at, or sending it by registered post addressed to, the residence or any office or place of business of the person on whom it is to be served, or, where a notice-book is maintained, by entry in the notice-book.

Payment of compensation for death has to be deposited by the employer with the Commissioner whose receipt shall be a sufficient discharge.

Where the amount of any lumpsum as compensation has been agreed, whether by way or redemption of a half-monthly payment or otherwise, a memorandum has to be sent by the employer to the Commissioner for registration.

If payment is not made within one month from the date it fell due the employer would be liable to pay interest and in case the delay is unjustified pay further amount by way of penalty subject to a maximum of 50% of the amount payable as ordered by the Commissioner.

Contracting

Section 12 : (1) Where any person (hereinafter in this section referred to as the principal) in the course of or for the purposes of his trade or business contracts with any other person (hereinafter in this section referred to as the contractor) for the execution by or under the contractor of the whole or any part of any work which is ordinarily part of the trade or business of the principal, the principal shall be liable to pay to any workman employed in the execution of the work any compensation which he would have been liable to pay if that workman had been immediately employed by him; and where compensation is claimed from the principal, this Act shall apply as if references to the principal were substituted for references to the employer except that the amount of compensation shall be calculated with reference to the wages of the workman under the employer by whom he is immediately employed.

(2) Where the principal is liable to pay compensation under this section, he shall be entitled to be indemnified by the contractor, or any other person from whom the workman could have recovered compensation and where a contractor who is himself a principal is liable to pay compensation or to indemnify a principal under this section he shall be entitled to be indemnified by any person standing to him in the relation of a contractor from whom the workman could have recovered compensation,] and all questions as to the right to and the amount of any such indemnity shall, in default of agreement, be settled by the Commissioner.

(3) Nothing in this section shall be construed as preventing a workman from recovering compensation from the contractor instead of the principal.

(4) This section shall not apply in any case where the accident occurred elsewhere than on, in or about the premises on which the principal has undertaken or usually undertakes, as the case may be, to execute the work or which are otherwise under his control or management.

Where the employer (referred to in the Section as Principal) contracts with any other person (referred to as Contractor) for the execution of the whole or part of any work which is ordinarily part of the business of the principal, the employer shall be liable to pay compensation to workmen employed by the contractor.

If the insured employer becomes insolvent his rights under the insurance policy are transferred to and vest in the workman who can recover the claim subject to the terms and conditions of the policy.

9.2 PUBLIC LIABILITY INSURANCE ACT, 1991

The Public Liability Insurance Act, 1991 imposes "no fault" liability in respect of use of hazardous substances as specified by the Act. The object of this Act is to provide through insurance immediate relief to persons affected due to "accident" while "handling" "hazardous substance" by the owners on "no fault liability basis". This has also been brought under Tariff. The definition of "Owner" is so comprehensive as to cover any person who owns or has control over any hazardous substance at the time of accident. This includes any Firm or its partners. Association or its members, Company or its Directors and all other persons associated and responsible to that Company in the conduct of their business.

Definitions

The various terms like "Accident", "Hazardous substances" as defined in Section 2 of the Act are given below :

"Accident" means an accident involving a fortuitous, sudden or unintentional occurrence while handling any hazardous substance resulting in continuous, intermittent or repeated exposure to death of, or injury to any person or damage to any property but does not include an accident by reason only of war or radioactivity.

"Handling" in relation to any hazardous substance, means the manufacture, processing, treatment, package, storage, transportation by vehicle, use, collection, destruction, conversion, offering for sale, transfer or the like of such hazardous substance.

"Hazardous Substance" means any substance or preparation which is defined as hazardous substance under the Environment (Protection) Act, 1986 and exceeding such quantity as may be specified by notification by the Central Government.

"Hazardous Substance" means any substance or preparation which, by reason of its chemical properties or handling is liable to cause harm to human beings, other living creatures, plants, micro-organism, property or the environment (as per the Environment (Protection) Act, 1986).

Maximum Liability

Any one accident : Minimum equal to Paid up Capital upto a maximum of Rs. 5 crores.

Any one year : Three times of 'Any one accident' limit subject to a maximum of Rs. 15 crores.

In case of claim/s exceeding the above statutory limit/s, it is to be met by the Environmental Relief Fund to be set up under Section 7A of the Act and managed by the Authority appointed by the Central Government.

The liability beyond the total of the insurance and the Relief/Fund is to be borne by the "Owner". Every owner , in addition to premium, has to pay to the insurer and equivalent amount to be credited to the said fund. However, the central government has powers to exempt any establishment from compulsory insurance, if a fund has been established and maintained for an amount not less than Rs. 5.0 crores or equal to the paid up capital of the establishment, in any nationalized bank for meeting liability under the act.

Schedule of Compensation

1. Reimbursement of medical expenses incurred upto a maximum of Rs. 12,500/- in each case.
2. For a fatal accident the relief will be Rs. 25,000/- per person in addition to reimbursement of medical expenses, if any incurred on the victim upto a maximum of Rs. 12,500/-.
3. For permanent total or permanent partial disability or other injury or sickness, the relief will be :
   (*a*) Reimbursement of medical expenses incurred, if any, upto a maximum of Rs. 12,500/- in each case and,
   (*b*) Cash relief on the basis of percentage of disablement as certified by an authorized physician. The relief for total permanent disability will be Rs. 25,000/-.
4. For loss of wages due to temporary partial disability which reduce the earning capacity of the victim, there will be a fixed monthly relief not exceeding Rs. 1,000/- per month upto a maximum of 3 months provided the victim has been hospitalized for a period exceeding 3 days and above 16 years of age.
5. In respect of damage to private property, upto Rs. 6,000/- per claim.
6. Apart from Public liability insurance Act policy, policies are also available to cover the legal liability of the insured against third parties for claims arising due to industrial accidents. Two different types of policies are available to cover accidents in industries like factories etc. and non industries like hotels, schools, exhibitions and storage tanks etc.

Claim Procedure

- ❑ The Insured has to give written notice to the company as soon as possible of any claim made against him (or any specific event or circumstance that may give rise to a claim being made against the Insured) which forms the subject of indemnity under the policy and shall give all such additional information as the company may require.
- ❑ Every claim, writ, summons or process and all documents relating to the event shall be forwarded to the Company immediately after they are received by the Insured, alongwith the claim form duly filled up.
- ❑ No admission, offer, promise or payment shall be made or given by or on behalf of the insured without the written consent of the company.
- ❑ The insured will have the right to take over and conduct in the name of the Insured in defense of any claim in case of voluntary public liability policies.
- ❑ In the event of liability rising under the policy or payment of a claim under the policy, the limit of indemnity per anyone year under the policy shall get reduced to the extent of quantum of liability to be paid or actual payment of such claim.
- ❑ No claim is payable under the policy unless the cause of action arises in India and the liability to pay claim is established against the Insured in an Indian Court. It is also to be understood that only Indian Law shall be applicable in such action.

Key Terms

- ✷ Negligence
- ✷ Compensation
- ✷ Temporary Disablement
- ✷ Accident
- ✷ In the Course of Employment
- ✷ Permanent Partial Disablement
- ✷ No Fault
- ✷ Hazardous Substance

References

- ★ *Bare Acts*
- ★ *Liability and Engineering Insurance*, IC79, Insurance Institute of India, Mumbai, 2000.
- ★ *www.ndc-nihfw.org*

Questions for Review

1. Write short notes on :

   (*a*) in course of employment

   (*b*) disablement

   within the meaning of Workman Compensation Act, 1923.

2. Explain the liability of the employer under the Workman Compensation Act, 1923. How compensation is arrived at under the Act.

3. Explain the liability of the "owner" under the Public Liability Insurance Act, 1991. What procedure is followed for claiming relief and the compensation under the Act.

CHAPTER 10 Miscellaneous Laws Concerning Insurance

10.1 INDIAN STAMP ACT, 1899

Definition

Section 2 of the act defines policy of insurance, policy of group insurance and policy of sea insurance.

(19) *"Policy of insurance"* includes :

(*a*) any instrument by which one person, in consideration of a premium, engages to indemnify another against loss, damage or liability arising from an unknown or contingent event;

(*b*) a life-policy, and any policy insuring any person against accident or sickness, and any other personal insurance;

(19A) *"Policy of group insurance"* means any instrument covering not less than fifty or such smaller number as the Central Government may approve, either generally or with reference to any particular case, by which an insurer, in consideration of a premium paid by an employer or by an employer and his employees, jointly, engages to cover, with or without medical examination and for the sole benefit of persons other than the employer, the lives of all the employees or of any class of them, determined by conditions pertaining to the employment, for amounts of insurance based upon a plan which precludes individual selection;]

(20) *"Policy of sea-insurance"* or *"sea-policy"* :

(*a*) means any insurance made upon any ship or vessel (whether for marine or inland navigation), or upon the machinery, tackle or furniture of any ship or vessel, or upon any goods, merchandise or property of any description whatever on board of any ship or vessel, or upon the freight of, or any other interest which may be lawfully insured in, or relating to, any ship or vessel, and

(*b*) includes any insurance of goods, merchandise or property for any transit which includes, not a sea risk within the meaning of clause (a), but also any other risk incidental to the transit insured from the commencement of the transit to the ultimate destination covered by the insurance.

Where any person, in consideration of any sum of money paid or to be paid for additional freight or otherwise, agrees to take upon himself any risk attending goods, merchandise or property of any description whatever while on board of any ship or vessel, or engages to indemnify the owner of any such goods, merchandise or property from any risk, loss or damage, such agreement or engagement shall be deemed to be a contract for sea-insurance;

Instruments Chargeable with Duty

According to *Section 3,* an instrument is to be chargeable with duty of the amount indicated in Schedule I to the Act which gives a list of instruments liable to stamp duty. The liability of an instrument to stamp duty is determined by the Act in force at the time the instrument was executed. Instruments not mentioned in this Schedule are not subject to duty.

Section 17 provides that all instruments chargeable with duty and executed by any person in India shall be stamped before or at the time of execution.

Section 3 : Subject to the provisions of this Act and the exemptions contained in Schedule I, the following instruments shall be chargeable with duty of the amount indicated in that Schedule as the proper duty therefor, respectively, that is to say-

(*a*) every instrument mentioned in that Schedule which, not having been previously executed by any person, is executed in India on or after the first day of July, 1899;

(*b*) every bill of exchange payable otherwise than on demand or promissory note drawn or made out of India on or after that day and accepted or paid, or presented for acceptance or payment, or endorsed, transferred or otherwise negotiated, in India; and

(*c*) every instrument other than a bill of exchange or promissory note mentioned in that Schedule, which, not having been previously executed by any person, is executed out of India on or after that day relates to any property situate, or to any matter or thing done or to be done, in India and is received in India:

PROVIDED that no duty shall be chargeable in respect of–(1) any instrument executed by, or on behalf of, or in favour of, the government in cases where, but for this exemption, the government would be liable to pay the duty chargeable in respect of such instrument;

(2) any instrument for the sale, transfer or other disposition, either absolutely or by way of mortgage or otherwise, of any ship or vessel, or any part, interest, share or property of or in any ship or vessel registered under the Merchant Shipping Act, 1894, or under Act 19 of 1938, or the Indian Registration of Ships Act, 1841, as amended by subsequent Acts.

Every instrument chargeable with duty executed out of India and not being a bill of exchange or promissory note, may be stamped within *three months* after it has been fist received in India [Sec. 18(1)]. Sec. 18 does not make an instrument which is not stamped within the time prescribed by this Section, inadmissible in evidence.

Such an instrument is impoundable and can be admitted in evidence on payment of stamp duty and penalty.

Policies of Sea-insurance

Section 7(4) : Where any sea-insurance is made for or upon a voyage and also for time, or to extend to or cover any time beyond thirty days after the ship shall have arrived at her destination and been there moored at anchor, the policy shall be charged with duty as a policy for or upon a voyage, and also with duty as a policy for time.

The object of Section 7 is to prevent loss of revenue which would occur if the business of sea-insurance were to be done on ships and not on formal stamped policies. Omission to issue stamped policies is made punishable under Sec. 66.

A contract of sea-insurance, which is expressed in the form of cover notes or slips, bearing date and insured against damages for 'all risks' is invalid and unenforceable as it is not expressed in a sea-policy.

Power to Reduce, Remit or Compound Duties

Sec. 9 deals with the power of the Government to remit, reduce, or compound duties in case of particular instruments or any particular class of instruments or groups of instruments.

Section 9(1)] : The government may, by rule or order published in Official Gazette,:

(*a*) reduce or remit, whether prospectively or retrospectively, in the whole or any part of the territories under its administration, the duties with which any instruments or any particular class or instruments, or any of the instruments belonging to such class, or any instruments when executed by or in favour of any particular class of persons, by or in favour or any members of such class, are chargeable, and

(*b*) provide for the composition or consolidation of duties in the case of issues by any incorporated company or other body corporate 30[or of transfers (where there is a single transferee, whether incorporated or not).]

Section 9(2) In this section, the expression "the government" means,:

(*a*) in relation to stamp-duty in respect of bills of exchange, cheques, promissory notes, bills of lading, letters of credit, policies of insurance, transfer of shares, debentures, proxies and receipts, and in relation to any other stamp-duty chargeable under this Act and failing within entry 96 of List I in Schedule VII to the Constitution, the Central Government;

(*b*) save as aforesaid, the State Government.

Cancellation of Adhesive Stamps

Section 12 deals with the cancellation of adhesive stamps. The object of cancellation is to prevent the same stamps from being used more than once.

Instruments Stamped with Impressed Stamps – How to be Written

Section 13 : Every instrument written upon paper stamped with an impressed stamp shall be written in such manner that the stamp may appear on the face of the instrument and cannot be used for or applied to any other instrument.

Instruments Executed in India

According to *Section 17,* all instruments chargeable with duty and executed by any person in India must be stamped before or at the time of execution.

It is sufficient if stamping and execution are part of the same transaction, so that it is permissible to stamp immediately after the execution of the document.

Instruments Executed out of India (Sec. 18)

Section 18 deals with the time of stamping of instruments other than bills of exchange and promissory notes executed out of India, [*i.e.,* instruments chargeable under Sec. 3(*c*)]. When any such instrument is received in India, it must be stamped within three months of its receipt in India [Sec. 18(1)].

Duties by Whom Payable

Section 29 names the persons by whom stamp duty is payable. It lays down that, in the absence of any agreement to the contrary, the expense of providing the proper stamp shall be borne–

(*a*) in the case of any instrument described in any of the following Articles of Schedule I, namely :

.........,No. 16. (Bottomry Bond),........ No. 56. (Respondentia Bond),..........No. 62(c). (Transfer of any interest secured by a bond, mortgage-deed or policy of insurance), by the person drawing, making or executing such instrument:

(*b*) in the case of a policy of insurance other than fire-insurance- by the person effecting the insurance:

(*bb*) in the case of a policy of fire-insurance- by the person issuing the policy:]

Obligation to Give Receipt in Certain Cases

Section 30 : Any person receiving any money, exceeding five thousand in amount, or any bill of exchange, Cheque or promissory note for an amount exceeding five thousand, or receiving in satisfaction or part satisfaction of a debt any movable property exceeding twenty rupees in value, shall, on demand by the person paying or delivering such money, bill, Cheque, note or property, give a duly stamped receipt for the same.

Any person receiving or taking credit for any premium or consideration for any renewal of any contract of fire-insurance, shall, within one month after receiving or taking credit for such premium or consideration, give a duly stamped receipt for the same.

Section 33 casts a duty upon Courts, arbitrators and public officers (except officers of police) to examine every instrument which is chargeable with duty, and is produced or comes before them in the performance of their functions, in order to ascertain whether it is duly stamped. If they are satisfied that the instrument is not duly stamped, they shall impound it.

Instruments not duly stamped in admissible in evidence, etc. (Sec. 35)

Section 35 contains a rule of procedure. According to it no instrument chargeable with duty shall be :

(*i*) admitted in evidence for any purpose by any person having by law or consent of parties authority to receive evidence, or

(*ii*) acted upon, or

(*iii*) registered, or

(*iv*) authenticated, by any such person or by any public officer, unless such instrument is duly stamped.

Collector's Power to Stamp Impounded Instruments (Sec. 40)

Section 40 deals with Collector's power to stamp any instrument impounded by him under Sec. 33 or an instrument sent to him under Sec. 38 (2), not being an instrument chargeable with a duty not exceeding ten paise only or a bill of exchange or promissory note. In such a case, he *shall* adopt the following procedure:

(*a*) If he is of opinion that the instrument is duly stamped, or is not chargeable with duty, he shall certify by endorsement thereon that it is duly stamped, or that it is not so chargeable, as the case may be [Sec. 40(1) (*a*)];

(*b*) If the is of opinion that the instrument is chargeable with duty and is not duly stamped, he shall require the payment of the proper duty, or the amount required to make up the same, together with a penalty of five rupees; or, if he thinks fit, an amount not exceeding ten times the amount of the proper duty or of the deficient portion thereof, whether such amount exceeds or falls short of five rupees [Sec. 40(1) (*b*)].

10.2 CONSUMER PROTECTION ACT, 1986

Insurance is a *service* and therefore it is covered by Section 2(e) of the Consumer Protection Act, 1986.

The Consumer Protection Act was passed in 1986 with a view to provide for better protection of the interests of the consumers. The Act makes provisions for the establishment of Consumer Protection Councils and other authorities such as Consumer Disputes Redressal Forums at the National, State and District levels for speedy and simple settlement of consumer disputes.

Aggrieved consumers can seek the following relief under Sec. 14 of the Act depending on the nature of relief sought by the consumer and the facts of case.

(*a*) removal of defects from the goods,

(*b*) replacement of the goods;

(*c*) refund of the price paid;

(*d*) award of compensation for the loss or injury suffered;

(*e*) removal of defects or deficiencies in the services;

(*f*) discontinuance of unfair trade practices or restrictive trade practices or direction not to repeat them;

(*g*) withdrawal of the hazardous goods from being offered to sale; or

(*h*) award for adequate costs to parties.

The Act recognises the right of the user other than the buyer also to sue the manufacturer by defining the word consumer to include user also. A summary of the provisions is given below :

- It empowers an individual consumer or a recognised consumer. Association whether the consumer is a member of such association or not to file a complaint in respect of affective goods or deficient services.
- It covers not only goods as defined under the Sale of Goods Act, 1930 but also services including services provided by public sector undertakings and government departments such as banking, financing, insurance, transport, processing, supply of electrical or other energy etc.
- It defines the rights of consumers.
- It provides for the establishment of advisory bodies at the Central and State levels to be known as Central Consumer Protection Council and the State Consumer Protection Councils with the object of promoting and protecting the rights of consumers.
- It provides for the establishment of quasi-judicial bodies for the redressel of the grievances of consumers at the District, State and Central levels known as District Forum, State Commission and National Consumer Disputes Redressal Commission
- It lays down the procedure to be followed in redressing consumer grievances and provides a time limit for the disposal of their complaints.
- It empowers the District Forum to issue orders to the opposite party to remove the defect from 'the goods or to replace the goods or to return the price or charges paid and or to pay compensation for any loss or injury suffered by the consumer due to the negligence of the opposite party, in respect of defective goods or deficient services.

- ❑ It empowers the District Forum, the State or the National Commission to enforce its order in the same manner as if it were a decree or order made by the Court, and in the event of its inability to execute it, to send such order to a court of competent jurisdiction for its execution.
- ❑ It empowers the forum or commission to impose a sentence of imprisonment of not less than one month extending to 3 years or with a minimum fine of Rs. 2,000/- extending upto Rs. 10,000/- or with both, for failure to comply with any order made by it.

The 1993 amendment has empowered the forum or commission to order payment of compensation by the complainant to the opposite party if the petition appears to be frivolous or vexatious in nature. The amount shall not be more than Rs. 10,000/-.

Consumer Defined

It defines *"Consumer"* as a person who :

(*i*) buys any goods for a consideration which has been paid or promised or partly paid and partly promised , or under any system of deferred payment and includes any user of such goods other than the person who buys such goods for consideration paid or promised or partly paid or partly promised, or under any system of deferred payment when such use is made with the approval of such person, but does not include a person who obtains such goods for resale or any other commercial purpose; or

(*ii*) hires or avails of any services for a consideration which has been paid or promised or partly paid and partly promised, or under any system of deferred payment and includes any beneficiary of such services goods other than the person who hires or avails of the services for consideration paid or promised or partly paid or partly promised , or under any system of deferred payment when such services are availed of with the approval of the first mentioned person.

Other Definitions

"Deficiency" means any fault, imperfection, shortcoming or inadequacy in the quality, nature and manner of performance which is required to be maintained by or under any law for the time being in force or has been undertaken to be performed by a person in pursuance of a contract or otherwise in relation to any service.

A *"service"* means service of service of any description which is made available to potential users and includes a provision of facilities in connection with banking, financing, insurance, transport, processing, supply of electrical or other energy, board or lodging or both, housing construction entertainment, amusement or the previewing of news or other information but does not include the rendering of any service free of charge or under a contract of personal service.

"Unfair trade practice" means a trade practice which, for the purpose of promoting the sale, use or supply of any goods or for the provision of any service, adopts any unfair method or unfair or deceptive practice including any of following practices, namely :

(*a*) false or misleading representation,

(*b*) bargain price

(*c*) offering of gifts, prize, contest etc.

(*d*) non compliance of product safety standard.

(*e*) hoarding or destruction of goods.

Complaint under the Act

Under the Act, *a complaint* means any allegation in writing made by a complainant in regard to one or more of the following :

- Any unfair trade practice as defined in the Act or restrictive trade practices like tie-up sales adopted by any trader.
- One or more defects in goods. The goods hazardous to life and safety, when used are being offered for sale to public in contravention of provisions of any law for the time being in force.
- Deficiencies in services.
- A trader charging excess of price.

Who can file a complaint?

The following can file a complaint under Sec. 12 of the Act :

- A consumer.
- Any voluntary consumer organisation registered under the Societies Registration Act, 1860 or under the Companies Act, 1956 or under any other law for the time being in force.
- The Central Government.
- The State Government or Union Territory Administrations.
- One or more consumers on behalf of numerous consumers who are having the same interest (Class action complaints).

It has been held that the wife of a deceased husband is a beneficiary and can claim compensation under the Consumer Protection Act, 1986 (Sushilaban Bupatrai Soni *vs.* New India Assurance Co. Ltd., 1996, 3 CPJ, Gujrat 404.

Where to file a complaint?

In the district forum if the value of services and compensation claimed is less than one lakh of rupees; before the state commission, if the value of the goods or services and the compensation claimed does of the goods or services and the state commission, the compensation does not exceed more than twenty lakhs of rupees. In the national commission, if the value of the goods or services and the compensation exceeds more than twenty lakhs of rupees.

Procedure under the Act

Procedures for filing complaints and seeking redressel are simple enough.

- ❑ There is no fee for filing a complaint before the District Forum, the State Commission, or the National Commission. (A stamp paper is also not required) There should be 3 to 5 copies of the complaint on plain paper.
- ❑ The complainant or his authorised agent can present the complaint in person.
- ❑ The complaint can be sent by post to the appropriate Forum / Commission.
- ❑ A complaint should contain the following information:
  - (*a*) The name, description and the address of the complainant.
  - (*b*) The name , description and address of the opposite party or parties, as the case may be, as far as they can be ascertained;
  - (*c*) The facts relating to complaint and when and where it arose;
  - (*d*) Documents, if any, in support of the allegations contained in the complaint.
  - (*e*) The relief which the complainant is seeking.
  - (*f*) The complainant or his authorised agent should sign the complaint.
  - (*g*) The complaint is to be filed within two years from the date on which cause of action has arisen.

On the receipt of the complaint, the District Forum has to refer a copy of the complaint to the opposite party mentioned in the complaint directing him to give his version of the case within a period of 30 days or such extended period not exceeding 15 days as may be granted by the Forum. In case the opposite party, on the receipt of the complaint referred to him denies or disputes the allegations contained in the complain, or omits or fails to take may action to represent his case within the time given by the District Forum, the District Forum has to proceed to settle the dispute in the manner provided in the Act.

To sum up, on the receipt of the complaint, the District Forum should:

- ❑ Give notice to the opposite party
- ❑ The notice should be accompanied with the copy of the complaint
- ❑ The opposite party should be given a minimum of 30 days to give his version

- The period of 30 days may be extended by the District Forum for the further period, but not exceeding 15 days.
- The District Forum should wait for a statutory period of 30 days from the date of notice for the version of the opposite party and should not order ex parte proceedings before the expiry of the minimum period of 30 days from the notice and
- Even if the opposite party fails to give his version within 30 days of the notice or the extended time, the complaint should be decided by the District Forum, after recording the evidence of the complainant on merits.

In case the complaint pertains to deficiency in service, the District Forum, as per the mandate of the Act should refer a copy of such complaint to the opposite party directing him to give his version of the cause within a period of 30 days or such extended period, not exceeding 15 days, as may be granted by the District Forum.

After the notice of the complaint to the opposite party, if the opposite party admits the claim of the complainant, the District Forum may pass the consent order in favour of the complainant provided the claim is justified on the basis of the documents and affidavits filed before the Forum. However, before passing such a consent order, the Commission has to satisfy itself, that there is no collusion and that the admissions have been made under no influence.

Section 13(2)(b) of the Consumer Protection Act lays down that if the opposite party does not respond to the notice sent to him by the Commission or denies or disputes the allegations made by the Complainant, the Commission shall have the power to decide the dispute on the basis of the evidence brought to its notice by the complainant and the opposite party, where the opposite party denies or disputes the allegation of the complainant or on the basis of the evidence supplied to it by the complainant, if the opposite party does not respond to the notice of the Commission.

On the other hand, if the complainant fails to appear on the day of hearing the District Forum has the power to either dismiss the complaint for default of decide it on merits. This is provided for in the Rules and not in the Act itself. The Commission also has the power to restore the complaint if sufficient reasons for non-appearance are given.

With regard to setting aside of ex parte orders, it has been held that if sufficient cause is shown for non-appearance of the parties, the Consumer Forum has the power to set aside the order passed ex parte.

Powers of District Forum

The Consumer Protection Act vests the District forum with the powers given to a Civil Court by the Code of Civil Procedure, 1908. These are:

- The power to summon and enforce the attendance of any defendant or witness and examining the witness on oath.

- ❑ The authority to order for discovery and production of any document or other material object producible as evidence;
- ❑ The power to receive evidence on affidavits;
- ❑ The power to requisition the report of the concerned analysis or test from the appropriate laboratory or from any other relevant source;
- ❑ The power to issue any commission for the examination of any witness.

Moreover, the Act says that the proceedings before the District Forum shall be deemed to be a judicial proceeding within the meaning of Section 193 and 228 of the Indian Penal Code. Hence, a person giving false evidence can be punished under the Penal Code. The power to proceed against a person for contempt of court is also provided for.

The proceedings of the District forum as per the Act has to be conducted by the President of the Forum and at least one member sitting together. The decision of the Forum has to be signed by the President and the other member or members sitting with him for the proceeding. If there is a split decision between the President and a member, the matter has to be referred to a third member for his opinion. The opinion of the majority then becomes the order of the Forum.

State Commission and Appeals

In case any person is aggrieved by the order of the District Forum, he may prefer an appeal against such order to the State Commission within a period of thirty days from the date of the order. The State Commission however has the power to entertain the appeal after the said period of thirty days if it is satisfied that there was sufficient reason not to file the appeal within the stipulated time.

The Consumer Protection Act, as mentioned earlier, provides for the setting up of a State Commission. This State Commission, as per the Act shall consist of a President, who shall be or has been a Judge of a High Court. There is a provision for two other members, one of whom has to be a woman. The State Commission has the jurisdiction to entertain complaints where the value of the goods or services and compensation, if any, claimed exceeds rupees five lakhs, but does not exceed rupees twenty lakhs. It also has the power to entertain appeals against the orders of any District Forum, within the State. It further has the authority to summon the records and pass appropriate orders in any consumer dispute pending before any District Forum in the State or which has been decided by any District Forum if it has failed to exercise a jurisdiction so vested or has acted in exercise of its jurisdiction illegally or with material irregularity. The same procedure that applies to District forums applies to the State Commissions also.

Any person aggrieved by an order made by the State Commission under its original jurisdiction has the right to prefer an appeal to the National Consumer Disputes Redressal Forum. The appeal has to be filed within a period of thirty days from the date of the order. It is however provided that the National Commission may allow the appeal after thirty days if it is satisfied that there was sufficient cause for not filing within that said period.

National Commission

The Consumer Protection Act provides for a National Consumer Disputes Redressal Forum. The forum consists of a President and four other members. The President has to be either a sitting or retired Judge of the Supreme Court.

The National Commission has the jurisdiction to entertain complaints where the value of the goods or services and the compensation, if any, claimed exceeds rupees twenty lakhs. It also has the jurisdiction to entertain appeals any orders of any State Commission. Further, it has the power to call for the records and pass appropriate orders in any consumer dispute pending or decided by any State Commission, where the State Commission has acted in excess of its jurisdiction or has failed to exercise the jurisdiction vested in it or has exercised jurisdiction illegally. The National Commission also has the powers that are vested in the Civil Court, as prescribed in Section 13, Consumer Protection Act.

A person aggrieved by the order of the National Commission has the right to appeal to the Supreme Court. The appeal has to be filed in the Supreme Court within thirty days of the order of the National Commission. The Supreme Court, however has the power to accept the appeal after thirty days if sufficient reasons are given for the delay. Moreover, the Act stipulates that if either of the parties do not appeal to the Appellate body, within the stipulated time, the order of the Forum shall be final.

Limitation Period

Limitation means a legally specified period beyond which an action cannot be brought, or a property right is not to continue. The Limitation Act provides for the period within which the suit has to be filed. In addition to this, some statutes prescribe a period of limitation for certain procedures.

Before the amendment in 1993, the limitation period for filing complaints before the various forums was governed by the Indian Limitation Act. However, in 1993, Section 24A was introduced, which specifies the Limitation period.

As per Section 24 A, the limitation period for filing a complaint before the District, State or National Commission is two years from the date on which the cause of action arises. However, as mentioned earlier the forums have the power to condone the delay if they feel that there was sufficient cause for the same. The reasons for condoning the delay has to be mentioned in the records.

It has been held that where the complainant claimed that he was busy in negotiating the claim with the insurance company and could not explain the delay, the claim is time barred (Tehri Hydro Development Corporation Ltd. *vs.* New India Assurance Co. Ltd., 2003, ICLD 318.

In a civil court, the suit is not maintainable unless and until the requisite court fee as per the Court Fees and Suit Valuation Act is affixed on the same. The Consumer Protection Act has done away with the requirement of a court fee.

Hence, a complaint can be filed in any of the forums without paying any court fees, which is very advantageous, unlike in the case of civil courts, where if the compensation being claimed is high, proportionate amount has to be paid as Court Fees.

However, to check that the bona fide complainant is not dragged into an appeal, vide rule 5 of the Supreme Court (First Amendment) Rules, 1990, for an appeal under Section 23 of the Consumer Protection Act before the Supreme Court, a fixed court fee of Rs. 250/- is payable. There is no court fee for an appeal to the State Commission against the order of the District Forum and to the National Commission against the order of the State Commission.

The District Forum, State Commission and the National Commission have the power to execute the orders passed by them in the same manner in which a Civil Court executes a decree. If they are not able to enforce the order, it can be sent to the court within the local limits of whose jurisdiction, in the case of a company, the registered office of the company is situated or in the case of an order against any other person, the place where the person concerned ordinarily resides or carries on business or personally works for gain is situated. On receipt of such order, the Court to which the order is sent has to execute it as if it is a decree or order sent to it for execution.

Remedy for Frivolous or Vexatious Complaints

If the District Forum, State Commission or the National Commission finds that a complaint is frivolous, they have the power to dismiss the complaint, but they have to give valid reasons for the same. Further, the complainant may be ordered to pay the costs, not exceeding Rupees Ten Thousand.

Penalties Imposed by the Act

Where a person against whom a complaint is made or the complainant fails to comply with the order of the District Forum, State Commission or the National Commission, such person may be imprisoned for a term which shall not be less than one month, but which may be extend to three years, or with fine which shall not be less than two thousand rupees, but which may extend to ten thousand rupees or both.

10.3 EMPLOYEE STATE INSURANCE ACT, 1948

The Employees' State Insurance Act, 1948, has been described as an Act "to provide for certain benefits to employees in cases of sickness, maternity and employment injury and to make provision for certain other matters in relation thereof "Under the Act, the Employees' State Insurance Corporation has been set up to administer the Insurance Scheme.

The Scheme is applicable to industrial employees as defined in the Act. The Act operated in certain industrial areas as notified by the Government from time to time. It is intended that the Act will be eventually extended to all industrial areas in the country. Under the scheme a fund is maintained consisting of contributions from the employees, employers and the Government.

From this fund the following expenses are met:

(*i*) Sickness benefit, maternity benefit, disablement benefit, dependants' benefit (death) and medical treatment

(*ii*) Establishment and maintenance of hospital, dispensaries, etc. for the benefit of the insured persons and their families.

(*iii*) Administration of the Scheme.

Some Important Definitions

In this Act, unless there is anything repugnant in the subject or context,:

(1) *"appropriate government"* means, in respect of establishments under the control of the Central Government or a railway administration or a major port or a mine or oil field, the Central Government, and in all other cases, the State Government;

(2) *"confinement"* means labour resulting in the issue of a living child or labour after twenty-six weeks of pregnancy resulting in the issue of a child whether alive or dead;

(3) *"contribution"* means the sum of money payable to the Corporation by the principal employer in respect of an employee and includes any amount payable by or on behalf of the employee in accordance with the provisions of this Act;

(6) *"Corporation"* means the Employees' State Insurance Corporation set up under this Act;

[(6A) *"dependant"* means any of the following relatives of a deceased insured person, namely, :

(*i*) a widow, a minor legitimate or adopted son, an unmarried legitimate or adopted daughter;

(*ia*) a widowed mother;

(*ii*) if wholly dependent on the earnings of the insured person at the time of his death, a legitimate or adopted son or daughter who has attained the age of eighteen years and is infirm;

(*iii*) if wholly or in part dependent on the earnings of the insured person at the time of his death, :

(*a*) a parent other than a widowed mother,

(*b*) a minor illegitimate son, an unmarried illegitimate daughter or a daughter legitimate or adopted or illegitimate if married and a minor or if widowed and a minor, (*c*) a minor brother or an unmarried sister or a widowed sister if a minor,

(*d*) a widowed daughter-in-law,

(*e*) a minor child of a pre-deceased son,

(*f*) a minor child of a pre-deceased daughter where no parent of the child is alive, or

(*g*) a paternal grand-parent if no parent of the insured person is alive,

(8) *"employment injury"* means a personal injury to an employee caused by accident or an occupational disease arising out of and in the course of his employment, being an insurable employment, whether the accident occurs or the occupational disease is contracted within or outside the territorial limits of India;]

(9) *"employee"* means any person employed for wages in or in connection with the work of a factory or establishment to which this Act applies and :

(*i*) who is directly employed by the principal employer on any work of, or incidental or preliminary to or connected with the work of, the factory or establishment whether such work is done by the employee in the factory or establishment or elsewhere; or

(*ii*) who is employed by or through an immediate employer on the premises of the factory or establishment or under the supervision of the principal employer or his agent on work which is ordinarily part of the work of the factory or establishment or which is preliminary to the work carried on in or incidental to the purpose of the factory or establishment; or

(*iii*) whose services are temporarily lent or let on hire to the principal employer by the person with whom the person whose services are so lent or let on hire has entered into a contract of service;

and includes any person employed for wages on any work connected with the administration of the factory or establishment or any part, department or branch thereof or with the purchase of raw materials for, or the distribution or sale of the products of, the factory or establishment or any person engaged as an apprentice, not being an apprentice engaged under the Apprentices Act, 1961, or under the standing orders of the establishment; but does not include :

(*a*) any member of the Indian naval, military or air forces; or

(*b*) any person so employed whose wages excluding remuneration for overtime work exceed such wages as may be prescribed by the Central Government:

PROVIDED that an employee whose wages excluding remuneration for overtime work exceed such wages as may be prescribed by the Central Government at any time after and not before the beginning of the contribution period, shall continue to be an employee until the end of that period;]

(10) *"exempted employee"* means an employee who is not liable under this Act to pay the employee's contribution;

(11) *"family"* means all or any of the following relatives of an insured person, namely, :

(*i*) a spouse;

(*ii*) a minor legitimate or adopted child dependent upon the insured person;

(*iii*) a child who is wholly dependent on the earnings of the insured person and who is :

(*a*) receiving education, till he or she attains the age of twenty-one years,

(*b*) an unmarried daughter;

(*iv*) a child who is infirm by reason of any physical or mental abnormality or injury and is wholly dependent on the earnings of the insured person, so long as the infirmity continues;

(*v*) dependent parents;

(12) *"factory"* means any premises including the precincts thereof :

(*a*) whereon ten or more persons are employed or were employed for wages on any day of the preceding twelve months, and in any part of which a manufacturing process is being carried on with the aid of power or is ordinarily so carried on, or

(*b*) whereon twenty or more persons are employed or were employed for wages on any day of the preceding twelve months, and in any part of which a manufacturing process is being carried on without the aid of power or is ordinarily so carried on.

but does not include a mine subject to the operation of the Mines Act, 1952 or a railway running shed;]

(13) *"immediate employer"*, in relation to employees employed by or through him, means a person who has undertaken the execution, on the premises of a factory, or an establishment to which this Act applies or under the supervision of the principal employer or his agent, of the whole or any part of any work which is ordinarily part of the work of the factory or establishment of the principal employer or is preliminary to the work carried on in, or incidental to the purpose of, any such factory or establishment, and includes a person by whom the services of an employee who has entered into a contract of service with him are temporarily lent or let on hire to the principal employer [4][and includes a contractor];

(13A) *"insurable employment"* means an employment in a factory or establishment to which this Act applies;]

(14) *"insured person"* means a person who is or was an employee in respect of whom contributions are or were payable under this Act and who is, by reason thereof, entitled to any of the benefits provided by this Act;

(14A) *"managing agent"* means any person appointed or acting as the representative of another person for the purpose of carrying on such other person's trade or business, but does not include an individual manager subordinate to an employer;]

(14AA) *"manufacturing process"* shall have the meaning assigned to it in the Factories Act, 1948;

(14B) *"mis-carriage"* means expulsion of the contents of a pregnant uterus at any period prior to or during the twenty-sixth week of pregnancy but does not include any mis-carriage, the causing of which is punishable under the Indian Penal Code;

(15) *"occupier"* of the factory shall have the meaning assigned to it in the Factories Act, 1948;

(15A) *"permanent partial disablement"* means such disablement of a permanent nature, as reduces the earning capacity of an employee in every employment which he was capable of undertaking at the time of the accident resulting in the disablement:

PROVIDED that every injury specified in Part II of the Second Schedule shall be deemed to result in permanent partial disablement;

(15B) *"permanent total disablement"* means such disablement of a permanent nature as incapacitates an employee for all work which he was capable of performing at the time of the accident resulting in such disablement:

PROVIDED that permanent total disablement shall be deemed to result from every injury specified in Part I of the Second Schedule or from any combination of injuries specified in Part II thereof where the aggregate percentage of the loss of earning capacity, as specified in the said Part II against those injuries, amounts to one hundred per cent or more;

(17) *"principal employer"* means :

(*i*) in a factory, the owner or occupier of the factory, and includes the managing agent of such owner or occupier, the legal representative of a deceased owner or occupier, and where a person has been named as the manager of the factory under the Factories Act, 1948; the person so named;

(*ii*) in any establishment under the control of any department of any government in India, the authority appointed by such government in this behalf or where no authority is so appointed, the head of the department;

(*iii*) in any other establishment, any person responsible for the supervision and control of the establishment;

(19A) *"seasonal factory"* means a factory which is exclusively engaged in one or more of the following manufacturing processes, namely, cotton ginning, cotton or jute pressing, decortication of groundnuts, the manufacture of coffee, indigo, lac, rubber, sugar including gur or tea or any manufacturing process which is incidental to or connected with any of the aforesaid processes and includes a factory which is engaged for a period not exceeding seven months in a year :

(*a*) in any process of blending, packing or repacking of tea or coffee; or

(*b*) in such other manufacturing process as the Central Government may, by notification in the Official Gazette, specify;

(20) *"sickness"* means a condition which requires medical treatment and attendance and necessitates abstention from work on medical grounds;

(21) *"temporary disablement"* means a condition resulting from an employment injury which requires medical treatment and renders an employee, as a result of such injury, temporarily incapable of doing the work which he was doing prior to or at the time of the injury;

(22) *"wages"* means all remuneration paid or payable, in cash to an employee, if the terms of the contract of employment, express or implied, were fulfilled and includes any payment to an employee in respect of any period of authorised leave, lock-out, strike which is not illegal or lay-off and other additional remuneration, if any, paid at intervals not exceeding two months], but does not include :

(*a*) any contribution paid by the employer to any pension fund or provident fund, or under this Act;

(*b*) any travelling allowance or the value of any travelling concession;

(*c*) any sum paid to the person employed to defray special expenses entailed on him by the nature of his employment; or

(*d*) any gratuity payable on discharge.

(23) *"wage period"* in relation to an employee means the period in respect of which wages are ordinarily payable to him whether in terms of the contract of employment, express or implied or otherwise.

Registration of Factories and Establishments

Section 2A : Every factory or establishment to which this Act applies shall be registered within such time and in such manner as may be specified in the regulations made in this behalf.

Applicability

1. All factories excluding seasonal factories employing 10 or more persons and working with electric power.
2. All factories excluding seasonal factories employing 20 or more persons and working without electric power.
3. Any establishment which the Government may specifically notify as being covered.
4. Shop employing 20 or more persons.

Eligibility

1. Any person employed for wages (upto Rs. 6,500) in or in connection with the work of a factory or establishment end.
2. Any person who is directly employed by the employer in a factory or through his agent on work which is ordinarily part of the work of the factory or incidental to purpose of the factory.

All Employees to be Insured

Section 38 : Subject to the provisions of this Act, all employees in factories or establishments to which this Act applies shall be insured in the manner provided by this Act.

Establishment of Employees' State insurance Corporation

Section 3 of the Act provides that :

(1) With effect from such date as the Central Government may, by notification in the Official Gazette, appoint in this behalf, there shall be established for the administration of the scheme of employees' state insurance in accordance with the provisions of this Act a Corporation to be known as the Employees' State Insurance Corporation.

(2) The Corporation shall be a body corporate by the name of Employees' State Insurance Corporation having perpetual succession and a common seal and shall by the said name sue and be sued.

Employees' State Insurance Fund

Section 26 deals with the establishment of Employees' State Insurance Fund (ESIF):

(1) All contributions paid under this Act and all other moneys received on behalf of the Corporation shall be paid into a fund called the Employees' State Insurance Fund which shall be held and administered by the Corporation for the purposes of this Act.

(2) The Corporation may accept grants, donations and gifts from the Central or any State Government, local authority, or any individual or body whether incorporated or not, for all or any of the purposes of this Act.

(3) Subject to the other provisions contained in this Act and to any rules or regulations made in this behalf, all moneys accruing or payable to the said Fund shall be paid into the Reserve Bank of India or such other bank as may be approved by the Central Government to the credit on an account styled the account of the Employees' State Insurance Fund.

(4) Such account shall be operated on by such officers as may be authorised by the Standing Committee with the approval of the Corporation.

Purposes for which the Fund may be Expended

Section 28 : Subject to the provisions of this Act and of any rules made by the Central Government in that behalf, the Employees' State Insurance Fund shall be expended only for the following purposes, namely:

(*i*) payment of benefits and provision of medical treatment and attendance to insured persons and, where the medical benefit is extended to their families, the provision of such medical benefit to their families, in accordance with the provisions of this Act and defraying the charges and costs in connection therewith;

(*ii*) payment of fees and allowances to members of the Corporation, the Standing Committee and the Medical Benefit Council, the regional boards, local committees and regional and local Medical Benefit Councils;

(*iii*) payment of salaries, leave and joining time allowances, travelling and compensatory allowances, gratuities and compassionate allowances, pensions, contributions to provident or other benefit fund of officers and servants of the Corporation and meeting the expenditure in respect of offices and other services set up for the purpose of giving effect to the provisions of this Act;

(*iv*) establishment and maintenance of hospitals, dispensaries and other institutions and the provisions of medical and other ancillary services for the benefit of insured persons and, where the medical benefit is extended to their families, their families;

(*v*) payment of contributions to any State Government, local authority or any private body or individual, towards the cost of medical treatment and attendance provided to insured persons and, where the medical benefit is extended to their families, their families including the cost of any building and equipment in accordance with any agreement entered into by the Corporation;

(*vi*) defraying the cost including all expenses of auditing the accounts of the Corporation and of the valuation of its assets and liabilities;

(*vii*) defraying the cost including all expenses of the Employees' State Insurance Courts set up under this Act;

(*viii*) payment of any sums under any contract entered into for the purposes of this Act by the Corporation or the Standing Committee or by any officer duly authorised by the Corporation or the Standing Committee in that behalf;

(*ix*) payment of sums under any decree, order or award of any Court or Tribunal against the Corporation or any of its officers or servants for any act done in the execution of his duty or under a compromise or settlement of any suit or other legal proceeding or claim instituted or made against the Corporation;

(*x*) defraying the cost and other charges of instituting or defending any civil or criminal proceedings arising out of any action taken under this Act;

(*xi*) defraying expenditure, within the limits prescribed, on measures for the improvement of the health and welfare of insured persons and for the rehabilitation and re-employment of insured persons who have been disabled or injured; and

(*xii*) such other purposes as may be authorised by the Corporation with the previous approval of the Central Government.

Contributions

Section 39

(1) The contribution payable under this Act in respect of an employee shall comprise contribution payable by the employer (hereinafter referred to as the employer's contribution) and contribution payable by the employee (hereinafter referred to as the employee's contribution) and shall be paid to the Corporation.

(2) The contributions shall be paid at such rates as may be prescribed by the Central Government:

PROVIDED that the rates so prescribed shall not be more than the rates which were in force immediately before the commencement of the Employees' State Insurance (Amendment) Act, 1989.

(3) The wage period in relation to an employee shall be the unit in respect of which all contributions shall be payable under this Act.

(4) The contributions payable in respect of each wage period shall ordinarily fall due on the last day of the wage period, and where an employee is employed for part of the wage period, or is employed under two or more employers during the same wage period, the contributions shall fall due on such days as may be specified in the regulations.

(5) (*a*) If any contribution payable under this Act is not paid by the principal employer on the date on which such contribution has become due, he shall be liable to pay simple interest at the rate of twelve per cent per annum or at such higher rate as may be specified in the regulations till the date of its actual payment:

PROVIDED that higher interest specified in the regulations shall not exceed the lending rate of interest charged by any scheduled bank.

(*b*) Any interest recoverable under clause (a) may be recovered as an arrear of land revenue or under sections 45C to 45-1.

Explanation : In this sub-section, "scheduled bank" means a bank for the time being included in the Second Schedule to the Reserve Bank of India Act, 1934 (2 of 1934).]

Benefits

Section 46 : (1) Subject to the provisions of this Act, the insured persons, their dependants or the persons hereinafter mentioned, as the case may be, shall be entitled to the following benefits, namely, :

(*a*) periodical payments to any insured person in case of his sickness certified by a duly appointed medical practitioner or by any other person possessing such qualifications and experience as the Corporation may, by regulations, specify in this behalf (hereinafter referred to as sickness benefit;

(*b*) periodical payments to an insured woman in case of confinement or miscarriage or sickness arising out of pregnancy, confinement, premature birth of child or miscarriage, such woman being certified to be eligible for such payments by an authority specified in this behalf by the regulations (hereinafter referred to as maternity benefit);

(*c*) periodical payments to an insured person suffering from disablement as a result of an employment injury sustained as an employee under this Act and certified to be eligible for such payments by an authority specified in this behalf by the regulations (hereinafter referred to as disablement benefit;

(*d*) periodical payments to such dependants of an insured person who dies as a result of an employment injury sustained as an employee under this Act, as are entitled to compensation under this Act (hereinafter referred to as dependants' benefit;

(*e*) medical treatment for and attendance on insured persons (hereinafter referred to as medical benefit; and

(*f*) payment to the eldest surviving member of the family of an insured person who has died, towards the expenditure on the funeral of the deceased insured person or, where the insured person did not have a family or was not living with his family at the time of his death, to the person who actually incurs the expenditure on the funeral of the deceased insured person (to be known as funeral expenses):

PROVIDED that the amount of such payment shall not exceed such amount as may be prescribed by the Central Government] and the claim for such payment shall be made within three months of the death of the insured person or within such extended period as the Corporation or any officer or authority authorised by it in this behalf may allow.

(2) The Corporation may, at the request of the appropriate government, and subject to such conditions as may be laid down in the regulations, extend the medical benefit to the family of an insured person.

Benefits Illustrated

1. Free medical treatment is offered to covered employees at hospital and dispensaries run by the ESI Corporation.

Benefits Table

Benefits	*Contributory*	*Duration*	*Rate*	*To Whom Payable*
1. (*a*) Sickness Benefit.	I.P. Should work for wages for 78 days in the corresponding C.P. (wef. 19-9-98).	91 days in any two consecutive B.P.	As per S.B.R.	Only to the insured person
(*b*) Extended sickness benefit for long term diseases like TB, leprosy, etc.	Continuous employment for the period of two years.	124 days which may be extended upto 309 days in specified chronic cases during a period of 3 yrs.	25% Above S.B.R.	Only to the insured person
(*c*) Enhanced sickness benefit (for under-going sterilization operation	Same as for Benefit (a)above	7 days for vasectomy & 14 days for tubectomy extended in cases of post-coperative complications etc.	Twice the S.B.R.	Only to the insured person
2. Disablement	No Conditions	In case of temporary (*a*) For temp. Only to disablement the disablement: as long injured 40% above person S.B.R. in case of permanent disablement: for life time.		
Explanation : Where more injuries than one are caused by the same accident, the rate of benefit payable under clauses (*c*) and (*d*) shall be aggregated but not so in any case as to exceed the FULL RATE and in cases of disablement not covered by clauses (*a*), (*b*), (*c*) and (*d*) at such rate, not exceeding the FULL RATE, as may be provided in the regulations.				
3. Dependent's Benefit (employment injury)	No condition	To the WINDOWS during life time until remarriage.	3/5 of the FULL RATE, if there are 2 or more windows, the amount payable to the windows shall be divided equally between the windows.	
		To the legitimate or adopted SON/S until he attains the age of 18 years.	2/5 of the FULL RATE, if there are 2 or more sons, the amount payable to the sons shall be divided equally between the sons. Subject to a min of Rs. 14/-.	

Benefits	Contributory	Duration	Rate	To Whom Payable
		To the legitimate or adopted unmarried Daughter/s until she attains the age of 18 yrs. or until marriage, whichever is earlier. In case the deceased person does not leave a widow or legitimate or adopted child. D.B. shall be payable to...		
		(a) Parent or grand parent, for life		3/10th of the FULL RATE
		(b) Any other male dependent, until he attains the age of 18 yrs.		2/10th of FULL RATE
		(c) Any other female dependent, until she attains the age of 18 yrs. Or until marriage whichever is earlier.		–do–

N.B. An insured person whose **Permanent Disablement** has been assessed as final and who has been awarded permanent disablement benefit at a rate not exceeding Rs. 1.50 per day may apply for a lumpsum payment and such amount shall be determined by multiplying the daily rate of permanent disablement benefit by the figure indicated in Co. 2 of the Schedule III of the Regulations.

Benefits	Contributory	Duration	Rate	To Whom Payable
4. Maternity Benefit	Payment of contribution for 70 days in one or two consecutive periods.	12 weeks of which not more than 6 weeks can precede the expected date of confinement.	Twice S.B.R. Subject to min of Rs. 20/- p.d.	Only to the insured person.
		6 weeks for miscarriage or for medical termination of pregnancy Addition payment for one month for Complications (pre or post) arising out of pregnancy.	Medical bonus of Rs. 250/- where ESI facility is not available.	

Benefits	*Contributory*	*Duration*	*Rate*	*To Whom Payable*
5. Medical Insured Benefit	No condition	From the date of entry of an employee into an insurable employment so long as he remains in insurable employment and three after for certain additional period.	Full Medical care including hospitalisation	Person as well as his/her Family Members as defined u/s 2(11) of the Act.
6. Funeral Expenses	No condition (*i.e.* merely by virtue of being an insured person)	One time lumpsum payment.	Not more than Rs. 1,500/-	To the eldest surviving member of the family of the deceased I.P. Or to the person who actually incurs the expenditure on the funeral of an I.P.
7. Rehabilitation Allowance	No condition	For each day of which I.P. remains admitted in Artificial Limb Center for fixation, repair or replacement of artificial limb.	Same as at 1(a) Upto to Rs. 15L for Rehabilitation.	Only to the I.P.
8. Medical Benefit to insured persons who ceases insurable employment on account of permanent.	No condition but an I.P. has to pay Rs. 10/- pm in lumpsum for one year in advance every year.	Till the date on which an I.P. would have attained the age of superannuation.	Medical Benefit	IP and spouse.
9. Medical Benefit to retired Insured Period	1. Insurable employment for a period of 5 years and 2. Payment of Office of the Contribution @ Rs. 15/- PM in lumpsum for one year in advance, each year.	Till the time yearly contribution is paid to the Concerned Office of the Corporation.	–	Insured person and his spouse

2. About 7/12th of employees normal wage will be payable to him by ESI during sickness.
3. Maternity benefit for 12 weeks of which not more than 6 weeks should be preceding confinement.
4. Injury during/in course of employment resulting in temporary/permanent disablement entities the covered employee to a regular payment to substitute his lost wages.
5. Death during course of employment entities specified dependents to a regular payment.
6. One time payment of Rs. 1,500 to help meet furneral expenses.

Other Benefits

Supply of special aids : Insured persons and members of their families are provided artificial limbs, hearing aids, artificial dentures, spectacles (for insured person only) and artificial appliances like spinal supports, cervical collars, walking callopers, crutches, wheel chairs and cardiac pace makers, dialysis/dialysis with kidney transplant etc. as part of medical care under the ESI Scheme.

Punishment for False Statements

Section 84 : Whoever, for the purpose of causing any increase in payment or benefit under this Act, or for the purpose of causing any payment or benefit to be made where no payment or benefit is authorised by or under this Act, or for the purpose of avoiding any payment to be made by himself under this Act or enabling any other person to avoid any such payment, knowingly makes or causes to be made any false statement or false representation, shall be punishable with imprisonment for a term which may extend to [six months], or with fine not exceeding [two thousand] rupees, or with both.

PROVIDED that where an insured person is convicted under this section, he shall not be entitled for any cash benefit under this Act for such period as may be prescribed by the Central Government.

Punishment for failure to pay contributions, etc.

Section 85 : If any person :

(*a*) fails to pay any contribution which under this Act he is liable to pay, or

(*b*) deducts or attempts to deduct from the wages of an employee the whole or any part of the employer's contribution, or

(*c*) in contravention of section 72 reduces the wages or any privileges or benefits admissible to an employee, or

(*d*) in contravention of section 73 or any regulation dismisses, discharges, reduces or otherwise punishes an employee, or (*e*) fails or refuses to submit any return required by the regulations, or makes a false return, or

(*f*) obstructs any Inspector or other official of the Corporation in the discharge of his duties, or

(*g*) is guilty of any contravention of or non-compliance with any of the requirements of this Act or the rules or the regulations in respect of which no special penalty is provided,

[he shall be punishable :

[(*i*) where he commits an offence under clause (*a*), with imprisonment for a term which may extend to three years but

(*a*) which shall not be less than one year, in case of failure to pay the employee's contribution which has been deducted by him from the employee's wages and shall also be liable to fine of ten thousand rupees;

(*b*) which shall not be less than six months, in any other case and shall also be liable to fine of five thousand rupees:

PROVIDED that the Court may, for any adequate and special reasons to be recorded in the judgement, impose a sentence of imprisonment for a lesser term;

(*ii*) where he commits an offence under any of the clauses (b) to (g) (both inclusive), with imprisonment for a term which may extend to one year or with fine which may extend to four thousand rupees, or with both.]

Enhanced punishment in certain cases after previous conviction

Section 185A : Whoever, having been convicted by a court of an offence punishable under this Act, commits the same offence shall, for every such subsequent offence, be punishable with imprisonment for a term which may extend to two years and with fine of five thousand rupees:

PROVIDED that where such subsequent offence is for failure by the employer to pay any contribution which under this Act he is liable to pay, he shall, for every such subsequent offence, be punishable with imprisonment for a term which may extend to five years but which shall not be less than two years and shall also be liable to fine of twenty-five thousand rupees.

The penal provisions may be summarised as follows:

Penal Provisions

1. *For employees' contribution :* Imprisonment for minimum 2 years to maximum 5 years and/or fine of Rs. 25,000/-.
2. *For employer's contribution :* Imprisonment for minimum 6 months to maximum 3 years and/or fine of Rs. 10,000/-.

Every employer has to the following documents as per the Act which shall at all time are ready for inspection.

Records to be kept Ready for Inspection

1. Attendance Register/Muster Roll.
2. Salary/Wage Register/Payroll.
3. EC (Employee's & Employer's Contribution) Statement.
4. Employees' Register U/R 32 (Form 7).
5. Accident Register U/R 66.
6. Return of Contribution (RC-Form 6).
7. Return of Declaration Forms (RDF-Form 3).
8. Receipted Copies of Challans.
9. Books of Account *viz.*, Cash/Bank, Expense Register, Sales/Purchase, Petty Cash Book, Ledger, Supporting Bills and Vouchers, a/w Delivery Challans (if any).

10.4 ARBITRATION ACT, 1940

Arbitration is a method whereby parties can resolve their disputes privately. It is known as an *alternative dispute resolution mechanism*. Instead of filing a case in a court, parties can refer their case to an arbitral tribunal, which is the forum where arbitration proceedings are conducted. The arbitral tribunal will consider the questions over which the parties are in conflict and will arrive at a decision. This decision is known as an 'award'.

In India, till the promulgation of the Arbitration and Conciliation Ordinance, 1996, which is now repealed and replaced by the Arbitration and Conciliation Act, 1996, with effect from 25th January 1996, the law relating to arbitration was governed principally by the Arbitration (Protocol and Convention) Act, 1937; the Arbitration Act, 1940 and the Foreign Awards (Recognition and Enforcement) Act, 1961.

Now these statutes stand repealed (Section 85) by the enactment of the 1996 Act. The object of the Act is to consolidate and amend the law relating to domestic arbitration, international commercial arbitration and the enforcement of foreign arbitral awards and for related matters.

Arbitration Agreement

Section 7 : (1) In this part "arbitration agreement" means an agreement by the parties to submit to arbitration all or certain disputes which have arisen or which may arise between them in respect of a defined legal relationship, whether contractual or not.

(2) An arbitration agreement may be in the form of an arbitration clause in a contract or in the form of a separate agreement.

(3) An arbitration agreement shall be in writing.

(4) An arbitration agreement is in writing if it is contained in :

(*a*) a document signed by the parties;

(*b*) an exchange of letters, telex, telegrams or other means of telecommunication which provide a record of the agreement; or

(*c*) an exchange of statements of claim and defence in which the existence of the agreement is alleged by one party and not denied by the other.

(5) The reference in a contract to a document containing an arbitration clause constitutes an arbitration agreement if the contract is in writing and the reference is such as to make that arbitration clause part of the contract.

Essentials of Arbitration Agreement

1. It must be in writing. [Section 7(3).
2. It must have all the essential elements of a valid contract.
3. The agreement must be to refer a dispute, present or future, between the parties to arbitration.
4. An arbitration agreement may be in the form of an arbitration.

Power of the Judicial Authority to Refer to Arbitration

Section 8 : Power to refer parties to arbitration where there is an arbitration agreement :

1. A judicial authority before which an action is brought in a matter which is the subject of an arbitration agreement shall, if a party so applies not later than when submitting his first statement on the substance of the dispute, refer the parties to arbitration.
2. The application referred to in sub-section (1) shall not be entertained unless it is accompanied by the original arbitration agreement or duly certified copy thereof.
3. Notwithstanding that an application has been made under sub-section (1) and that the issue is pending before the judicial authority, an arbitration may be a commenced or continued and an arbitral award made.
4. There must be a valid and subsisting agreement between the parties.
5. The matter about which a suit has been filed should be within the scope of the arbitration agreement.
6. The party asking for the stay must have applied at the earliest opportunity, *i.e.*, before submitting his first statement on the substance of the dispute.

7. The application must be made to the judicial authority before which the proceedings are pending.
8. The application must be accompanied by the original arbitration agreement or by a duly certified copy thereof.
9. The judicial authority must be satisfied that there is no sufficient reason why the matter should not be referred.

Composition of Arbitration Tribunal

An arbitrator is a person selected by mutual consent of the parties to settle the matters in controversy between them. A person appointed to adjudicate the difference between two or more parties is called an arbitrator. An arbitrator is a tribunal chosen by the consent of the parties. The person who is so appointed must also give his consent to act as an arbitrator.

Number of Arbitrators

The parties are free to determine the number of arbitrators provided that such number shall not be an even number. If the parties fail to make the determination the arbitral tribunal shall consist of a sole arbitrator. (Section 10)

Appointment of Arbitrators

A person of any nationality may be an arbitrator, unless otherwise agreed by the parties. The parties are free to agree on a procedure for appointing the arbitrator or arbitrators. (*Section 11*)

Challenge Procedure

The parties are free to agree on a procedure for challenging an arbitrator. [*Section 13(1)*]

Replacement of Arbitrator

Where the mandate of an arbitrator terminates, a substitute arbitrator shall be appointed according to the rules that were applicable to the appointment of the arbitrator being replaced. [*Section 15(2)*]

Death or Insolvency of a Party to the Arbitration Agreement

Death of a party (*Section 40*)

An arbitration agreement shall not be discharged by the death of any party thereto either as respects the deceased or as respects any other party, but shall in such event be enforceable by or against the legal representative of the deceased. [*Section 40(1)*]

The mandate of an arbitrator shall not be terminated by the death of any party by whom he was appointed. [*Section 40(2)*]

Insolvency (Section 41) : A contract entered into by a person who is declared insolvent might contain an arbitration clause. If the Official Receiver or Assignee adopts the contract, then such clause is enforceable by or against him.

Equal Treatment of Parties

The parties shall be treated with equality and each party shall be given a full opportunity to present his case. (Section 18)

Place of Arbitration

Section 20(1) provides that parties are free to agree on the place of arbitration.

Court Assistance in taking Evidence

Application : The arbitral tribunal, or a party with the approval of the arbitral tribunal, may apply to the Court for assistance in taking evidence. [*Section 27(1)*].

Particulars of Application : The application shall specify :

(*a*) the names and addresses of the parties and the arbitrators;

(*b*) the general nature of the claim and the relief sought;

(*c*) the evidence to be obtained, in particular :

(*i*) the name and address of any person to be heard as witness or expert witness and a statement of the subject-matter of the testimony required;

(*ii*) the description of any document to be produced or property to be inspected. [*Section 27(2)*].

Settlement

Section 30 provides that :

(1) It is not incompatible with an arbitration agreement for an arbitral tribunal to encourage settlement of the dispute and, with the agreement of the parties, the arbitral tribunal may use mediation, conciliation or other procedures at any time during the arbitral proceedings to encourage settlement.

(2) If, during arbitral proceedings, the parties settle the dispute, the arbitral tribunal shall terminate the proceedings and, if requested by the parties and not objected to by the arbitral tribunal, record the settlement in the form of an arbitral award on agreed terms.

(3) An arbitral award on agreed terms shall be made in accordance with section 31 and shall state that it is an arbitral award.

(4) An arbitral award on agreed terms shall have the same status and effect as any other arbitral award on the substance of the dispute.

Form and Contents of Arbitral Award

Section 31 deals with Arbitral Award. It provides that :

(1) An arbitral award shall be made in writing and shall be signed by the members of the arbitral tribunal.

(2) For the purposes of sub-section (1), in arbitral proceedings with more than one arbitrator, the signatures of the majority of all the members of the arbitral tribunal shall be sufficient so long as the reason for any omitted signature is stated.

(3) The arbitral award shall state the reasons upon which it is based, unless,:

(*a*) the parties have agreed that no reasons are to be given, or

(*b*) the award is an arbitral award on agreed terms under section 30.

(4) The arbitral award shall state its date and the place of arbitration as determined in accordance with section 20 and the award shall be deemed to have been made at that place.

(5) After the arbitral award is made, a signed copy shall be delivered to each party.

(6) The arbitral tribunal may, at any time during the arbitral proceedings, make an interim arbitral award on any matter with respect to which it may make a final arbitral award.

(7) (*a*) Unless otherwise agreed by the parties, where and in so far as an arbitral award is for the payment of money, the arbitral tribunal may include in the sum for which the award is made interest, at such rate as it deems reasonable, on the whole or any part of the money, for the whole or any part of the period between the date on which the cause of action arose and the date on which the award is made.

(*b*) A sum directed to be paid by an arbitral award shall, unless the award otherwise directs, carry interest at the rate of eighteen per centum per annum from the date of the award to the date of payment.

(8) Unless otherwise agreed by the parties, :

(*a*) the costs of an arbitration shall be fixed by the arbitral tribunal;

(*b*) the arbitral tribunal shall specify, :

(*i*) the party entitled to costs,

(*ii*) the party who shall pay the costs,

(*iii*) the amount of costs or method of determining that amount, and

(*iv*) the manner in which the costs shall be paid.

Explanation : For the purpose of clause (a), "costs" means reasonable costs relating to, :

(*i*) the fees and expenses of the arbitrators and witnesses,

(*ii*) legal fees and expenses,

(*iii*) any administration fees of the institution supervising the arbitration, and

(*iv*) any other expenses incurred in connection with the arbitral proceedings and the arbitral award.

Termination of Proceedings

Section 32 : (1) The arbitral proceedings shall be terminated by the final arbitral award or by an order of the arbitral tribunal under sub-section (2).

(2) The arbitral tribunal shall issue an order for the termination of the arbitral proceedings where, :

(*a*) the claimant withdraws his claim, unless the respondent objects to the order and the arbitral tribunal recognises a legitimate interest on his part in obtaining a final settlement of the dispute,

(*b*) the parties agree on the termination of the proceedings, or

(*c*) the arbitral tribunal finds that the continuation of the proceedings has for any other reason become unnecessary or impossible.

(3) Subject to section 33 and sub-section (4) of section 34, the mandate of the arbitral tribunal shall terminate with the termination of the arbitral proceedings.

Arbitration Clause in Insurance Policies

Arbitration clause is generally found in insurance policies. It is a time saving and cost saving method of claims settlement. The arbitration condition in fire and motor insurance policies currently in use in India reads :

"If any difference shall arise as to the quantum to be paid under this policy, (liability being otherwise admitted) such difference shall independently of all other questions be referred to the decision of an arbitrator, to be appointed in writing by the parties in difference, or if they cannot agree upon a single arbitrator to the decision of two disinterested persons as arbitrators of whom one shall be appointed in writing by each of the parties within two calendar months after having been required so to do in writing by the other party in accordance with the provisions of the Arbitration Act, 1940, as amended from time to time and for the time being in force. In case either party shall refuse or fail to appoint arbitrator within two calender months after receipt of notice in writing requiring an appointment the other party shall be at liberty to appoint sole arbitrator; and in case of disagreement between the arbitrators, the difference shall be referred to the decision of an umpire who shall have been appointed by them in writing before entering on the reference and who shall sit with the arbitrators and, preside at their meetings.

It is clearly agreed and understood that no difference or dispute shall be referable to arbitration as hereinbefore provided, if the Company has disputed or not accepted liability under or in respect of this Policy.

It is hereby expressly stipulated and declared that it shall be a condition precedent to any right of action or suit upon this policy that the award by such arbitrator, arbitrators or umpire of the amount of the loss or damage shall be first obtained."

10.5 LOK ADALATS

The enactments or legal aid boards of state governments establish Lok Adalat (Lok Nyayalaya). It settles dispute through conciliation and compromise. Lok Adalat accepts the cases which could be settled by conciliation and compromise, and pending in the regular courts within their jurisdiction. As per Chapter XI of the Lok Nyayalaya Rules, 1986, special provisions are made to settle amicably the cases pending before MACT.

Since April 1985, Lok Adalats have been exclusively organised for settlement of motor third party claims. Although the concept of Lok Adalat was very much vogue since early years. This form was made available for settlement of Motor Third Party claims under the initiative of former Chief Justice of India, Shri. P.N. Bhagwati.

The First Lok Adalat was held in Chennai in 1986. The Lok Adalat is presided over by a sitting or retired judicial officer as the chairman, with two other members, usually a lawyer and a social worker. There is no court fee. If the case is already filed in the regular court, the fee paid will be refunded if the dispute is settled at the Lok Adalat. The procedural laws, and the Evidence Act are not strictly followed while assessing the merits of the claim by the Lok Adalat.

The primary requisite for seeking relief in Lok Adalat is that both parties in dispute should agree for settlement and its decision is binding on the parties to the dispute and its order is capable of execution through legal process. No appeal lies against the order of the Lok Adalat.

Lok Adalats have been successful in settling huge number of Third Party claims referred by Motor Accident Claim Tribunal (MACT). Except matters relating to offences, which are not compoundable, a Lok Adalat has jurisdiction to deal with all matters. Matters pending or at pre-trial stage, provided a reference is made to it by a court or by the concerned authority or committee, when the dispute is at a pre-trial stage and not before a Court of Law it can be referred to Lok Adalat.

Legal Services Authorities Act was promulgated in 1987, which aimed to organise Lok Adalat to secure that the operation of legal system promotes justice on the basis of an equal opportunity. The Act gives statutory recognition to the resolution of disputes by compromise and settlement by the Lok Adalats.

According to Legal Services Authorities (Amendment) Act 1994, Lok Adalat settlement is no longer a voluntary concept. By this Act, Lok Adalat has got statutory character and has been legally recognised.

Constitution of Lok Adalats

Section 18 : **Organisation of Lok Adalats :** (1) Every State Authority or District Authority or the Supreme Court Legal Services Committee or every High Court Legal Services Committee or, as the case may be, Taluk Legal Services Committee may organise Lok Adalats at such intervals and places and for exercising such jurisdiction and for such areas as it thinks fit.

(2) Every Lok Adalat organised for an area shall consist of such number of :

(*a*) serving or retired judicial officers; and

(*b*) other persons,

of the area as may be specified by the State Authority or the District Authority or the Supreme Court Legal Services Committee or the High Court Legal Services Committee, or as the case may be, the Taluk Legal Services Committee, organising such Lok Adalats.

(3) The experience and qualifications of other persons referred to in clause (b) of sub-section (2) for Lok Adalats organised by the Supreme Court Legal Services Committee shall be such as may be prescribed by the Central Government in consultation with the Chief Justice of India.

(4) The experience and qualifications of other persons referred to in clause (b) of sub-section (2) for Lok Adalats other than referred to in sub-section (3) shall be such as may be prescribed by the State Government in consultation with the Chief Justice of the High Court.

(5) A Lok Adalat shall have jurisdiction to determine and to arrive at a compromise or settlement between the parties to a dispute in respect of :

(*i*) any case pending before; or

(*ii*) any matter which is falling within the jurisdiction of, and is not brought before, any court for which the Lok Adalat is organised:

Provided that the Lok Adalat shall have no jurisdiction in respect of any case or matter relating to an offence not compoundable under any law.

Section 19 : 1. Central, State, District and Taluk Legal Services Authority has been created who are responsible for organising Lok Adalats at such intervals and place.

2. Conciliators for Lok Adalat comprise the following :

A. A sitting or retired judicial officer.

B. Other persons of repute as may be prescribed by the State Government in consultation with the Chief Justice of High Court.

Reference of Cases

Section 20 : Cases can be referred for consideration of Lok Adalat as under:

1. By consent of both the parties to the disputes.
2. One of the parties makes an application for reference.
3. Where the Court is satisfied that the matter is an appropriate one to be taken cognisance of by the Lok Adalat.
4. The principles of justice, equity, fair play and other legal principles shall guide compromise settlement.
5. Where no compromise has been arrived at through conciliation, the matter shall be returned to the concerned court for disposal in accordance with Law.

Effect of the Orders

Section 21 : After the agreement is arrived by the consent of the parties, award is passed by the conciliators. The matter need not be referred to the concerned Court for consent decree.

1. ***Award of Lok Adalat :*** (1) Every award of the Lok Adalat shall be deemed to be a decree of a civil court or, as the case may be, an order of any other court and where a compromise or settlement has been arrived at, by a Lok Adalat in a case referred to it under sub-section (1) of Section 20, the court-fee paid in such case shall be refunded in the manner provided under the Court Fees Act, 1870 (7 of 1870).

(2) Every award made by a Lok Adalat shall be final and binding on all the parties to the dispute, and no appeal shall lie to any court against the award.

Proceedings to be Recognised as Judicial

Every proceedings of the Lok Adalat shall be deemed to be judicial proceedings for the purpose of summoning of witnesses, discovery of documents, reception of evidences, requisitioning of Public record etc.

Powers of Lok Adalats

Section 22 : (1) The Lok Adalat shall, for the purposes of holding any determination under this Act, have the same powers as are vested in a civil court under the Code of Civil Procedure, 1908 (5 of 1908), while trying a suit in respect of the following matters, namely :

(*a*) the summoning and enforcing the attendance of any witness and examining him on oath;

(*b*) the discovery and production of any document;

(*c*) the reception of evidence on affidavits;

(*d*) the requisitioning of any public record or document or copy of such record or document from any court or office; and

(*e*) such other matters as may be prescribed.

(2) Without prejudice to the generality of the powers contained in sub-section(1), every Lok Adalat shall have the requisite powers to specify its own procedure for the determination of any dispute coming before it.

(3) All proceedings before a Lok Adalat shall be deemed to be judicial proceedings within the meaning of Sections 193, 219 and 228 of the Indian Penal Code (45 of 1860) and every Lok Adalat shall be deemed to be a civil court for the purpose of Section 195 and Chapter XXVI of the Code of Criminal Procedure, 1973(2 of 1974).

Ombudsman

Ombudsman traces its history to Sweden way back in 19th century and it literally means an authority that is empowered to investigate individual complaints against public authorities, departments etc. Later it has been adopted in many countries including UK, Australia etc.

In India the idea of insurance ombudsman was first mooted in the year 1998. Central government by the powers conferred on it by sub section (1) section 114 of insurance act 1938 has set up an ombudsman specifically for Insurance sector. Main objective of insurance ombudsman is redressal and settlement of disputes arising between insured and insurer. Insurance ombudsman is a quasi-judicial body established for speedy settlement of disputes in fair, impartial and judicial manner.

Any individual policyholder (including a sole proprietor but not partnerships or companies) or his legal heir can approach the Insurance Ombudsman for complaints in respect of policies on personal lines of business.

Personal lines of business include coverage under Personal Accident policies, Mediclaim, insurance of property of the individual such as motor vehicles, household articles etc. There is no fee or charge required to be paid and there is no requirement to approach the Ombudsman through a lawyer. However, before approaching Ombudsman, a representation should be made to the insurance Company. If no reply is received within one month or the reply is not satisfactory, the Ombudsman can be approached. The maximum limit for the amount under dispute for which the Ombudsman can entertain is Rs. 20 lakhs and Complaints can be made to Ombudsman within one year of the rejection by insurer of the representation of the complainant or the insurer's final reply to the Complainant's representation.

Types of Complaints

The insurance ombudsman may consider or receives the complaints regarding:

- Partial or total repudiation of claims

- Delay in settlement of claims
- Legal construction of policy (policy wordings)
- Premium paid or payable
- Non-issue of insurance documents to customers after receipt of premium.

An insurance ombudsman cannot act on :

- Any complaint which falls outside the territorial limits of the ombudsman
- Any complaint where the claims amount is more than 20 lakhs.
- Any dispute/issue/complaint which is under trial in any other judicial or quasi-judicial body.
- Where the complaint is not regarding personal lines of business.
- Where the complaint is filed by any artificial judicial person
- Any complaint which is lodged after one year from the date of issue of first reply by the insurer.

Procedure for Redressel

1. The insured has to apply in writing to the Insurance Ombudsman under whose jurisdiction the insurer falls. A complaint may be filed either by the insured or his legal heirs and should clearly state the name and address of the insurer against whom the complaint is made, nature and circumstances giving rise to dispute, nature of loss sustained by the complainant and relief sought from Insurance Ombudsman.
2. The complainant has to substantiate his claim with all the documentary evidences.
3. The Insurance Ombudsman would first act as a mediator to settle the grievance on a mutually agreeable basis. This mediation process would be for a maximum of one month. After hearing both the parties Insurance Ombudsman may pass an award, which if acceptable to the complainant, is sent to insurer for final execution. Insurer has to comply with the award within 15 days and it has to be informed to the Insurance Ombudsman.
4. If the grievance is not settled on a mutually agreeable basis, Insurance Ombudsman gives a speaking award within a period not exceeding three months. If the complainant is not satisfied with the award, he can appeal in any other forum or court, however such facility is not available to the insurer.
5. An award passed by the Insurance Ombudsman has to be complied with, by the insurer within the 15 days. However, no action lies if the insurer opts for non-compliance of the award because he no judicial powers for the execution of award compared to other judicial systems like consumer forums, civil courts etc.

No advocates are allowed to represent insurer/ complainant to argue their respective cases. Further Insurance Ombudsman being a non-judicial authority, does not have the powers of summoning particular persons/witness and examining them on oath. Another specific feature of Insurance Ombudsman is that it can pass award for *ex-gratia* settlement of disputes, while such powers of exgratia settlement are not vested with other redressal mechanisms such as consumer courts etc.

Key Terms

- Policy of Insurance
- Policy of Group Insurance
- Policy of Sea-Insurance
- Adhesive Stamps
- Impressed Stamps
- Impounded Instruments
- Deficiency
- Service
- Unfair Trade Practice
- Complaint
- District Forum
- State Commission
- National Commission
- Dependant
- Employment Injury
- Employee
- Exempted Employee
- Family
- Immediate Employer
- Permanent Partial Disablement
- Permanent Total Disablement
- Temporary Disablement
- Wages
- Employees' State Insurance Fund
- Arbitration
- Arbitration Tribunal
- Award
- Lok Adalas
- Insurance Ombudsman

References

- N.D. Kapoor & Rajni Abbi, *General Law*, Sultan Chand & Sons, 1991.
- *www.indiainfoline.com*
- Avtar Singh, *Law of Insurance*, Eastern Book Company, 2005.
- *www.bimaonline.com*
- *orientalinsurance.nic.in*
- *on-lyne.com*
- *invert.economictimes.indiatimes.com*

Questions for Review

1. What is the consequence of an instrument requiring to be stamped under the Indian Stamp Act, 1899 not being duly stamped?
2. Define the various types of policies as per Section 2 of Indian Stamp Act, 1899.
3. Define "Consumer" and "Deficiency in Services" as per the provisions of Consumer Protection Act, 1986. What is the redressal mechanism available to the insured (consumer) under the Act.
4. Write short notes on :

   (1) False Complaints

   (2) Limitation Period

   under the Consumer Protection Act, 1986.
5. Define the following terms as per Employees State Insurance Act, 1948.

   (*a*) Dependent

   (*b*) Contribution

   (*c*) Family

   (*d*) Permanent Partial Disablement

   (*e*) Permanent Total Disablement

   (*f*) Principal Employer
6. Write short notes on :

   (*a*) Registration of Factories and Establishment

   (*b*) Employees State Insurance Fund
7. List the various benefits to employees under the Employees State Insurance Act, 1948.
8. What is an arbitration agreement? What matters may be referred for arbitration?
9. What are the powers and duties of arbitrator? When may the Cowet remove an arbitrator?
10. Write short notes on :

    (*a*) Arbitration Clause in Insurance Policies

    (*b*) Lok Adalats

    (*c*) Insurance Ombudsman